The Latino Christ in Art, Literature, and Liberation Theology

QUERENCIAS SERIES
Miguel A. Gandert and
Enrique R. Lamadrid, Series Editors

Querencia is a popular term in the Spanish-speaking world that is used to express a deeply rooted love of place and people. This series promotes a transnational, humanistic, and creative vision of the US-Mexico borderlands based on all aspects of expressive culture, both material and intangible.

Also available in the Querencias Series:

Sisters in Blue / Hermanas de azul: Sor María de Ágreda Comes to New Mexico / Sor María de Ágreda viene a Nuevo México by Enrique R. Lamadrid and Anna M. Nogar

Aztlán: Essays on the Chicano Homeland, Revised and Expanded Edition edited by Francisco A. Lomelí, Rudolfo A. Anaya, and Enrique R. Lamadrid

Río: A Photographic Journey down the Old Río Grande edited by Melissa Savage

Coyota in the Kitchen: A Memoir of New and Old Mexico by Anita Rodríguez

Chasing Dichos through Chimayó by Don J. Usner

Enduring Acequias: Wisdom of the Land, Knowledge of the Water by Juan Estevan Arellano

Hotel Mariachi: Urban Space and Cultural Heritage in Los Angeles by Catherine L. Kurland and Enrique R. Lamadrid

Sagrado: A Photopoetics Across the Chicano Homeland by Spencer R. Herrera and Levi Romero

The LATINO CHRIST *in*
ART, LITERATURE, *and*
LIBERATION THEOLOGY

Michael R. Candelaria

UNIVERSITY OF NEW MEXICO PRESS • ALBUQUERQUE

© 2018 by the University of New Mexico Press
All rights reserved. Published 2018
Printed in the United States of America

Library of Congress Cataloging-in-Publication Data

Names: Candelaria, Michael R., author.
Title: The Latino Christ in Art, Literature, and Liberation Theology /
Michael R. Candelaria.
Description: First [edition]. | Albuquerque: University of New Mexico Press, 2018. |
Includes bibliographical references and index. |
Identifiers: LCCN 2017005434 (print) | LCCN 2017033243 (e-book) |
ISBN 9780826358806 (e–book) | ISBN 9780826358790 (printed case: alk. paper)
Subjects: LCSH: Christianity and the arts—Latin America. | Jesus Christ—Art. |
Jesus Christ—In literature. | Liberation theology.
Classification: LCC BR115.A8 (e-book) | LCC BR115.A8 C36 2018 (print) |
DDC 232.089/68—dc23
LC record available at https://lccn.loc.gov/2017005434

Cover illustration: Salvador Dalí,
Christ of St. John of the Cross, 1951.
© CSG CIC Glasgow Museums. Glasgow, Scotland, 2017.
Composed in Adobe Garamonde Pro

This book is dedicated to Azariah, Tahlia, and Hadasah Cohen.

CONTENTS

ILLUSTRATIONS

ACKNOWLEDGMENTS

I would like to thank the following people who helped with this publication in various capacities at the University of New Mexico: Mercedes Nysus and Mary Domski of the Philosophy Department, John Bussanich and Monica Lopez in the Religious Studies Program, and Enrique Lamadrid, professor emeritus, and Tobias Duran, retired, of the Center for Regional Studies. I want to express my appreciation to the following people for their help in acquiring images and permissions: Rebecca Fawcett at the Hood Art Museum; Akiko Yoshida at the Fukuoka Art Museum in Fukuoka, Japan; Michelle Burton of Marquette University's Haggerty Art Museum; Winnie Tyrell in Glasgow; Robbi Siegel at Art Resources, New York; and J'Aimee Cronin from Artist Rights Society. Above all, I want to express gratitude to Zac Candelaria for the countless times he let me run my ideas by him.

Introduction

According to Luke's Gospel, Jesus had sent his disciples throughout the towns and villages of Galilee proclaiming the good news of the Kingdom of God. When they returned, he asked them, "Who say the people that I am?" The disciples replied, "John the Baptist; but some say Elias; and others say, that one of the old prophets is risen again." Jesus responded, "But who say ye that I am?" Peter replied, "The Christ of God" (Luke 9:18, 20). Responses to that question from Iberia and Latin America suggest an imaginary Spanish or Latino Christ. Brazilian modernist painter Oswald de Andrade, in his *Anthropophagite Manifesto*, mentions the social construction of the Latin American Christ: "From the French Revolution to Romanticism, to the Bolshevik Revolution, to the surrealist revolution . . . we continue on our path. We were never catechized. We sustained ourselves by way of sleepy laws. We made Christ be born in Bahia or in Belem, in Para. But we never let the concept of logic invade our midst" (Ades 1989, 134). Years earlier in Spain, Miguel de Unamuno, along similar lines, recalls that a Portuguese writer, Guerra Junqueiro, remarked to him many times that the Spanish Christ came from Tangiers (Mackay 1932, 95). Although Junquiero alludes to the impact of the Islamic faith on Spanish Catholicism, the sentiment expressed emphasizes the constructive and relativistic nature of the Spanish/Latin American (Latino) Christ.

However interesting the question may be concerning the degree to which Islam influenced Spanish Catholicism, this book aims at drawing a bead on the diverse and unconventional ways prominent Latina/o writers and artists represent Christ in art, literature, and theology.

Why the Latino Christ? A cursory examination of recent cultural studies of the figure of Jesus in American culture or of representations of Christ in the history of Western Civilization reveals a veritable absence of Hispanic/Latino representations of Christ. *Jesus through the Centuries: His Place in the History of Culture* by Yale Church Historian and Nobel Prize honoree Jaroslav Pelikan offers a breathtaking cultural history of representations of Jesus in Western civilization from the first century to the twentieth. Pelikan examines a great diversity of Christian images in Byzantine, Latin, German, Italian, Dutch, British, American, Jewish, and black art, theology, literature, and church history. Published in 1985 at a time when Latin American liberation theology was gaining worldwide attention, Pelikan's book appeared between the assassination of Archbishop Oscar Romero (1980) and the murders of the six Jesuit priests, including the liberation theologian Ignacio Ellucaria (1989). Yet the book does not even allude to Latin American liberation theology, not even in the chapter entitled The Liberator. In this chapter, he discusses Dostoevsky, Tolstoy, Gandhi, Martin Luther King Jr., and even Abraham Lincoln. Pelikan does not mention Gustavo Gutiérrez, Leonardo Boff, or Jon Sobrino, liberation theology's torchbearers, who directly addressed the problem of an authentic Latin American Christology. In 1985, the Vatican silenced Leonardo Boff and summoned Gutiérrez to Rome. Both events garnered international attention in the news media.

Of the eighteen color illustrations in the book, there is only one Iberian image—that of a Greek expatriate, El Greco, *The Savior*, which hangs at the Museo del Greco in Toledo, Spain. To his credit, Pelikan devotes one and a half pages to the Spanish mystical tradition, discussing the Christ mysticism of Fray Luis de León and St. John of the Cross. In a companion volume, *The Illustrated Jesus through the Centuries*, Pelikan includes a few Hispanic/Latino images of Jesus including Orozco, Dalí, Velásquez and one or two others that fill, to some extent, the glaring lacunae in the first book. Nonetheless, the impression remains that Iberia and Latin America are peripheral to the history of the West and insignificant to the self-understanding of the successive epochs of Western culture.

Paul C. Burns edited the book *Jesus in Twentieth-Century Literature, Art, and Movies* partly to supplement Pelikan's weak chapter on twentieth century cultural expressions of Christ. Burns describes this chapter of Pelikan's book as "his most general and hence least effective chapter" (Burns 2007, 3). Burns selects ten exemplifications of modern works including Nino Ricci's *Testament*, Norman Mailer's *Gospel*, José Saramago's *The Gospel of Jesus Christ*, Bulgakov, Kazantzakis, and Scorsese, D. H. Lawrence, Chaim Potok, Al Aqqad's Muslim Jesus, Dan Brown's *The Da Vinci Code*, and Mel Gibson's *The Passion of the Christ*. There is no investigation of Hispanic/Latina/o writers and filmmakers, although, on close inspection, one ought to consider José Saramago Latino for the purposes of this book.

In his illuminating historical cultural study of American Christology, *American Jesus: How the Son of God became a National Icon*, Stephen Prophero readily confesses at the outset that he is willfully neglecting the Hispanic Jesus. He reasons that there are so many expressions of the American Jesus that "one book cannot obviously cover them all. So this project is by necessity selective and by

admission idiosyncratic" (Prophero 2004, 14). He offers no justification for omit-
ting the Latino Christ specifically. What criteria of selection could dispose of the
Hispanic Jesus? Spanish missionaries evangelized Pueblo Indians with the help of
the Crucifix before Cotton Mather proclaimed America the new Israel. New Mexican Spanish settlers irrigated farms in the desert Southwest before the first Anglos
tasted maize and smelled roast turkey. Spanish holds the distinction of the first
European language established in this country.

Richard Wightman Fox addressed the significance of Jesus in American culture in a book entitled *Jesus in America: A History*. His wide-ranging and historically comprehensive study begins with the first settlers and continues into the
twentieth century. Fox, unlike Prophero, begins his chronological study with the
Spanish Catholic Jesus of the sixteenth and seventeenth centuries in the context of
the Spanish/Native American encounter and the subsequent evangelizing and
missionary efforts of religious orders in the Southwest. After this promising beginning, the narrative quickly shifts to the New England Puritans and the historical
development of Anglo and, to some extent, black Christianity. The Hispanic Jesus
fades from American history just as American history marginalizes Hispanics
from national concerns.

Latina/o theology commits the error of paying scant attention to its cultural
expressions of Christ. An eight-page chapter is devoted to *Jesus* in Aponte and de
la Torre's *Handbook of Latina/o Theologies*. After providing a summary of Latina/o
treatments of Christ, Michelle González concludes this article by claiming that
Latina/o Christologies are in need of critical development (González 2006, 22).
Nestor Medina's book, *Mestizaje: Remapping Race, Culture, and Faith in Latina/o
Catholicism* (2009), dedicates five chapters to Latino Catholicism; not one of them
deals with Jesus/Christ.[1] Ada María Isasi-Díaz and Fernando F. Segovia's collection of theological essays, *Hispanic/Latino Theology: Challenge and Promise* (1996),
examines the sources, theological locus, and expression of Hispanic/Latino theology. Not a single chapter commits an extensive study to the theme of Jesus/Christ.
Arturo J. Bañuelos's *Mestizo Christianity: Theology from the Latin Perspective* (1995)
brings together essays by leading Latina/o theologians on methodology, popular
religiosity, Latina voices, social ethics, and spirituality. Again, there is no chapter
devoted exclusively to a study of Jesus/Christ.

This book attempts to fill a glaring lacuna overlooked for unknown reasons.

---

1 A right slash separating the two names *Jesus* and *Christ* indicates that *Jesus* refers to the
historical Jew of flesh and bone who lived in the first century CE and that *Christ* refers to
all the imaginary constructions about the significance and identity of Jesus, including
those of the New Testament.

Standard theological texts about Christ and culture take scant notice of Hispanic/
Latina/o Christologies. On the other hand, Latina/o theologians fail to deal extensively with a Latina/o Christology. Both sides generally approach the idea of Christ
traditionally. By contrast, this book is a study of unconventional cultural expressions of Christ in Latina/o art and literature.

This work regards theology and philosophy as types of literature. On one level,
well-written theological and philosophical texts are literary in terms of style, deliv-
ery, originality, creativity, and thought-provoking content that makes a reader not
only think, but feel. On another level, theology and philosophy, generally, are
forms of fiction, largely products of a fertile human imagination of the way the
world could be—just like literature. This is probably truer of theology than of
philosophy because theology deals with the supernatural imaginary. Philosophy,
too, trades in the imaginary with its discourse on possible worlds and the use of
indefinable words like *existence*, *being*, and *reality*. Experimenting with a dizzying
array of logic, philosophers spin new worlds and weave elegant, sophisticated fab-
rics by which they clothe semantic meaning, express ontological designs about
abstract objects, represent slippery ethical principles, and tailor fashions in aesthetics and socio-political thinking. As literature, philosophy and theology yield
an interesting array of stories, plots, and images of ways the world might be.

Thinking about unconventional images of Christ in Hispanic/Latina/o culture, certain historically important figures—Spanish, Latin American, and US
Hispanic—stand out because of the unconventional and provocative nature of
their respective representations of Christ. Among them are Salvador Dalí's nuclear
mystical Christ, Orozco's Christ chopping down his own cross, Miguel de Unamuno's Quixote-Christ, Jorge Luis Borges's fictional Christ in fantastic short stories, Richard Rojas's secular humanistic Christ, and Latin American liberation
theology's Christ the Liberator. US Latina/o contributions to unconventional
images include the mestizo Christ and Chicana feminist substitution of the Aztec
goddess Coatlicue for the Catholic Christ. Andres Serrano's controversial photo,
Piss Christ, certainly counts as unconventional, but because of its highly scandalous and potentially offensive nature does not receive extensive treatment in this
book. Anthropological, folkloric, historical, and sociological studies of various
aspects of popular religion give ample treatment to particular images of Christ in
churches, chapels, domestic altars, pilgrimage sites, and so on. Interesting as these
studies may be, the focus of this book is largely on the works of Latina/o writers of
international repute—artists and writers who have seen what others could not and
have made visible what is invisible to the vast majority.

More specifically, this book focuses on outliers in art, literature, and theology.

"Outliers" refers to the artists, poets, writers, and theologians whose work stands out from the conventional, the everyday, and the traditional. Outliers stretch our imagination, test our credulity, probe the limits of our sensibilities, open our eyes to see what has not been seen or what we do not want to see. Among the outliers in this book, as I mentioned, are some of the most brilliant stars in the Spanish and Latin American firmament: the Spanish painter Salvador Dalí, Mexican muralist José Clemente Orozco, the Argentine writer Jorge Luis Borges, the Spanish existentialist Miguel de Unamuno, the Brazilian theologian Leonardo Boff, and the Mexican philosopher José Vasconcelos. Among these stars are others of lesser luminosity whose twinkling deserves some contemplation and reflection in both senses of the term. These include New Mexican author, painter, and priest Fray Angélico Chávez; Argentine writer, historian, and political leader Ricardo Rojas, who authored the spiritual classic *The Invisible Christ*; Mexican-American theologian Virgilio Elizondo; and Chicana feminist, poet, and writer Gloria Anzaldúa, author of the Chicana classic, *Borderlands/La Frontera*.

In no way does this book purport to deal with representative Spanish, Latin American, and Hispanic/Latina/o writers and artists. The manner in which gifted artists and writers imagine Christ is worthy of consideration for its own sake, apart from any consideration of their status as cultural representatives. Artists, writers, philosophers, and theologians and their work featured in this book are not representatives of the Latina/o/Hispanic world but exemplifiers who project some of the disparate values of their polyvalent cultural life forms.

While this book is not intended as a theological work, historical theology and modern biblical scholarship will shed light on theological and biblical references that appear in the work of the writers and artists under discussion. Art, philosophy, aesthetics, philosophy of religion, and hermeneutics play important roles alongside historical theology in informing description, interpretation, and evaluation of content. Generally, a quasi-historical materialism provides a loose framework for understanding society and history.

For the purposes of this work, two regulative ideas apply methodologically to construct a heuristic framework for interpretation. First, representations of Jesus/Christ result from projections of human self-understanding. Second, images of Jesus/Christ express some ideal or idea.

Concerning the first assumption, Jaroslav Pelikan's thesis in his book *Jesus through the Centuries* asserts that images of Christ in art are reflections of human self-understanding. Freud articulated this idea in his theory about the origins of religion in *The Future of an Illusion*. In effect, Freud hypothesized that the idea of God originates in the childhood need for the father to protect and provide. In adulthood, people still have these needs, but only a more powerful father figure can fulfill them, and thus people project their wishful needs or fantasies on a heavenly screen, creating "Our Father which art in heaven." Freud, however, did not originate this idea; he derived it from the German Hegelian philosopher Ludwig Feuerbach's book *The Essence of Christianity*. Feuerbach argues that the idea of God is simply the projection of the idea of man stripped of defects and shortcomings and endowed with unlimited powers. Whether or not these atheistic statements of the psychological origins of the idea of God are true is not a burden of this book. What matters here is the recognition that ideas of God and Christ and other religious figures mirror psychological projections of human needs, desires, concerns, anxieties, values, ideals, self-understanding, hopes, and material conditions of life. Therefore, representations of Christ in art, literature, and theology are projections of human self-understanding and thus offer insight into an artist's cares, concerns, anxieties, desires, hopes, fears, ideals, and values as well as those of his or her culture and times. From another angle, these images as perceived by others in all times and places reflect the psychology and culture of the percipients—those doing the seeing, reading, and hearing.

Regarding the second regulative idea, that images of Christ represent some idea, José Clemente Orozco once said that art always begins with an idea: "In every painting, as in any other work of art, there is always an IDEA, never a story. The ideas are the point of departure, the first cause of the plastic construction, and it is present all the time as energy-creating matter" (Elliott 1980, 59). Orozco could mean that an idea is the initial spark for a painting. Alternatively, he may intend to convey the concept that the real content of a work of art is an idea. There is no contradiction between these alternative meanings. Emphasis falls on the latter. The term *idea* is ambiguous and can mean thought, concept, plan, ideal, form, pattern, and so on. An idea is a concept or thought about some object, material or abstract. Thus, an idea is a representation of some object (object is used here in a broad sense to include things, persons, and events). To say that art represents an idea seems redundant. Art, at least art about religious figures, represents some idea, symbolizes something. Art represents, expresses exemplifies, or shows an idea about some object. Art represents an idea through a material medium—painting, sculpture, literature, music, and so on.

An idea defined in this way appears subjective and private, whereas art appears objective and public. Idea and art appear incommensurable; However, it is only in appearance. Metaphorically, art is the outer and idea is the inner, or to put it another way, art manifests the idea by making the idea perceptible. Before art takes material form, it exists conceptually in the mind of the artist. The idea of art, a conceptual entity, can be expressed propositionally. One may object that art represents by providing an image of some object—a mountain, a cloud, an animal, a plant, a human being, and so forth. Art represents or expresses an idea about some object through sight, touch, or hearing. In doing so, the idea gives the why, the wherefore, and the finality of the art. Moreover, with every artistic idea there is an accompanying feeling. Dalí's *Christ of St. John of the Cross* conveys the idea of unity of spirit and matter, and emanates beauty. Orozco's New School mural *Future Homecoming of the Worker* evokes a sense of hopefulness.

Some theories of art deny the validity of the representation theory. Instead of representation, they claim that art affords viewers a particular kind of aesthetic experience depending on the kind of image under consideration. Art, then, is not about representation but about a certain type of experience. Several critical questions come to mind. Whose experience? Does the mere viewing or contemplation of art stimulate an experience like the experience the artist undergoes while creating? Are the aesthetic experiences of all percipients of a work of art similar in quality? The answers to these questions appear subjective and are probably limited to first-person reports. Problematically, these kinds of reports are unreliable and at best can only provide knowledge of a report and not of an experience. Whose experience is paramount in evaluating the quality of the aesthetic experience, the artist's or the viewer's? Frankly, each person has privileged access only to his or her own subjective experience. Moreover, the ability to make sense of that experience depends on levels of competence in art appreciation, knowledge about art history, degree of sensitivity to the nuances of the aesthetic qualities of experience, depth of self-understanding, and understanding of one's formative context.

A formalist will object that the work of art stands alone and represents nothing external to it. Of course, this is a valid angle to take. To consider a work of art on its own merits, disregarding everything extraneous to the immediate form of the object, may possess intrinsic value. Objectively, artworks stand alone whether in display at a private home, museum, gallery, wall, cupola, or vault. Each work is ontologically independent, existing in its own world independent of environment. Being on loan for special exhibits in other cities or countries does not affect the ontological status of an aesthetic object. A work of art may be reproduced and appear as a poster, an illustration for a flyer, as an image on a T-shirt, or as an illustration in a book. Still the aesthetic object stands independent of any form of reproduction or type of location.

However, a work of art does not appear spontaneously in a vacuum. It is the product of human hands made in the circumstances of a particular community and at a specific time in history. In addition, an artistic creation is the crystallization of human creativity at a specific moment in the life of the artist and in the evolution of humanity at different developmental and evolutionary stages of life. From this perspective, then, a work of art reflects the values, cares, concerns, anxieties, ideologies, and self-understanding of the human individual, community, and culture of a particular socio-historical context. Collectively these make up the conditions both necessary and sufficient for the possibility of projection, externalization, objectification, representation, expression, interpretation, analysis, and evaluation.

Settling on representation or expression narrows the scope and sharpens the focus on whatever idea a particular representation is conveying. To the extent that art represents an idea, art is symbolic. This is particularly true of religious art or art featuring symbols drawn from religion or mythology. In this book, our concern is with the symbolic meaning of representations of Christ, the idea represented by Christ as a symbol in art, literature, and theology. Representations of Christ are symbols, and symbols convey meanings. One mistaken view is that pictures represent by resemblance or similarity. A picture represents an object by resembling it. More specifically, in this context, resemblance takes place when the form and figure of the picture looks like or calls to mind the original. A picture, one may say, captures the look of the object. At the most superficial level, this is what pictorial representation means. Thus, a painting of Jesus giving the Sermon on the Mount represents that moment by resembling Jesus giving the Sermon on the Mount. However, consider Matthias Grünewald's *Resurrection of Christ* in the Isenheim altarpiece or William Blake's watercolor, *Christ's Resurrection*. There is a remarkable likeness between the two images. How can we determine that they resemble the Resurrection of Christ, either fictionally or historically? Most people would be surprised to learn that there is no account of the Resurrection in the Gospels. Necessarily, artists' representations of the Resurrection are entirely imaginary. Even if a fictional or historical account of the Resurrection existed, this would still be the case. However picturesque or inspirational, an imaginary creation like a painting is the visual representation of an idea. To suggest that the idea simply conveys the belief that Christ rose from the dead is too facile and superficial. The representation must be about something other than what the image is ostensibly about; otherwise, the representation is self-referential. Not every representational art symbolizes an idea, but artistic renderings of religious figures do by the very nature of their function.

Religious symbols, moreover, are notoriously multivalent. The ambiguity of religious symbols raises problems of interpretation similar to the philosophical problem of the indeterminacy of translation. Interpretations are multiply realizable partly because meanings depend on context. Controversies about two recent works of art will serve as examples of mutivalency, ambiguity, and indeterminacy of translation.

On July 10, 2015, Bolivian President Evo Morales presented Pope Francis with a replica of a wooden sculpture originally carved by Bolivian artist and Jesuit priest Luis Espinal featuring Christ crucified on a hammer and sickle. Some people condemned the gift saying that it represented an attempt to manipulate God. Jerry Ryan, writing for *Commonweal*, a Catholic periodical, felt offended by the gesture, calling it "clumsy and controversial." For him, the gesture implied that Espinal, a champion of democracy, was a Marxist priest, a label Ryan could not countenance. Ryan claims that when questioned about the gift, Pope Francis responded that the world brands as Marxists those who live by the Beatitudes; it is not surprising that the powerful would have crucified Christ as a Marxist. Ryan accepted the justice of the Pope's remarks (Ryan 2015).

Consider the example of Andres Serrano's controversial photo, *Piss Christ* (1986). The glossy photo shows a plastic crucifix attached to a wooden cross submerged in liquid that looks like urine. Some reports state that Serrano claimed that the amber liquid is his urine. Serrano submerged objects in milk, blood, and urine to obtain certain effects in his photography. First exhibited in 1986 at the Stux Gallery, the photo first drew negative national attention when exhibited at the Southeastern Center for Contemporary Art in 1989. Conservative US senators, on learning that the National Endowment for the Arts awarded money to Serrano for his 1989 exhibit, demanded cutting funding to the NEA. Senator Helms denounced Serrano as an artist, calling him a jerk. Senator D'Amato tore up a print copy of the photo on the floor of the US Senate. New York Representative Michael Grimm called on President Obama to denounce the blasphemous image exhibited in New York in 2012 (Starnes 2012).

In "NEA's Cloudy Future," Jennifer Johnson says that the mass media is misleading the public about Serrano's work and its relation to the NEA. She writes, "Most of what you think you know about Andres Serrano and his now infamous photograph 'Piss Christ,' for example, is probably false" (Johnson 2013). Serrano, contrary to widespread misunderstanding, did not intend to make an offensive statement about Christ or Christianity. His work descries the cheapening and commercialization of Christianity in the modern era. In an interview published in the *Huffington Post*, when asked about the controversial photo, Serrano said that the crucifix is a symbol that has lost its true meaning: the horror of what a man endured, tortured, nailed to a cross, shed his blood, and probably other bodily fluids. If people are offended, they are probably getting closer to the true meaning of the cross. Serrano identifies himself as a Christian artist and his work stands in relationship with his faith (Okafor 2014).

As these two examples demonstrate, a depiction of Christ, whether a wood carving of Christ crucified on a hammer and sickle, or a photo of a plastic crucifix submerged in urine, can elicit contrary and oppositional feelings as well as inspire conflicting interpretations. These examples serve as a cautionary note warning us not to jump to conclusions about any given interpretation or to accept any particular feelings as those the work of evokes. A work of art in itself may appear without life and static; however, in interaction with human beings in varying contexts, artworks are dynamic and socially living entities.

Religious depictions of Christ, whatever the content, convey some essential idea about Christ. What is this essential idea? The body of Jesus or the humanity of Jesus is the principal clue. Assuming that personality is the expressive essence of a human being, then it follows that the meaning behind the symbol is personality. Different artists treat different aspects of the human personality exemplified in the images of Jesus.

In the history of Christian art, images of Christ typically depict a young human male, bearded or clean-shaven, longhaired or short, blond or dark-haired, and so on. Early Christians resorted to nonhuman images—fish, anchor, lamb, cross—to represent Christ or the Christian faith. However, the most enduring, emotional, memorable, and sympathetic images of Christ are those of the body of Jesus. Every stage of Jesus' life yields a different Christ—the child Christ appears in the mythology of the Spanish world as the Santo Niño de Atocha. The tragic figure at the trial of Pontius Pilate, the *Ecce Homo*, in Latin America and the American Southwest takes on the form of Jesús Nazareno, the Nazarene. Of course, the most popular representation of Christ throughout the Spanish-speaking world is *Cristo crucificado*, the crucified Christ. People venerate Christ's dead corpse, the recumbent Christ, an image that Miguel de Unamuno found repulsive. Representations of Christ carved in wood, painted on canvases or the hoods of low-rider cars, inked as tattoos on shoulders, chests, and backs. Prisoners draw detailed images of Christ, preferably with a crown of thorns, with black ink on *paños* (handkerchiefs). Images appear on cheap plastic molds, prints, posters, and, occasionally, by some purported miracle, on tree trunks struck by lightning, rock formations, tortillas, ribs, and other food items. Consider, then, the human body or the image of the human body as a symbol of the spiritual, as incongruous as it sounds. The human body is also a symbol, a field of representation, "a veil that covers that which is beyond all forms" (Rojas 1929, 47).

Taking humanity as a clue to uncovering the meaning of the representations of

Christ leads to a methodological question that serves as the basis for a heuristic principle of interpretation. Do representations of Christ summon a universal concept of humanity or evoke a particular vision of humanity? Imagine a scale running between two ends. One end stands for universal humanity, the other end signals a particular instance of humanity, for example, an individual, an ethnic group, or a nation, and so on. Representations of Christ can swing between these two ends. One objective, then, is to determine the degree of universality or particularity of the symbolism of humanity represented by a particular artistic or literary image of Christ.

This book explores Iberian, Latin American, and US Hispanic representations of Christ, in short, the "Latino Christ." The choice of the appellation *Latino* is stipulatory for the purposes of this book. This book begins with a chapter on Salvador Dalí. Four of the main works from Dalí's nuclear mystical period discussed in this book include the two versions of *The Madonna of Port Lligat* (1949, 1950), the *Christ of St. John of the Cross* (1951), and *Crucifixion* (*Corpus Hypercubus*) (1954). Early in his childhood, Dalí displayed an avid interest and prodigious talent in drawing and painting. By 1929, influenced by Joan Miró, René Magritte, and others Dalí began his foray into surrealism. André Breton, leader of the surrealist movement in Paris, welcomed Dalí into the fold, recognizing in him a fellow traveler in the world of art and ideas. Hostilities later tore them apart. For one, Dalí's overblown ego drove him to unseat Breton as the leader of the surrealists.

Sigmund Freud tremendously influenced Dalí. From Freud's oneirological work, *Interpretation of Dreams*, Dalí discovered the unconscious to be a rich trove of normally inaccessible truths about hidden beliefs, desires, fears, and insecurities that function as the principal motivators of human action. Not only that, but also the dream and myth (considered a collective dream), become conduits of spiritual truth bridging the distance between rationality and irrationality, offering fruitful and bizarre sources for art. Influenced by Freud and Jacques Lacan, Dalí developed a method he called the paranoid-critical method that characterized his surrealist paintings, drawings, writings, and so-called art objects. The basic purpose of the method aimed at giving familiar objects unfamiliar meaning using double images, dreamscapes, myth, sexuality, and so on.

News of the atomic explosions at Hiroshima and Nagasaki shocked Dalí and transformed his thinking and sensibility about art and his role as an artist. Discovery of the nature of the atom and the subatomic world convinced Dalí of the correctness of his intuitions about the spiritual nature of matter and the substantial nature of spirituality. His metaphysics affirmed neither idealism nor materialism but affirmed a *tertium quid*, the unity of spiritual and material reality. To convey to the world his new understanding of reality, Dalí integrated his paranoid-critical method with his basic knowledge of quantum physics, and with a Spanish Catholic type of mysticism, and chose as his painterly method the classical technique in painting already foreshadowed early in his career. The overall result is the nuclear mystical style exemplified in his paintings between 1945 and 1955. During this period, the image of Christ functions as the center of gravity for his new vision as represented in *The Madonna of Port Lligat, Christ of St. John of the Cross*, and *Crucifixion (Corpus Hypercubus)*. Dalí's image of Christ expresses complexity of semantic content connoting mystical, metaphysical, and psychological ideas.

A Franciscan priest from Santa Fe, New Mexico, Fray Angélico Chávez, wrote a poem, "The Virgin of Port Lligat" (1955) as an ode to Dalí's 1950 *Madonna of Port Lligat*. Chávez envisioned his poem as part of a duet accompanying Dalí's painting. Taking up Dalí's metaphysics of a unitary reality—spiritualized matter and materialized spirit—Chávez attempts to domesticate Dalí's painting by rehabilitating its meaning in light of traditional Catholic dogma about the virgin birth and the incarnation. Chávez frames the structure and the semantics of his poem with a sort of template consisting of three superimposed images, Dalí's *Madonna of Port Lligat*, the Sphinx's riddle, and the atomic and astronomical description of the world. In short, the infant Christ, the poem's center of gravity, the fusion of the Cosmic *Logos* and the molecules of the Virgin, emerges from the Virgin's womb, a mystic portal, as the answer to the Sphinx's riddle. In the end, Chávez, despite his glorification of the unity of the spiritual and the material, tends toward the spiritualization of Christ in his interpretation of the Song of Mary or *Magnificat* with which he closes the poem. He interprets the last words of the poem, "He gives the hungry good things," as referring to the Eucharist, the central sacrament of the Catholic Church. Chávez's beautiful verse misses Dalí's idea and, thus his poem is more of a duel with Dalí than a duet.

The Mexican muralist José Clemente Orozco largely treats the Christ motif more obliquely than Dalí and Chávez, but his style is expressionist. The third chapter explores the murals of Orozco, primarily focusing on the murals painted in Mexico at the Escuela Nacional Preparatoria, and the US murals at Pomona College, the New School in Manhattan, and at Baker Library at Dartmouth College. Of particular interest is the last panel at Baker Library, *Modern Migration of Spirit*, showing an eschatological Christ as Creator-Destroyer, already instantiated in his Prometheus mural at Pomona College, and in the figure of Quetzalcoatl, who occupies two panels in the pre-Columbian series of the west side of the north wall at Baker Library. The significance of this theme expresses Orozco's pessimistic attitude toward the possibility of humankind's salvation and redemption and conveys an elitist understanding of the mass/elite dialectic.

From Orozco's pessimism, the discussion shifts to the paradoxically optimistic yet tragic yearning for eternal salvation that haunted Spanish existentialist writer Miguel de Unamuno. Throughout his life, Unamuno struggled to reconcile the tension between his religious beliefs and rational skepticism. Finding no satisfactory solution, he resolves to live pragmatically as if his beliefs were true, in order to make them true. In this chapter, the focus is on the unfolding of the vitally practical theme of living faith as if it were true. This theme is explored in his modern existential classic *The Tragic Sense of Life*; an essay to a friend titled "Mi religión"; the Pascal-inspired *The Agony of Christianity*; and his disconcerting novella, *San Manuel the Good, Martyr*; and brief references to his other works, like the poem "El Cristo de Velásquez," which glorifies the dying but not dead Christ.

Unamuno deeply longed for personal immortality, but his intellect refused him license to believe in it. Reason undermined his faith. Thus, he resolved to live with this inner contradiction, to resign to the agonistic struggle between his head and his heart. Given his intellectual and emotional travail, it is no wonder that he sees Don Quixote as the paradigm of the Spanish Christ.

Jorge Luis Borges, the subject of the next chapter, unlike Unamuno, is not desirous of immortality; in fact, the very idea of living an unending life strikes fear in him. He does not see Christ as an immortalizer. He does not look upon Christ with the eyes of faith, but the Christ-figure, as a rhetorical figure in the Western literary imagination, sufficed to inspire two short stories that deliver shocks to the nervous systems of Christian believers. In "Three Versions of Judas" (1944), the narrator explores the attempts of a fictive theologian to correct the role of Judas Iscariot in salvation history. "The Gospel According to Mark" (1970) parallels Christ's passion in the Argentine Pampas, where a young man from Buenos Aires meets an unexpected fate at the hands of backward and illiterate ranch hands. Since Borges treats philosophical and theological literature as fiction, it follows for him that Christ is a fictional figure whose variations are almost endless.

Next, a little known spiritual classic, *The Invisible Christ*, written by Argentine historian and political leader Ricardo Rojas, takes the form of a dialogue between the author and an unnamed provincial bishop. The dialogue begins with the observation of the thematic difference between and European representations of the Trinity in art. The author deftly moves the conversation from the absence of an official image of Christ and the plasticity in the representation of Christ in the history of Western religious art, to the question about these images intend to represent. At the end of the short dialogue, the author surprises with a bold and simple message about the key to universal liberation.

Latin American theologians since the 1970s have struggled to construct a viable image of Christ the liberator as key to a genuine Latin American Christology, one that would be relevant to Latin Americans and express an authentic Latin American being. To do so, they take the historical Jesus as the point of departure for getting at an accurate biography as the basis for a Christology. Curiously, even though they turn to the historical Jesus to avoid the pitfalls of abstract conceptualization of Christ, they end up with fantastic conceptions of Christ. Along the way, we will examine a critical problem in theology, philosophy, and literature—the problem of hermeneutics. Hermeneutics is the art and science of the interpretation of historical texts, especially ancient ones. How can readers in the twenty-first century with a rationalistic outlook and scientific worldview understand the views of ancients writing from a pre-scientific perspective? The problem of hermeneutics suggests that no definite profile of the historical Jesus is forthcoming.

The final chapter examines the concept of the mestizo Christ constructed by the Mexican American priest Virgilio Elizondo, inspired by José Vasconcelos's classic, *The Cosmic Race*. Vasconcelos envisioned Latin America as the birthplace of a new race, the mestizos, the hybrid offspring of Spaniards and Native Americans. He writes that the mestizos are the forerunners of a cosmic race who would recapitulate the best biological, cultural, and spiritual traits of all the races and usher in a utopian age whose ruling principles would be love and beauty. *Mestizaje* is the process of interracial marriage, hybridity, and synthesis that brings about the new race. Chicana and Chicano writers have appropriated this concept to construct an authentic and meaningfully appropriate ethnic identity. In her modern classic, *Borderlands/La Frontera*, Gloria Anzaldúa traces the dynamics of mestizo consciousness that takes its point of departure not in the mestizo Christ but in the chthonic deities of the Aztecs.

Completing the final chapter, an excursus focuses on the philosophical debate on Hispanic/Latino identity by the US Hispanic philosophers Jorge Gracia and Linda Martin Alcoff. For Gracia, the 1492 encounter between Spain and America sets in motion a chain of historical events that collectively supply the factor unifying Hispanic Americans, thus accounting for their ethnic identity and his preference for the ethnic name *Hispanic* over *Latino*. Alcoff disagrees with Gracia and dates the origins of Hispanics/Latina/os in the 1898 Spanish–American War. She also argues that *Latino* is a better name than *Hispanic* because it has more political resonance and epistemic value.

CHAPTER ONE

Salvador Dalí

Nuclear Mystical Christ

R eading about the nuclear explosion in Hiroshima on August 6, 1945, Salvador Dalí was shaken to the core, not so much for the unimaginable scale of the horror and exponential number of deaths, but for the revelatory power issuing from unlocking the hidden laws of nature in the disintegration of the atom, revealing the "spiritualization" of matter. Dalí struggled to draw a line of demarcation between the rational and the irrational until, for the first time, he saw a transformative vision revealed as if he were an eighth-century Hebrew prophet, in his case a revelation of the ultimate and substantial unity of the spiritual and the material. From this mystical theopoetic vision, he created a style of art that integrated the classical techniques of Renaissance oil painting, rigorous draftsmanship, paranoiac criticism, Spanish Catholic mysticism, and the spirituality of the material world thanks to the atomic structure of matter uncovered by nuclear physics—nuclear mysticism. During this phase of his artistic development, in the late 40s and 50s, Dalí painted some of his most beautiful religious paintings, most notably *The Madonna of Port Lligat*, *Christ of St. John of the Cross*, and *Crucifixion (Corpus Hypercubus)*, among others.

A brief overview of Dalí's life and works up to the nuclear mystical period of 1948–1955 will prove enlightening to an exploration of the aforementioned works. Focus will fall on Dalí's search for a painterly identity in his youth, his uneasy tension with André Breton, leader of the surrealist movement, over the rational and irrational in art, and the basic features of the paranoiac critical method developed during his surrealist period.

Salvador Dalí i Domènech was born May 11, 1904, in Figueras, Catalonia. As a precocious child he showed an avid interest and gave evident promise as an artist. Ramon Pitchot, an impressionist artist and friend of Pablo Picasso, took the promising artist under his wing and introduced him to impressionist painting. Pepito Pichot, also a family friend, persuaded Dalí's father to allow his son to take drawing lessons from Professor Juan Nuñez at the Municipal School of Drawing in

Figueras. At an early age, Dalí found inspiration in the artists Diego Velásquez, Francisco Goya, El Greco, Albrecht Dürer, Leonardo da Vinci, and Michelangelo. Through his admiration for them, he developed an ardent enthusiasm and life-long appreciation for the classical methods in painting, which he would revive and practice during his nuclear mystical period.

Dalí's father, a lawyer and a free thinker, kept a well-stocked library where Dalí read and studied philosophy. Dalí recalls reading Voltaire and Nietzsche. Reading Voltaire's *Philosophical Dictionary* gave him a dull feeling. Nietzsche, by contrast, awakened him from his spiritual malaise. Nietzsche's quick-witted barbs and athe-istic denunciations moved Dalí to doubt his schoolteacher's claim that God did not exist: "My first dose of Nietzsche shocked me profoundly. In black and white, he had had the audacity to affirm: 'God is dead!' What? I had just learned that God did not exist, and now someone informed me that he had died. My first doubts were born" (Dalí 1986, 7).Whatever doubts Dalí had about God's existence vanished by the time of his nuclear mystical period. For, he goes on to say, "It is true that Nietzsche, instead of driving me further into atheism, initiated me into the questions and doubts of pre-mystical inspiration, which was to reach its glori-ous culmination in 1951 when I drew up my Manifesto . . . Nietzsche awoke in me the idea of God" (Dalí 1986, 8).

Surprisingly, Dalí's middle-class father did not discourage his son's artistic aspirations. His father's intuitive belief in his son's artistic potential trumped his paternal doubts and allowed his son to matriculate at the Fine Arts Academy of Madrid in September 1921. There the young Dalí soon joined a radical group of students, including the poet Federico García Lorca and the future filmmaker Luis Buñuel—an ultraist (anti-modernist) group influenced by Dadaism.

The twentieth century had opened with great optimism about civilization and exuberant hope in real human progress, but the violence, chaos, massive death, and destruction wrought by the Great War dashed the high expectations. The first war fought with extensive modern technology revealed the dark side of reason. Betrayed by rationality, Dadaists gave iconoclastic vent to deepening alienation, inspiring unconventional modes of art like surrealism. The fashions of art inspired by Dadaism influenced the remarkable personalities of Federico García Lorca and Luis Buñuel as well as Dalí.

With Buñuel, Dalí co-produced the first surrealist film, *Un Chien Andalou*, remembered for its horrific opening scene showing a girl's eye sliced by a sharp razor. Dalí and Buñuel set out to create an antisymbolist film, boasting that noth-ing in the film is symbolic.

Along the way, Dalí picked up futurist and cubist influences from André

Derain, Paul Cézanne, Pablo Picasso, and Georges Braque. Dalí, like many of his contemporaries, tried his hand at Cubism, producing his cubist *Purist Still Life* (1924), *Self-portrait* (1926), and *Venus and Sailor* (1926). A student walkout blamed on him in 1923, resulted in Dalí's suspension from the academy. Coincidentally, in Mexico a few years earlier, José Clemente Orozco also participated in a student strike, walking out of the Art Academy of San Carlos, showing a spiritual kinship between the two, probably owing to the crisis in art education. Later Dalí took part in anarchist activism directed against General Primo de Rivera, which led to the artist's arrest and incarceration. By the time of his final expulsion from the academy, Dalí had assured himself of a promising career as an artist with his student and mixed exhibitions and a notable 1925 one-man show in the Dalmau Gallery in Barcelona. The latter exhibition won Dalí positive critical reviews especially for his *Girl Standing at the Window*. Picasso, in particular, admired Dalí's painting *Girl Seated Seen from the Rear*. Also exhibited at the Dalmau show were Dalí's pencil drawing, *Portraits of the Artist's Father and Sister* (inspired by the drawing techniques of the French artist Ingres) and the cubist painting, *Venus and Sailor*. Exhibiting different styles from neoclassical to Cubism, Dalí's paintings show an enthusiastic artist exploring, experimenting, and searching for a painterly identity.

Most people are unaware that Dalí was a prolific writer as well as a painter. He published regularly in the monthly issue of *L'Amic de les Arts*, a habit carried on well after he joined the surrealist movement in 1929. Dalí also published in Lorca's review, *Gallo*, which in April 1928 published the Catalan *Anti-Artistic Manifesto* promoting the conceptual viewpoints of Dadaism, futurism, and ultraism and criticizing Catalan art for its lack of modernity (Ades 1982, 41). Dalí authored several autobiographical books including the controversial *The Secret Life of Salvador Dalí*, translated into English and published in 1942, the reading of which led George Orwell to condemn it; *Diary of a Genius* (1965); and *The Unspeakable Confessions of Salvador Dalí* (1976). An enthusiastic writer, Dalí produced essays, poetry, manifestos, and lectures on a wide variety of themes: philosophy, architecture, poems, paintings, photography, film, music, surrealism, sex, love, memory, dreams, paranoid-criticism, and nuclear mysticism. Dalí also experimented with surrealist art objects, the most memorable of which is probably his "Lobster Telephone." Of his writings the following titles are noteworthy: "The Conquest of the Irrational" (1935), "The Tragic Myth of Millet's *L'Angelus*: Paranoid-Critical Interpretation" (1963), "50 Secrets of Magic Craftsmanship" (1948), and "Mystical Manifesto" (1951).

At the 1929 exhibition at the Galerie Goemans in Paris, Dalí's *The Sacred Heart* provoked barbed criticism and offended certain religious sensibilities, including that of his father. In *La gaceta literaria*, Eugenio d'Ors reacted in disgust to Dalí's "impure" art, referring specifically to the drawing. The graffiti-like picture shows a black outline of Christ raising his right hand in benediction, a halo circumscribes his head, and in the center of his chest, a crown of thorns topped by a cross rings a faint outline of a heart. In French cursive script across the image, Dalí wrote, "Sometimes I spit with pleasure on the portrait of my mother." Two different interpretations come readily to critics. First, Dalí is saying that he takes pleasure at spitting on his mother's portrait. The second interpretation scandalizes Christians because it attributes the words to Jesus speaking about his own mother. Dalí's father, offended that the young painter directed such words to his dead mother, disowned him. Later when Dalí painted the beautiful *Christ of St. John of the Cross*, he may have done so out of regret for his earlier scandalous painting *Sacred Heart* (Fanés 2007, 154–55).

In other respects, too, 1929 was a fateful year for Dalí. The last issue of the surrealist journal, *La Revolution Surrealiste*, reproduced two of Dalí's paintings, *Accommodations of Desire* and *Illumined Pleasures*. The most provocative painting of this period was the *Dismal Sport* (*Le Jeu Lugubre*) whose scatological feature, a man wearing soiled pants, offended his friends and colleagues, especially scandalizing his soon-to-be lover, Gala. Paul Éluard, the French surrealist poet, his Russian wife Gala, René Magritte, the painter, and his wife visited Dalí in Cadaqués. The visit by prominent French surrealists in effect welcomed Dalí into the surrealist fold, but only André Breton could say who was a surrealist. Looking back, Breton said that Dalí "insinuated himself into the movement." However, more consequentially, Dalí fell in love with Gala, Éluard's wife. When Éluard left Cadaqués for Paris, Gala remained with Dalí. She later divorced Éluard and married Dalí in a civil ceremony in 1934. She became his muse, his goddess, his divine Madonna. One cannot underestimate Gala's influence on Dalí's art and life. In 1949 and 1950, he painted two versions of Gala as a Madonna with the divine infant. She was a frequent model, subject, and muse for his art.

Surrealism emerged from the same psycho-sociological matrix that made Dadaism possible, the setting free of unconscious irrational forces in response to an increasingly rationalized and mechanized world (Shanes 2010, 25). By the late 1920s surrealism entered the Spanish art scene largely because of articles about Joan Miró in *L'Amic de les Arts* (1927–1928). At the time, surrealism probably influenced Picasso. Dalí familiarized himself with other surrealist artists including Yves Tanguy, Max Ernst, André Masson and Jean Arp, and Giorgio de Chirico.

Before joining the surrealists, Dalí immersed himself in surrealist or pre-surrealist literature and discovered a deep spiritual kinship with the likes of the Marquis de Sade and the Comte de Lautréamont. When offered the opportunity, Dalí gladly illustrated Lautréamont's psychologically unsettling *Chants del Maldoror*. When he moved to Paris in 1930, Dalí effectively joined the surrealist movement championed by Breton, writer, poet, and founder of surrealism, who wrote a preface to the catalogue of Dalí's first one-man show in Paris in November 1929. The conflict in Dalí's and Breton's relationship was largely caused by authoritarian egos. Dawn Ades provides an illuminating discussion about the unraveling of their relationship, which began after 1936. At one level, the rivalry between Georges Bataille and Breton initiated the opposition between Dalí and Breton because, to the latter's consternation, Dalí identified more with Bataille and with Bataille's review *Documents* than with Breton and his journal. Bataille, in particular, rejected the antimaterialist idealism of Breton even though Breton subscribed to dialectical materialism. Dalí ultimately did not join forces with Bataille; motivated by an outsized ego and his unrestrained hubris, Dalí aspired to replace Breton as leader of the surrealist movement in Paris. Other surrealist dissidents turned away from Breton, including Joan Miró, Dalí's fellow Catalan. Breton resisted Dalí's determined and unabashed attempts to inject a dose of religion into surrealism (Ades 1982, 124).

Ades insightfully identifies three reasons for the contention between Breton and Dalí: First, Dalí was indifferent to the social and political aims of the surrealists. Second, Dalí changed his attitude toward religion, becoming more Catholic and mystical. The third and most fundamental difference lay in their opposing attitudes about the relationship between consciousness and the unconsciousness, rationality and irrationality, reality and unreality. Breton sought to reconcile the apparent contradictions between reality and the forces of imagination, dreams, and the unconscious. In particular, Breton sought to resolve the opposition between reality and dream, and out of the antithesis to create a synthesis of "surreality" in which the scope of reality is expanded to include the irrational. Dalí, by contrast, wanted to keep the rational and the irrational apart, essentially rebelling against reality in favor of the irrational (Ades 1986, 98–100).

From Dalí's rivalry with Breton and Breton's vision of surrealism emerge the essential features that define Dalí's attitude during his nuclear mystical period. More about this later. For now, consider the paranoid-critical method that he cobbled together, appropriating elements from Sigmund Freud and Jacques Lacan.

Dalí's paranoid-critical method is characteristic of his surrealistic period and continued in his nuclear mystical period. It originates with his discovery of Sigmund Freud's psychoanalytic imagery in *The Interpretation of Dreams* (1900). Dalí

read the book after its translation into Spanish in 1925. Following Freud, he takes
the dream and imagination to be central to thought. Freud argues that dreams
contain a repository of images expressing commonly repressed elements of the
human psyche that, rightly analyzed, unlock the mysterious sources of individual
and collective behavior. Jacques Lacan, a Freudian disciple associated with the
surrealists in the early 1930s, influenced Dalí's interest in paranoia as a means of
undermining the meanings of ordinary objects and familiar images. A prime
example of Dalí's paranoid-critical method is evident in his use of double images,
exemplified in his paintings, *Invisible Sleeper, Horse, Lion* (1930), *The Slave Market
with the Disappearing Bust of Voltaire* (1940), and *The Great Paranoiac* (1936).
Dreamlike settings, Freudian in inspiration, already characterized works by Chirico and Max Ernst. Ernst's *Pietà or Revolution by Night*, in particular, cast a spell
over Dalí (Ades 1982, 70).

Myths resemble dreams and function, psychoanalytically, like collective
dreams. Dalí naturally turned to myths, legends, and sagas as dreamlike irrational
sources of insight into the human condition and invested them with meanings
drawn from psychoanalysis: Narcissus, Leda and the Swan, William Tell, Abraham and Isaac, Lot's wife, and so on. For Dalí, Jesus Christ, too, functions as a
mythical figure. Appropriating the concept of myth in a Freudian manner allowed
Dalí to dissect the content of myths into two kinds: the manifest content and the
latent content. The manifest content of the dream is what the dream is about on
the apparent surface. Latent content is what the dream is really conveying at a
deeper level. For example, the manifest content of the "flying dream" is apparently
about the individual flying through the air. At the latent level, the dream may be
about the desire to be free from social constraints, laws, and conventional rules.

In particular, the themes of William Tell and Jean Millet's *L'Angelus* are fertile
sources for the application of Dalí's method of paranoid criticism as "an attempt at
'the critical and systematic objectification of delirious associations and interpretation,' drawing on his interest in psycho-analysis and demonstrating in a more general way the relationship between perception and mental states" (Ades 1982, 120).
Dalí expressed the theme of the Swiss legend William Tell many times in drawings and paintings, including *William Tell* in 1930 followed by *The Old Age of
William Tell* and *The Youth of William Tell* (1931), then the *Enigma of William Tell*
(1933). Dalí's reading of the legend of William Tell, a Swiss hunter, expert at the
crossbow, forced to save himself and his son only if he can shoot an arrow through
an apple sitting on top of his son's head, forces a tortured Freudian interpretation
involving sex. Dalí interprets the William Tell myth in an oedipal reversal wherein
the father symbolically castrates his son (Ades 1982, 89).

Another potent example of the paranoid-critical method, this time from art and not myth—although art is a kind of myth—is Dalí's employment of Jean Millet's *L'Angelus* as an ambiguous motif for exploring the theme of sexuality. Millet's *L'Angelus*, an early Dalí childhood icon, provides the grist of a sacred French trope for Dalí's ever-churning, irrepressible psychoanalytic mill. Dalí discovers in *L'Angelus* the "maternal variant of the immense and atrocious myth of Saturn, Abraham, the Eternal Father with Jesus Christ and William Tell himself, devouring their own sons" (Ades 1982,36). Many versions of *L'Angelus* materialized from Dalí's brush including *Angelus*, 1932, *Gala and the Angelus of Millet Preceding the Imminent Arrival of the Conical Anamorphosis*, 1933, *Atavism at Twilight* 1933–1934, among others.

Integrating the term "paranoia" into surrealist theory, Dalí first used the term "paranoid-critical" in 1933 in an essay entitled "*Le Surrealisme au Service de la Revolution, 'L'Ane pourri'* (the Rotten Donkey)" For Dalí, the difference between paranoia and hallucination lies in the voluntary nature of the former. Dalí believed that through paranoid criticism it would be possible to "systematize confusion and contribute to the total discreditation of the world of reality" (Dalí 1982, 121). Paranoid criticism is a delirium of interpretation in which images, ideas, events are causally related with a central ideal meaningful to the interpreter but meaningless to an outsider.

Dalí's essay "The Conquest of the Irrational" (1935), an exposition of another essay, "Latest Fashions of Intellectual Excitement for the Summer of 1934," explains the origin of the paranoid-critical method as a "spontaneous method of irrational knowledge based upon the interpretive-critical association of delirious phenomena" (Dalí 1998, 267). Common images, as mentioned earlier, have a double figuration. Behind the appearance of any object or image lurks a hidden essence, Kant's thing in itself, potentially full of rebellious representational power. Consequently, a Dalí image yields multiple simultaneous representations, showing that there are other worlds besides the one called reality. In the "Conquest of the Irrational," Dalí writes that the painterly aim "is to materialize the images of concrete irrationality with the most imperialistic furor of precision, so that the world of imagination and concrete irrationality may be of the same objective clearness . . . as that of the external world of phenomenal reality" (Dalí 1998, 265).

For the journal, *Minotaur I*, April 1933, Dalí wrote the essay "Paranoid-Critical Interpretations of the Obsessive Image of Millet's *Angelus*" and a short book, *The Tragic Myth of Millet's Angelus*, explaining his paranoid-critical method. Dalí reports that in 1962 the image of *L'Angelus* suddenly appeared to his mind "completely modified and charged with such latent intentionality" revealing itself to him as "the pictorial work that is the most disturbing, the most enigmatic, the most dense, and the richest in unconscious thoughts ever to have existed" (Dalí 1998, 283).

Dalí applies the paranoid-critical method to *L'Angelus* uncovering its latent universal message. He intentionally distorts and deliberately misinterprets obvious visual cues so that the viewer will see things that are not there, "re-reading objects or images whose meaning is conventionally accepted, in order to probe for a new, invariably surrealist and always Dalian, meaning concealed within it" (Bradley 1999, 16). Ades describes Dalí's paranoid-critical method "as the ability of the artist to perceive different images within a given configuration" (Ades 1982, 119).

Dalí's book *The Tragic Myth of Millet's Angelus* mingles fiction, autobiography, and psychoanalysis. His mythical reading of *L'Angelus* undermines the traditional Christian reading of a peasant couple quietly at prayer at the end of a day's work. He uses the paranoid-critical method to see things that are not there—more than a "secret enactment of an anguished family scenario, painted over by Millet" (Dalí 1976, 154). He recognizes in the scene an ambivalent attitude toward sex, fear of castration, the female as an agent of sex and death, her stillness a prelude to violence. Dalí looks behind the appearances of the image to find what is lurking underneath the still and silent man and woman. Dalí's sexually charged writing style describes Millet's peasant woman as "exhibitionist eroticism of a virgin in waiting" and likens her position to that of a praying mantis on the verge of fatally attacking her mate. Is the man the woman's son or husband using his hat to hide his sexual virility? Dalí, unashamed to flout society's taboos, like incest, imagines the man as the woman's son. It follows of course that for Dalí the wheelbarrow exudes erotic symbolism. He recalls a nineteenth-century American cartoon satirizing *L'Angelus*: "There is a woman holding her husband's feet in her hands and pushing him ahead like a wheel barrow, he holding a wheel between his two hands, while his rigid sex organ becoming an actual tool plows the earth and his balls appear as two cacti" (Dalí 1976, 155). As will be evident, eroticism, characteristic of the paranoid-critical method, persists in Dalí's religious paintings of the nuclear mystical period.

Civil war in Spain and Nazi aggression drove Dalí and Gala to the United States, where they stayed for the remainder of World War II. Shanes, Dalí art historian, believes that Dalí's work was richer before his move to America, noting that Dalí's pictures became banal, more rational, symbolic, and illustrative (Shanes 2010, 47–8). George Orwell criticized Dalí after reading Dalí's *Secret Life*, writing in his essay "Benefit of Clergy" (1944), "One ought to be able to hold in one's head simultaneously the two facts that Dalí is a good draughtsman and a disgusting human being" (Shanes 2010, 48).

By the time Dalí returned to Europe, Breton had expelled him from the surrealist movement, enraged by Dalí's mocking portrayal of Lenin in the painting, *The Enigma of William Tell*. Moreover, Dalí's lack of enthusiasm for Marxism and unadulterated admiration for Franco further alienated Breton (Shanes 2010, 53). In a vengeful spirit, Breton disparaged Dalí in his 1941 essay, "Artistic Genesis and Perspective of Surrealism," saying that Dalí's "ultra-retrograde technique revealed a cynic indifference and panic that he saved temporarily by vulgarization" (Breton 1965, 75–76). Franco, for his part, conferred on Dalí the distinguished Cross of Isabel the Catholic, Spain's highest honorary award for civilians, in 1964. Dalí broke decisively with Breton when the latter would not accept a mystical component to surrealism.

By 1948, Dalí's formal ties with the surrealists no longer existed. However, the paranoid-critical method that characterized his surrealistic period, by his own admission, remains central in his nuclear mystical period. The use of mythical figures continues to play a predominant role in the religious symbols of the Madonna and Jesus. Port Lligat's land- and seascape replaces the generalized flat non-descript dreamscapes of the surrealist painting. The paranoid-critical method of taking of familiar symbols and imparting to them unfamiliar aspects connect the work of the nuclear mystical period with his earlier surrealistic vision.

THE NUCLEAR MYSTICAL PERIOD

The dawning of the nuclear age, with all its sublime horror, boldly introduced its world-destroying potential in 1945, forever dangling like Damocles' sword over the collective head of an anxious humanity. Dalí personally felt its impact as a transformative force inspiring a new vision and inaugurating a new period of artistic expression for him.

> The atomic explosion of August 6, 1945, shook me seismically. Thenceforth, the atom was my favorite food for thought. Many of the landscapes painted in this period express the great fear inspired in me by the announcement of that explosion, I applied my paranoia-critical method to exploring the world. I want to see and understand the forces and hidden laws of things, obviously so as to master them. To penetrate to the heart of things, I know by intuitive genius that I have an exceptional means: mysticism, that is to say deeper

intuition of what is, immediate communication with the all, absolute vision
by grace of truth, by grace of God. Stronger than cyclotrons and cybernetic
computers, in a moment I get through to the secrets of the real, but only
facing the landscape of Port Lligat will this conviction become certainty and
my entire being catch fire with the transcendental light of that high place.
(Dalí 1976, 216)

From the Freudian inner world of the unconscious, Dalí turned to Werner
Heisenberg and the mysterious realm of quantum physics for insight into the
secret of material reality: "Besides, to me, a paroxymist possessed by imperialist
definition, there is nothing in the world that looks so sweet, pleasant, restful, and
even gracious as the transcendental irony which is supposed by Heisenberg's
principle of incertitude" (Dalí 1986, 41). Heisenberg's principle of uncertainty was
a revelation for Dalí, securing his long-held intuition that spirit is the ultimate
stuff of the universe: "If the physicists are producing anti-matter, let it be allowed
to the painters, already specialists in angels to paint it. . . . Today the exterior
world—that of physics—has transcended the one of psychology. My father today
is Dr. Heisenberg" (Dalí 1998, 366).

Dalí's ontological metaphysics describes a fundamental unity of matter and
spirit, reason and unreason, science and religion, waking and dreaming, and consciousness and unconsciousness.[2] For Dalí, nuclear science indubitably confirmed
the philosophical insights of his intellectual heroes Ramon Llull and Raymond
Sebonde. In the physics of the quantum realm, Dalí discovered the spiritualized
material for the application of his paranoid-critical method. At the same time, he
convinced himself that the only style of painting capable of adequately representing the new reality would be the Renaissance technique, an ideal method not only
for capturing cosmic unity in art, but also for reviving Spanish mysticism. With
his new tools and novel vision, he felt well equipped to battle against the crass
materialism of the age and the bad taste and technique of modern art: "It was in
this state of intense prophecy that I understood that the means of pictorial expression had been invented once and for all with maximum perfection and efficiency
during the Renaissance, and that the decadence of modern painting came from
the skepticism and lack of faith resulting from mechanistic materialism. I, Dalí,

2 By "spirit," Dalí means the traditional notion of the supernatural stuff of the universe.
To make it more palatable for the contemporary reader, "spirit" should be interpreted as a
metaphor for thought.

by restoring currency to Spanish mysticism, will prove the unity of the universe through my work by showing the spirituality of all substance" (Dalí 1976, 217).

An atomic understanding of matter, revival of the classical painting technique, and a return to Spanish mysticism complemented by the paranoid-critical method combine to form a new Dalian aesthetic style characterizing the paintings of his nuclear mystical period. From this period, four particular paintings stand out for the purposes of this work—*The Madonna of Port Lligat* (1949), *The Madonna of Port Lligat* (1950), *Christ of St. John of the Cross* (1951) and *Crucifixion (Corpus Hypercubus)* (1954).

THE MADONNA OF PORT LLIGAT, 1949

At the beginning of his nuclear mystical period, Dalí painted two images of the Madonna and Child, a recurring theme popular with the Italian renaissance artists. The first *Madonna of Port Lligat* (figure 1.1) was presented to Pope Pius IIX in 1949, and a final version was painted in 1950 and first exhibited in 1952. With respect to the first version presented to the Pope on November 23, 1949, Dalí makes it clear in one of his autobiographies that the image is that of Gala, his wife: "The box I had carried contained the effigy of Gala as the Madonna of Port Lligat, which I had shown to the sovereign pontiff" (Dalí 1986, 152). Of course, he did not explain this to the Pope. Dalí probably intended to demonstrate that he was no longer anticlerical and hoped to earn a special dispensation to marry Gala in the church. She was, after all, divorced from Paul Éluard, the surrealist poet.

On first glance, primary colors pop out of the painting, giving it a pedestrian quality, a quality one finds in poster art—Shanes calls it kitsch. Gala in the pose of the Madonna fills the center of the picture naturally, suggesting a triangular composition, a triangle within a rectangle. The form of the rectangle appears as six disconnected parts of an apse, a semicircular domed vault. Immediately, one uncomfortably notices a split from the back of her head to the top of her forehead. In one of the preparatory drawings, the Madonna's head is split wide open, an aspect that he finally minimized. The void in the Madonna's chest represents the void in an atom as Dalí understood it. Dalí forms a rectangular hole hollowed out of her chest, simultaneously conveying the impression of a window that looks out at the sea from an interior domestic scene and the immateriality of the Madonna's body. In front of and just above the portal in her chest, her hands come together in the form of prayer, but the palms face the viewer. Just below the praying hands, the seascape appears through the portal. Her arms are detached from her shoulders, suggesting the spirituality of the physical body. The infant Jesus, framed by

FIGURE 1.1   Salvador Dalí, *The Madonna of Port Lligat*, 1949. The Haggerty Museum of Art, Marquette University, © Salvador Dalí, Fundació Gala-Salvador Dalí, Artists Rights Society, New York, 2017.

the Madonna's rectangular portal, hovers above a floating pillow and casts a shadow on the Madonna's lap, hinting at solidity. Duplicating the portal in the Madonna, a smaller rectangular hole in Jesus' chest also appears as a portal within a portal through which one sees only the water of the Bay of Port Lligat. By contrast, the Madonna's portal offers a more robust vision where sky and water meet to form a small segment of the implacable horizon, a glimpse of the numinous boundary thinly separating heaven and earth.

Simulating the nontangential particles in atomic space, everything in the painting floats, defying gravity to emphasize the spiritual nature of material objects: "The floating figures and His fragmented imagery derive from his interest in nuclear physics. Fragmentation symbolizes dematerialization, disintegration, and the spiritualization of matter. Modern physics has revealed to us increasingly the dematerialization which exists in all nature and that is why the material body of my Madonna does not exist and why in place of a torso you find a tabernacle 'filled with Heaven.' But while everything floating in space denotes spirituality it also represents our concept of the atomic system—today's counterpart of divine gravitation" (Descharnes and Néret 2001, 458).

Above the Madonna's head dangles an egg hanging from the concave side of a conch shell, an idea Dalí probably acquired from Piero della Francesca's *Madonna and Child Enthroned* (1472) in the Brera Museum, Milan. Piero's painting depicts a conch with an ostrich egg hanging down at the end of a string over the head of the Madonna. In the medieval period, people believed that the ostrich egg, fertilized by the rays of the sun, symbolized the Immaculate Conception (Shanes 2010, 216). Piero's painting also depicts a seated Madonna in a domed Gothic vault. A low pedestal stretches below the feet of the Madonna, partly graced by the hem of her dress. Two lemons, symbols of fidelity, lie on top of the pedestal to the viewer's right side. On the opposite side lies a piece of cloth pocked with indistinguishable marks. Seashells, a conch shell, a sea urchin shell, and a plate featuring a fish float in the air to the right of the Madonna.

For the setting, Dalí chose the landscape of the cove at Port Lligat, where Dalí and Gala settled after their return from New York in 1948. The barrenness of the setting recalls the surrealistic space of a dream world. In the background, at the center of either side of the painting, stand the imposing rock formations characteristic of Port Lligat.

What is the subject matter or idea represented by *The Madonna of Port Lligat*? Is Dalí rendering a representation of the Virgin Mary and the Infant Christ? Some viewers may think that is exactly what Dalí is depicting. Fray Angélico Chávez, the New Mexican priest, for instance, wrote an ode to *The Madonna of Port Lligat* complete with a commentary informed by traditional Catholic dogma. From another perspective, the painting is about Gala as the mother of God and Dalí as the infant. Dalí frequently spoke about Gala as a deity, his own personal divinity. Moreover, it is not farfetched to think that Dalí would depict himself as Jesus. Looking closely at the infant Jesus, one notices the downward direction of the face, away from the viewer. In fact, neither of his Christs in *Christ of St. John of the Cross* and *Christus Hypercubus* show the face. More than one art critic and historian has concluded from this that Dalí intends for the Christ not to be anonymous but to represent Dalí. One may object that the face of Christ in Dalí's *Last Supper* is in full view and it is not the face of Dalí. Nobody ever accused Dalí of consistency. There is no rule that Dalí had to keep to one idea. Jim Wallis, in his discussion of *The Madonna of Port Lligat* makes a similar observation: "Interestingly, the artist claimed that this new version of *The Madonna of Port Lligat* was 'completely changed' and that the central subject was not the Madonna, but Christ. Scholars have pointed to Dalí's association with his depictions of Christ, but usually in reference to the mature images of the figure crucified. Here I am interested in the idea of the Christ Child as the 'reborn' Dalí, who, as he claimed, was led to his new direction, and thus in a way mothered, by Gala-Madonna" (Wallis 2008, 46).

Artists in fifteenth-century Florence chose as their motif the image of the seated Madonna and Child. Renaissance artists often included in their paintings of the Madonna objects known to symbolize proleptically the foreshadowing the Passion of Christ. In the 1949 version, there is no evident sign of the Passion; however, in the 1950 version of *The Madonna of Port Lligat*, considered next, a broken loaf of bread appears in the infant Jesus' portal, symbolic of the Eucharist and signifying the broken body of Jesus at his Crucifixion.

THE MADONNA OF PORT LLIGAT, 1950

The Madonna of Port Lligat of 1949 is only a study for the more stylized, detailed, and polished version of *The Madonna of Port Lligat* of 1950 (figure 1.2). Blue is still the dominant hue, but it is subdued by a grey tone. Dalí's completed version maintains the same structural composition but the hues are cooler. Grayish blue creates a monochromatic atmosphere, yielding a subdued mood. Certainly, the color scheme expresses a more mystical and serious mood than the cruder sketch of 1949.

In the upper corners, parted curtains signify a revelatory disclosure of the spiritual essence of the earthly scene unveiled at Port Lligat, where the rock formations in the background float eerily above the sea. Hands clasped in prayer, the

FIGURE 1.2   Salvador Dalí, *The Madonna of Port Lligat*, 1950. The Fukuoka Art Museum, Kyushu, © Salvador Dalí, Fundació Gala-Salvador Dalí, Artists Rights Society, New York, 2017.

Madonna's arms form a triangle with the infant's arms, her head is no longer split down the middle as in the 1949 version, and her arms are attached to her shoulders, yielding a greater semblance of unity. Folds of her dress no longer touch the cabinet-style pedestal; instead, a bare foot makes a shy appearance. As mentioned above, the piece of broken bread in the hollow of the infant Jesus suggests the idea of communion bread.

Bread is a common enough motif in Dalí's paintings that the interpreter may be easily tempted to resort to a religious interpretation. As a precautionary note, the art critic should be aware that Dalí relates that he once stuck a piece of bread under his foreskin so that it would acquire a strong, musty, seminal smell. Bread is not always a symbol of Christianity in his work. Dalí makes bread the central object of his 1926 painting, *Basket of Bread*, featuring the sheer black background favored by the Spanish painter Francisco de Zurbarán, one of Dalí's favorite painters. In 1945 he painted a similar picture with the same title but, curiously, with only a broken half of bread. In a scene from the unfinished film *Babaouo*, glass panels in a lit box show bicyclists crisscrossing, carrying loaves of bread on top of their heads (Ades 1982, 201). By contrast, his 1952 *Eucharistic Still Life* prominently displays bread as a religious objet d'art. Because Dalí's bread motif seems ambiguous, interpreters should refrain from making hasty religious conclusions.

A rhinoceros, an ambiguous symbol of both sexuality and chastity, stands inside the left hand compartment of the pedestal. One cannot overestimate the significance of the rhinoceros horn for Dalí. On July 5, 1952, the poet Loten presented a rhinoceros horn to Dalí, who then excitedly told Gala, "This horn is going to save my life." Commenting on his painting *Crucifixion* (*Corpus Hypercubus*), Dalí writes, "Today that statement is beginning to come true. Painting my Christ, I notice that he is composed of rhinoceros horns. Like a man possessed, I paint every fragment of the anatomy as if were the horn of a rhinoceros. When my horn is perfect, then—and only then—the anatomy of the Christ is equally perfect and divine. And, when I notice that each horn implies another upside down, I start painting them interlaced" (Dalí 1986, 36). Dalí, expressing his love of mathematics, claimed that the rhinoceros horn naturally instantiates the logarithmic spiral, a curve Dalí esteemed as perfect, enhancing the horn's symbolic power.

On the right-hand side of the middle ground, two angelic figures, reminiscent of Gala, represent a transformation from the cuttlefish shells on the opposite side, adding a dynamic quality of motion to the composition. A child similar to the one portrayed in this painting appears in Dalí's earlier painting, *Myself at Age Six When I Thought I Was a Girl Lifting with Extreme Care the Skin of the Sea to Observe a Dog Sleeping in the Shadow of the Water*. In this version, the child is older and plays a larger role in the composition, drawing attention somewhat from the Madonna. Dalí identifies himself with the child. Robert Descharnes and Gilles Néret claim the image is appropriated from the sixteenth-century painting *The Martyrdom of Saint Cucuphas* by Ayne Bru (Museu Nacional d'Arte de Catalunya, Barcelona) (Wallis 2008, 47). Regarding his *Mystical Madonna*, Dalí ironically claims that it had no association with any religious idea (Dalí 1976, 218). One wonders if the same applies to the two versions of his *Madonna of Port Lligat*. However, what does it mean to depict a religious symbol without religious meaning? One should consider that a religious symbol remains a religious symbol independent of the intention of the artist.

From the religious symbolism of the Madonna and Child, Dalí turned his attention to the symbol of the Crucified Cross.

CHRIST OF ST. JOHN OF THE CROSS

Anticipating the unveiling of his painting, *Christ of St. John of the Cross* (April 15, 1951), Dalí wrote his "Mystical Manifesto," which sets forth in convoluted and obfuscatory language his philosophy of nuclear mysticism, a unity of nuclear science and mysticism, a philosophy of art and a metaphysics mixed with typical Dalian braggadocio. Proclaiming himself no longer a surrealist but a mystic, he unabashedly extolls himself as one of the greatest of Catalonian geniuses, alongside Raymond Sebonde, the medieval author of *Theologia Naturalis*, and Antoni Gaudí, father of the Mediterranean Gothic. Sebonde wrote his book on natural theology as a polemic against Duns Scotus's separation of reason and faith, arguing that God gave humankind two books of knowledge—the Bible and book of nature. Michel de Montaigne, at his father's request, translated the *Theologia Naturalis* and wrote a book in defense of Sebonde, *Apology for Raymond Sebonde*, published as the twelfth essay in Book II of his *Essays*.

Dalí's hall of fame includes the non-Catalonians Ramon Llull, thirteenth-century philosopher from Majorca, and Juan de Herrera, seventeenth-century architect and mathematician, from Cantabria, not Catalonia. By combining his paranoid-critical method with mathematics and mysticism, Dalí boasted that he could save modern painting. Modern art, according to Dalí, suffers from a decrepit degeneration due to the absence of classical technique, a de-emphasis on draftsmanship, and a turning to primitive culture for inspiration. Dalí's Eurocentric elitist attitude rejected primitive art forms—pre-Renaissance and African—as appropriate sources of aesthetic models for modern painting. A few modern artists escape his invective—Willem de Kooning, Marcel Duchamp, and Georges

Mathieu. Particularly impressed by the latter's photography, Dalí perceived that photography's mirroring of reality promised the possibility of recovering realism and restoring it to the modern artistic age that unjustifiably revels in mechanical representations of the world. Dalí seems not to have regarded photography as a mechanical way of representing the world.

By mysticism, Dalí did not insist on traditional religious mysticism alone but a mystical attitude integrated with the general knowledge of quantum physics. Mysticism is an aesthetic experience of ecstasy before a nuclear world. Dalí's example of a mystical artist is Donato Bramante, the architect who designed St. Peter's Basilica. Another major example of Bramante's architecture is the Tempietto de San Pietro in Montoria, whose aesthetics Dalí describes in typically Dalian fashion as "a spasm of a long and rigorous inquisitorial process." For Dalí, form is an inquisitorial process working on matter.

Sixteenth century Spanish mystic St. Teresa de Ávila also inspired Dalian mysticism. She describes the paths of perfection that penetrates into the deepest part of the spiritual castle of the soul. Mysticism for Dalí is not a method or process for attaining union with God, but an ecstatic experience that opens the world of the artist to unveil a reality that others cannot see. Words fail him even in the desperately effusive and vain attempt to find the right words that only he can find with his imaginative vocabulary. As he describes it, mystical ecstasy is supercheerful, explosive, disintegrated, supersonic, undulatory, corpuscular, and ultra-gelatinous. In the state of mystical ecstasy, the artist can see the "immanently corpuscular" nature of the world. Consequently, Dalí can realistically paint a child on the beach lifting the skin of the sea to unveil a sleeping libidinous dog. Modern science, for Dalí, confirms the revelatory character of St. Teresa's militant Spanish Catholic mysticism showing the constantly disintegrating character of matter proves "the spirituality of all substance." Dalí writes that mysticism is a "paroxysm of joy" possible for the ultra-individualist who affirms the human "heterogeneous tendencies within the absolute unity of ecstasy" (Dalí 1998, 365).

By accentuating the artist's mystical experience, Dalí seems to limit the experience of mystical ecstasy to the artist in the act of painting, drawing, sculpting, designing, and composing. One wonders whether the experience of mystical ecstasy is also attainable for the viewer in the right state of mind. Is mystical ecstasy an aesthetic experience only available to the artist? However, the transcendent beauty of Dalí's *Christ of St. John of the Cross* seems to emanate from the painting, making it the apparent source aesthetic experience.

There is much controversy as to the source of Dalí's *Christ of St. John of the Cross*. Jonathan Wallis writes that in the summer of 1948, while Dalí and Gala lived at Port Lligat, Dalí met Father Bruno de Jesus-Marie, a Carmelite monk, who talked to him about St. John of the Cross and showed him a reproduction of a drawing of Christ on the cross purportedly by the mystic (Wallis 2008, 38). Wallis, however, is aware that Dalí attributed the source of the work to a vision he purportedly experienced while in San Diego, California: "seeing of the Christ drawn by St John of the Cross that determined the geometric composition of a circle within a triangle which 'aesthetically' assumed up all my previous experiments. . . . I PUT MY CHRIST IN THAT TRIANGLE" (Fanes 2000, 49).

Mathematically inclined, Dalí attributed the geometrical aesthetics to the golden section. In his "50 Secrets of Magic Craftsmanship," addressed to young artists, especially American ones, he encourages them to use geometry for the mathematical scaffolding of the infrastructure of their paintings. He warns them of critics who reject geometry applied to painting. "Do not hesitate at that moment to answer them promptly that, on the contrary, it is in order not to think and reflect upon them that you make use of the properties, unique and of a natural magic, derived from the wise use of the golden section, and called the "*divina proporzione* by Luca Pacioli" (Dalí 1998, 361).

Dalí admitted that St. John's drawing served as the initial model for his painting confirmed by his dream in California. Motivated by his negative reaction to Matthias Grünewald's *Crucifixion* (figure 1.3), Dalí expressed a desire to paint a beautiful Christ. Dalí specifically said that his painting *Christ of St. John of the Cross* would be the most beautiful ever of the crucified Christ, in contrast to Grünewald's depiction of the ugly Christ: "I want my next Christ to be a painting containing more beauty and joy than anything that will have been painted up to the present. I want to paint a Christ that will be the absolute contrary in every respect to the materialist and savagely anti-mystical Christ of Grünewald's *Crucifixion*" (Dalí 1976, 217).

Matthias Grünewald (1470–1528) best known for his Isenheim Altarpiece (1550), painted in a more expressive style than the traditional classic style characteristic of the Renaissance (figure 1.3). Incidentally, twentieth-century surrealists identify Grünewald as one of their precursors. Originally painted for the Monastery of St. Anthony at Isenheim, specializing in the treatment of plague victims, the painting shows plague sores covering Jesus' decrepit and mangled body. Numerous thorns in the flesh enhance the agony of Jesus' suffering. Gravity inexorably and painfully pulls down the weight of his body, bending the wooden crossbars of the cross. Jesus' head hangs down awkwardly, his neck bent in a tortured position. His bearded face exudes no beauty, only ugliness. Meant to identify Jesus with those who suffer, the earthly, concrete materiality of Jesus' agonized

FIGURE 1.3   Matthias Grünewald, *Crucifixion, Isenheim Altarpiece*. Overall view (wings closed): Martyrdom of St. Sebastian, the Crucifixion, Saint Anthony the Great; prendella, the Deposition of Christ, 1512–1516. Oil and tempra on wood. Inv. 88RP139, © Musée d'Unterlinden. Dist. RMN. Grand-Palais/Art Resources.

body obscures any underlying spirituality and mysticism, as far as Dalí is concerned. In his *Unspeakable Confessions of Salvador Dalí*, Dalí writes agonistically, "Give me ecstasy! . . . The ecstasy of God and man. Give me perfection, beauty, so I may look it in the eyes. Death to the academic, to the bureaucratic formulas of art, to decorative plagiarism, to the feeble aberrations of African art. Help me, Saint Teresa of Avila!" (Dalí 1976, 217)

Dalí's *Christ of St. John of the Cross* (figure 1.4) passed through a lively history of its own, independent of the painter. Glasgow Museums acquired the painting in 1952 for the sum of £8,200 and found it a home at the Kelvingrove Art Museum. Controversy brewed among the Scottish over the amount paid, considered by some to be too much for a painting. Critics, sounding like Judas, complained that the money should have been given to the poor. Tragedy struck in 1961 when a visitor slashed the painting. Fortunately, art restorers repaired the tear. In 1993, the painting was moved to the St. Mungo Museum of Religious Life and Art, where it hung until it returned to its home at the Kelvingrove Art Museum in 2006. Under pressure from its citizens, the Spanish government offered the astronomical sum of $127 million to buy back the painting. Scotland rejected the generous offer in a magnanimous gesture to the Scottish people, who had adopted the painting as national art.

This large canvas, measuring 205 centimeters by 116 centimeters, shows Christ on the cross from a nonconventional viewpoint (figure 1.4). The angle suggests the perspective of a dying patient lying in bed as the crucifix is placed before the face for a blessing. Some critics objected to the angle of the crucifix, noting that it was heterodox. Dalí answered to the objection, writing,

> One of the first objections to this painting came from the position of the
> Christ, that is, the angle of the vision and the tilting forward of the head. This

FIGURE 1.4   Salvador Dalí,
Christ of St. John of the Cross, 1951.
© CSG CIC Glasgow Museums.
Glasgow, Scotland, 2017.

objection from the religious point view fails from the fact that my picture was
inspired by a drawing made of the Crucifixion by St. John of the Cross
himself. . . . This painting so impressed me the first time I saw it that later in
California, in a dream, I saw the Christ in the same position, but in the
landscape of Port Lligat, and I heard voices which told me, "Dalí, you must
paint this Christ." The next day, I started the painting. . . . In this second
dream, I saw again my picture without the anecdotal attributes but just the
metaphysical beauty of Christ God. . . . My principal preoccupation was that
my Christ would be beautiful as the God that he is. (Descharnes 2001,
441–42)

Dalí's mastery of chiaroscuro technique frames the white Christ figure against
the background of an impenetrable black darkness reminiscent of Diego
Velásquez's *Christ Crucified* (1632). A light source from the upper right diffuses a
soft golden light on the body of Jesus, causing a dynamic interplay between the
illuminated flesh and the dark shadows formed by the defined muscular features
of his sculpted anatomical structure. Christ is juxtaposed with the cove of Port
Lligat. Below the crucified Christ, barely perceptible rays of the sun pierce through
the darkness with a light parting the resisting clouds of dawn or twilight. At the
horizon, a patch of blue sky silhouettes the rocky formations of Port Lligat, enclos-
ing the dark blue waters of the bay. At the bottom of the painting, there are the
fishermen of Port Lligat, a boat, and a dock. The figure at the bottom right corner
of the painting is a tribute to Velásquez, using a figure from the latter's study for
the *Surrender of Breda* (1635). The figure standing next to the boat is from Louis Le
Nain, *Peasants in Before a House* (1642). Originally, Dalí had intended to depict
actual fishermen of Port Lligat, but in a second dream of St. John of Cross's drawing of the crucified Christ, Dalí saw Le Nain's image of the French peasant and
decided to use that instead. Jesus' hands and feet are not nailed to the cross as one
traditionally sees in depictions of the crucified Christ. His hands and feet are
detached from the cross. Dalí's Christ is not the suffering Christ of Miguel de
Unamuno, but a highly spiritualized mystical but apparently human Christ freed
from the constraints of physical forces. Floating in the sky, Jesus' ethereal Crucifixion recalls the docetic theology and gnostic Christianity that denied the materiality of Jesus' body. The author of I John probably had docetic doctrine in mind
when he wrote, "That which was from the beginning, which we have heard, which
we have seen with our eyes, which we have looked upon, and our hands have han-
dled, of the Word of life" (1 John 1:1).

Dalí exemplifies his mystical aesthetics in the image *Christ of St. John of the*

Cross, but the nuclear feature is only hinted at by the defiance of gravity. He does not depict the fragmentation of matter as in his *Madonna of Port Lligat* (1949) or even in the more explicit disintegration of matter as in the *Exploding Raphaelesque Head* painted the same year.

Just as Ramon Llull saw in mathematics a divine language, Dalí recognized in physics not only a language for making sense of matter, but a language to make sense of spiritual reality. His painting is a medium, a type of language, for communicating with God or more properly about God. Hence, it is not surprising to find Dalí turning to post-Euclidean geometry to express the unity of the spiritual and the physical in the four dimensional spatial form of the hypercubus in his 1954 painting *Crucifixion (Corpus Hypercubus)*.

CRUCIFIXION (CORPUS HYPERCUBUS)

On his return home to Cadaqués from a subsequent visit to New York (1953), Dalí announced that he was going to paint an exploding Christ that was going to be his great metaphysical work of the summer. Writing about the principal sources of inspiration for his painting *Crucifixion (Corpus Hypercubus)* (figure 1.5), Dalí identifies them as mathematician and architect Juan de Herrera, Llull, Velásquez, and Zubarán.

An octahedral hypercube constitutes the form of the cross, a figure informed by Juan de Herrera's Treatise of Cubic Form. Captivated by the mysteries of the hypercubic form, Dalí invited some young physicists for a visit to talk about its properties. He reports, "Some young researchers specializing in nuclear physics came to see me today. They left again, intoxicated, having promised me to send the cubic crystallization of salt photographed in space. I should like salt—symbol of incombustibility—to work like me and Juan de Herrera on the question of the *Corpus Hypercubus*" (Dalí 1965, 98).

Dalí's Christ levitates before a polyhedron known as a hypercube or tesseract. A cube unfolds into six squares; a tesseract unfolds from a cube into eight cubes. A tesseract is a four-dimensional analogue of the cube. Humans cannot perceive a hypercube, but they can describe a three-dimensional analogue of it. The fourth dimension in post-Euclidean geometry is not the fourth dimension of space-time relativity, but a fourth dimension of space.

A large painting, the *Crucifixion (Corpus Hypercubus)* is similar in dimensions to the *Christ of St. John of the Cross*, measuring 194.3 centimeters by 123.8 centimeters. Painted in 1954, it now hangs in the Metropolitan Museum of Art. Christ, at the center of the composition is a cross-like figure composed of cubes, alternating

FIGURE 1.5   Salvador Dalí, *Crucifixion (Corpus Hypercubus)*, 1954. © Artists Rights
Society, New York. Oil on canvas, 76 1/2 × 48 3/4 in. (194.3 × 123.8 cm). Gift of the
Chester Dale Collection, 1955 (55.5). Image copyright: © The Metropolitan Museum
of Art. Image source: Art Resource, New York. © Salvador Dalí, Fundació
Gala-Salvador Dalí, Artists Rights Society, New York, 2017.

between light and dark tones of brown, hovering above a black-and-white tiled floor resembling a chessboard. On closer inspection, the tiles in the center are in the shape of an unfolded cube with one missing side. An avid admirer of Johannes Vermeer, Dalí may have gotten this idea of the black-and-white tile floor from Vermeer's *The Art of Painting* (1860), which features a similar floor pattern. In the bottom left, Gala, dressed in papal vestments, looks up at Christ in adoration. Port Lligat provides the background scene for a sun setting against a dark and brooding cloudy sky. No part of Christ's body touches the cross. There are no nails in the hands or feet. A small triangular metallic colored piece of cloth barely covers his crotch. A bright light from the right of the figure floods photons to illuminate Christ's body and cast shadows of Christ's arms onto the horizontal cubes of the cross, accentuating three dimensionality. By contrast, Gala's figure barely casts a faint shadow. The sun is not the source of light, for it can be seen setting in the distance between the mountains of Port Lligat. Dalí evokes the idea of a transcendent source of light for divinity. Convinced that *Crucifixion* (*Corpus Hypercubus*) was perfect, Dalí reported that he was afraid to start anything new (Dalí 1986, 90).

A debate rages over whether Dalí's mysticism rang true. Was Dalí religious? Were his paintings of the Madonna and Christ religious paintings? Dalí, in a postscript to the epilogue of his autobiography, *The Secret Life of Salvador Dalí*, writes a painfully honest confession: "At this moment I do not yet have faith, and I fear I shall die without heaven." Yet a few lines before these tragic words Dalí proclaims boldly, "One thing is certain: nothing, absolutely nothing, in the philosophic, esthetic, morphological, biological, or moral discoveries of our epoch denies religion. On the contrary, the architecture of the temple of the special sciences has all its windows open to heaven." Dalí's heaven is not that of the typical Christian, a paradise inhabited after death. He says that when he first saw a woman's "depilated armpit" and when he looked down from the Muli de la Torre, he was seeking heaven. "Heaven," he says, is "in the bosom of the man who has faith" (Dalí 1942, 400).

Does Dalí's mysticism imply that he held faith in God? Descharnes reports a personal conversation with Dalí in which Dalí told him that he wanted to communicate with God. Dalí shared his belief that "God is probably the substance that physicists seek" (Descharnez 2001, 424). A desire to communicate with God does not presuppose faith in God. Desire could be rooted in a conscious fantasy of an imaginary object. In any case, Dalí suggested a physicalist concept of God when he surmised about the substance that physicists seek. Still the concept is thoroughly metaphysical, for identifying God with physical substance expresses a pantheistic concept of God.

Dalí did admit, according to Descharnes, that atheists could paint great works of religious art, but warned of dangers when atheists paint religious art: "better an artist whose religious genius matches his artistic genius" (Descharnes 2001, 444–45). Dalí claimed that by the time of *Christ of St. John of the Cross*, he substituted religious mysticism for surrealism. Shanes is not charitable when he doubts the integrity of Dalí's spirituality: "Usually Dalí's late mysticism does not ring true, and this is not surprising, for the painter himself was anything but a fervent believer in God, let alone a mystic. But in works like this he did successfully project some modicum of religious belief, while avoiding his more usual tendency to make such offerings look like something out of a Hollywood movie" (Shanes 2010, 230). For this reason, there is no discussion of Dalí's *The Sacrament of the Last Supper* (1955) in this book.

According to Amanda Lear (a longtime friend of Dalí and Gala), in a roundtable conversation at "The Dalí Renaissance: An International Symposium" at the Philadelphia Museum of Art (April 10–11, 2005), Dalí used himself as a model for Christ in *Christ of St. John of the Cross* (Taylor 2008, 213). She insisted that Dalí painted himself as the crucified one. At the same symposium, Ultra Violet, actor and longtime friend, adamantly agreed, stating that Dalí had no faith, he was not a Christian, and was "irreverent as far as God and Jesus Christ were concerned" (Taylor 2008, 213).

Jonathan Wallis, by contrast, regards Dalí's turn to religion and spirituality as genuine, claiming that St. John of the Cross not only served as an inspiration for the painting, but that Dalí's spirituality was also inspired by his talk with Father Jesus de Marie, a Carmelite monk and authority on mysticism. Wallis maintains that it was Father Jesus who initially showed Dalí the drawing by St. John of the Cross at the Convent of the Incarnation at Ávila. Wallis seems convinced that this encounter secured the depth of Dalí's mysticism in his work. "I would like to suggest that, in addition to leading directly to the painting *Christ of Saint John of the Cross*, this encounter with the life and work of the Catholic mystic influenced Dalí's ideas and work more meaningfully than has previously been considered" (Wallis 2008, 38).

Dalí's religious paintings of his nuclear mystical period undoubtedly testify to some kind of commitment to the Catholic faith and perhaps represent penance for earlier antireligious works, such as the scandalous *The Sacred Heart*, shown at the 1929 exhibition at the Galerie Goemans in Paris (Fanés 2006, 154–55). Dalí may also have regretted his insensitive identification of Jesus with the Comte de Blangis. Dalí's and Luis Buñuel's production of the 1930 film, *L'Age d'Or*, shows the Comte de Blangis leaving an orgy scene. Dalí wrote a synopsis of the film handed out to spectators stating, "The Comte de Blangis is clearly Jesus Christ" (Fanés 2006, 171).

Who is to say whether Dalí had faith, including Dalí? If faith is the subjective grasping of something uncertain as if it were the truth, then faith is subjective uncertainty. What matters is not the integrity of Dalí's religious faith, mysticism, or spirituality, but Dalí's representations of Christ. On this, two points are in order. First, aesthetic monism describes Dalí's view of reality expressed in his painting during the nuclear mystical period. Aesthetic monism is an axiological ontology and an ontological aestheticism. Aesthetic monism exalts beauty as the highest value in the universe and affirms that the ontological oneness or unity of spirit and matter—the spirituality of substance and the substantiality of spirit. Christ's spirituality emanates from the physicality of the human mode of reality. Essentially, human nature is spirit and matter unified and inseparable. Second, Dalí's Christ is the projection of Dalí's own self-understanding. Above all, Dalí's Christ probably represents the apotheosis of Dalí.

On the surface, Dalí's nuclear mystical Christ exemplifies the humanity of a traditional religious symbol. A critical eye perceives a stasis, a moment in the uneasy oscillation between the humanization and dehumanization of religious art. Between the infant and the suffering adult exists a vast gulf, a nothingness, a void, an absence of what could be. For the Spanish imagination, what matters for the mythical imagination is the innocence of infancy, all potential, no guilt, no regrets, and the symbolization of universal suffering. A contradiction seems to exist between innocence and suffering. A question rises before the mind's eye. How does what begins in innocence and purity end in suffering and death? Juxtaposing images is the work of irony. Ironic juxtaposition presents an apparent unity. Suffering and innocence constitute an apparent unity. The unity is only apparent because suffering and innocence are aspects, parts of a whole that together do not complete the whole. Humans look back in their own life to a lost innocence, so lost that it does not exist, for there is no memory. On the other hand, humans look to the future but not forward looking, not in anticipation only in expectation of suffering to come. Horizontally, people can see innocence and suffering around them as separate valences, occasionally properties of the same individual. Christ represents the occasional coming together of innocence and suffering. However, the innocence of an infant and the innocence of Christ are not the same. The innocence of a child is a forced innocence, a moral state not chosen. The innocence of Christ purportedly results from choice. Which innocence is the purest? Dalí cannot decide. He chooses both. In choosing both, he establishes an insurmountable distance between the two. The result is a false unity.

Dalí images of the infant Christ and the crucified Christ express beauty but the universal judgment of beauty rings false because the images exhibit a tension between a universality of significance and a particular concretization. In this case, Grünewald's Christ, although repulsive, attains universality because suffering characterizes the human condition. This universality emanates through the ugliness of the body in pain. Dalí's Christ transcends suffering, because suffering nullifies beauty. The body in suffering drives away all thought of the beautiful. Determined to show the beauty in the unity of matter and spirit, Dalí required a Christ who did not suffer. Dualistic ontology frightened Dalí, as dualism repels a certain type of person. The person who yearns for unity rejects the paradoxes that dualism yields. From whence comes the demand for unity? The only answer can be that of alienation. The experience of alienation implies separation, fragmentation, and the sense of incompleteness. Perceived as an illness, alienation needs a cure. The cure is a reconciliation of parts into a whole, a union of separate opposites into a seamless unity, knowledge without mystery, being with one substance, good without evil, beauty without ugliness, and heaven shorn of hell.

Theologically, Dalí's Christ is reminiscent of Docetism, an early Christian movement that denied the integrity of Jesus' humanity. *Docetism* derives from the Greek *dokein* meaning "to seem" or "to appear." The Docetics attributed evil to matter and goodness to spirit. God, who is spirit, cannot take on a human body because the body is evil. Therefore, Jesus appeared human but in reality existed only as a phantom because as a spiritual being, he could not take on a real human body contaminated by evil. The author of the John and I John purposely wrote to attack an early version of Docetism. John 1:1 opens the Gospel with a prologue or hymn to the Logos: "In the beginning was the Word [Logos], and the Word [Logos] was with God, and the Word [Logos] was God." The prologue closes with a bold affirmation of the physicality of Christ, "And the Word [Logos] was made flesh, and dwelt among us" (John 1:14). St. Ignatius of Antioch, one of the earliest postapostolic fathers, attacked Docetism as heretical, for if God did not become fully human in Jesus, then Christ's resurrection and ascension did not occur and, hence, there is no salvation. In subsequent chapters, Docetism recurs frequently in Latino representations of Christ. This is clearly the case with Fray Angélico Chávez, a Franciscan priest from New Mexico, who wrote an ode to Dalí's *Madonna of Port Lligat*.

CHAPTER TWO

Fray Angélico Chávez
"The Virgin of Port Lligat"

F ive thousand four hundred miles away from Port Lligat, in Santa Fe, New
Mexico, a Hispanic Franciscan friar, poet, writer, priest, and painter was
inspired by Dalí's 1950 painting, *The Madonna of Port Lligat*. Fray Angélico
Chávez wrote an ode entitled "The Virgin of Port Lligat," celebrating the cosmic
unity of the spiritual and material represented by the Dalian nuclear mystical Virgin Mary and Child. Significantly, Chávez lived a few miles away from the Trinity
Site, now Los Alamos, New Mexico, where the atomic bomb was developed; and
White Sands, New Mexico, where the bomb was tested. Chávez, feeling a kinship
with the spirit of Dalí's nuclear mysticism, wrote his poem celebrating the unity of
spirit and matter figuring, like Dalí, that the nuclear age confirmed the oneness of
the natural and supernatural.

Whatever commonalities and shared beliefs Chávez believed bonded him to
Dalí, in reality, Dalí and Chávez offered radically different expressions of the
infant Jesus and the Madonna. Chávez assumed that he possessed an epistemolog-
ically privileged insight into the symbolism of Dalí's painting. Chávez's theo-
poetical interpretation challenged Dalí's secularization of the image and imputed
traditional Catholic significance to it in an attempt to rescue the dogmatic symbolism of the Virgin and Child motif. Chávez imposed his own inquisitorial process on Dalí's portrayal.

This chapter's concern is with the explication and evaluation of Chávez's poem,
"The Virgin of Port Lligat," in light of Dalí's painting. Chávez employs Biblical
symbols and alludes to or quotes Bible verses in his poem. In the supplementary
commentary he wrote to accompany his poem, Chávez employs a typical Catholic
evangelical interpretation of scripture and applies it to explicate the theological
content of his poem, and indirectly, that of Dalí's image. By giving a Biblically
based theological interpretation, he makes himself vulnerable to criticism from
the standpoint of modern Bible scholarship. Accordingly, this chapter will also
assess Chávez's use of scripture in the light of scientific Biblical criticism.

Manuel Ezequiel Chávez was born April 10, 1910 in Wagon Mound, New Mexico, son of Fabián Chávez and María Nicolasa Roybal de Chávez. He was educated in Mora, New Mexico, by the Sisters of Loretto. According to Ellen McCracken's excellent biography of Chávez, *The Life and Writing of Fray Angélico Chávez: A New Mexico Renaissance Man* (2009), followed here, he was an avid reader at a young age. He read the Santa Fe newspaper *El nuevo mejicano*, *National Geographic Magazine*, his family's encyclopedia, and Spanish primers. When he was a young child, the family moved to San Diego. There, after visiting the Franciscan mission founded by Fray Junípero Serra, young Chávez dreamed of becoming a Franciscan monk. At fourteen, he took the first steps to realize his dream of moving to Cincinnati to study at a Catholic seminary for the priesthood. As an Hispano from New Mexico immersed in a largely German American community, he sought to minimize his cultural distance and alienation by improving his command of English through reading classic works in English. He became so proficient that he assumed the post of editor of the seminary paper, *Brown and White*, the venue for his first published story, "A Desert Idyll" (February 1928). A prolific writer and artist while in seminary, and throughout his life, he wrote short stories, essays, produced drawings, and paintings. Securing his ethnic identity became a great source of frustration and preoccupation. He took pains to explain that he was not Mexican but Hispano, a New World descendant of Spanish forebears. This concern remained a motif of many of his writings throughout his life.

While living in Mora and later in Cincinnati, Chávez spent his summers in Santa Fe with his aunt. There he came under the influence of Santa Fe writers and artists such as Alice Corbin; William Penhallow Henderson, Corbin's husband; Mary Austin; D. H. Lawrence; Willa Cather; Carl Sandburg; and Robert Frost. Artists included John Sloan, Gustave Baumann, and B. J. O. Nordfeldt. Enthusiastically participating in their meetings, he found community of similar spirits sharing their romantic interest in the desert southwest.

In 1929, he entered the novitiate and took the name Fray Angélico Chávez. He adopted the name "Angelico" from the Italian Medieval painter Fra Angelico. Becoming a Franciscan may have been his way of connecting with New Mexico's past since Franciscan missionaries were among the first settlers there (Garcia 2000, 27). He took his BA from Duns Scotus College in 1933 and studied theology at Oldenberg until 1937, the year of his ordination in Santa Fe and first post in Peña Blanca. During World War II, he volunteered in the Army out of a sense of patriotic duty, serving as a military chaplain in the Philippines and Germany. After his service, he worked as an archivist and historian for the Santa Fe archdiocese. He developed a scholarly reputation as a historian of Southwestern and especially of colonial New Mexican history, writing twenty-three books and over six hundred other pieces in his career. He focused on New Mexican Hispanic Catholicism and its role in fostering positive ethnic identity in a society ruled by Anglos. In his writing, he draws on popular religious traditions and reappraises the roles of the French American archbishops Lamy and John Salpointe, and the Hispano priests Padre Martinez and Padre Gallegos. Chávez exalts a vision of traditional Hispanic culture in New Mexico as heir to Spanish culture in resistance to Anglo incursion. Chicano historian Mario T. García depicts Chávez as one of the first Chicanos writing oppositional literature: "Chávez's focus on religion was a way of asserting ethnic identity and opposing a growing Anglo-American historical presence that was pushing Chávez's subjects to the margins" (García 2000, 27). Chávez, however, did not self-identify as a Mexican American.

Among his many books, Chávez wrote *Origins of New Mexico Families: A Genealogy of the Spanish Colonial Period* (1954), which traces family lines from the seventeenth through the eighteenth centuries. Chávez sought to establish a continuity between twentieth-century Hispano families and the Spanish-speaking *pobladores* (settlers). Like many New Mexican Hispanos, Chávez attempted to convince Anglos that New Mexican Hispanos are not Mexicans, in the hope that Anglos would stop treating Hispanos as foreigners or immigrants. The same motive appears to be the main reason for his other books. In 1954, he wrote a fictionalized autobiography of a New Mexican statue of the Virgin Mary with the title *La Conquistadora: The Autobiography of an Ancient Statue*. The work grew out of a book published in 1948 called *Our Lady of Conquest*, itself an outgrowth of an article appearing in the *New Mexico Historical Review* (1848), "*Nuestra Señora del Rosario, La Conquistadora*." Chávez argues that La Conquistadora in Santa Fe is the same statue that Fray Alonso de Benavides brought to New Mexico in 1625. Don Diego de Vargas, who led the reconquest of New Mexico in 1692–1693 after the 1680 Pueblo Revolt, refers to the statue as Our Lady of the Conquest (Leal 2000, 39). Celebrating the role his familial ancestors played in the formation of New Mexico, Chávez wrote *Chávez, A Distinctive American Clan of New Mexico* (1989).

Chávez wrote his first novel, *Guitars and Adobes*, as an alternative ethnic reading to Willa Cather's *Death Comes for the Archbishop*. Cather's narrative focuses on the role played by the French in New Mexico; Chávez shifts the focus to the role of Hispanos. In his story, a particular guitar comes down from the Reconquista but curses to death all who play it. Adobe, an indigenous New Mexican construction material, by contrast, stands as a symbol of life. Chávez looks at fictional narrative as a field of cultural conflict over ethnic identity and cultural self-assertion (García 2000, 28). As an aside, in this paper García wrongly identifies Chávez as a Chicano, a moniker that the latter probably never self-identified with, since he presented himself as Spanish or Hispano.

Fray Angélico Chávez announced his resignation from the Franciscan Order and the Catholic Church on June 30, 1971, ostensibly for theological differences, but in reality as an act of moral indignation and protest. In his view, the Franciscan Order and the Catholic Church treated Hispanics as an inferior people. He labelled the church's treatment of Hispanics "ecclesiastical colonialism and his historical research seems to support his complaint" (McCracken 2009, 54–5).

After seeing a picture of Dalí's 1950 *Madonna of Port Lligat* in *Life* magazine, Chávez composed a devotional poem to the Virgin based on it. The ode was first published in *Spirit*, a poetry magazine (1956). At T. S. Eliot's prompting, Chávez published the poem in book form with a black and white reproduction of the painting on the cover and as the frontispiece in 1959. In a typescript for a future edition, Chávez set the title as, "A Dalí-Chávez Duet: *The Madonna of Port Lligat*—A painting by Salvador Dalí, *The Virgin of Port Lligat*—Ode by Fray Angélico Chávez" (McCracken 2009, 380).

In the front matter to his poem, Chávez writes, probably to shield himself from criticism, that "the ideas developed here are not necessarily those of the artist." Chávez, however, enthusiastically adopts metaphysical elements from Dalí's nuclear mysticism, especially the unity of spirituality and materiality, but deviates from Dalí's idiosyncratic views in significant ways, as will be made evident.

Importantly, Chávez dedicates the poem to the medieval scholastic philosopher John Duns Scotus (1266–1308). Probably more than a nod to his alma mater, Duns Scotus College, the dedication is a homage to the Franciscan philosopher whose philosophy Chávez admired. In some ways, the dedication is unsurprising. Duns Scotus championed the Franciscans against the Thomists. From the perspective of Chávez's ministerial status and theological training, the dedication to Duns Scotus is understandable. Ironically, Chávez's philosophical and theological metaphysics is inconsistent with Scotus's metaphysics. By contrast, Dalí's favorite medieval philosophers, Ramon Llull and Raymond Sebonde, took philosophical positions opposite those of Duns Scotus. Like all scholastic philosophers, Llull, Sebonde, and Duns Scotus tried to resolve the apparent antinomy between reason and faith. Where Duns Scotus separated faith and reason, relegating faith to the supernatural realm and reason to the natural plane, reflective of Thomas Aquinas's distinction of planes and hierarchy of orders, Llull and Sebonde, on the other hand, sought to reconcile faith and reason in genuine unity. For instance, Sebonde regarded both nature and the Bible as joint revelations from God. In the poem, ironically, Chávez celebrates the unity of the spiritual and the natural, following Llull and Sebonde, not Duns Scotus to whom the ode is dedicated.

Educated at Oxford, Duns Scotus taught philosophy at Cambridge and Paris, holding to a sharp line of demarcation between the natural and the supernatural. As a philosopher, he was primarily concerned with metaphysical questions about God, being, existence, matter, and form. He is known for his emphasis on individuality, individuation, or *haeccitas*, the "thisness" of particular things against the realist claim that universals, the properties or qualities of things—whiteness, hardness, smoothness, and so on—are objectively real, existing independently of the objects they characterize. Emphasizing the will as a faculty superior to reason, he stressed faith and practical activity. Faith, not reason, is the source of the church's beliefs. Duns Scotus is at loggerheads with Dalí's medieval scholastic hero Ramon Llull, who sought a synthesis between faith and reason, going so far as to contrive a rudimentary type of calculating machine of movable squares by which to derive Christian doctrines logically. His computational ideas influenced Gottfried Wilhelm Leibniz and Jorge Luis Borges.

In addition to the dedicatory, a bracketed note by the author reveals that he purposely ignores the "strictly private symbols" of the rhinoceros horn and the shell with dangling egg, significant erotic symbols for Dalí. Chávez dismisses them as trivial, oddly referring to them as "minute details." By ignoring their erotic symbolism, Chávez misses the point of Dalí's divinization of the erotic nature of Gala, who not only acts as a model for the Virgin, but stands in place of the Virgin. Dalí, by his own admission, divinized Gala. For him, she was the veritable Madonna.

The rhinoceros horn is not a "minor detail," but a highly charged and ambiguous symbol found in many of Dalí's paintings from the 1950s, representing both sexuality, because of the phallic appearance, and chastity. Dalí crudely informs the public that he celebrates the date July 27, 1952, because on that day that he defecated feces in the shape of rhinoceros horns (Dalí 1986, 51). Study of Freud led Dalí to constant introspection of his thoughts, experiences, and childhood. By introspection, Dalí arrived at the conclusion that he had been painting rhinoceros horns all his life. He reports that, at the age of ten, he prayed before a table made of a rhinoceros horn. Looking back at his work, Dalí claims that he was stupefied at the number of times a rhinoceros appears in his work (Dalí 1986, 43). What appealed to Dalí in the rhinoceros horn is the logarithmetic spiral, ubiquitous in nature and expressing perfection because no matter its size its proportional form remains unchanged. In the summer of 1955, he claims to have discovered that "in the junctions of the spirals that form the sunflower there is obviously the perfect curve of the rhinoceros horn." At a wildly popular lecture at the Sorbonne, he asserted that the rhinoceros horn is a natural example of the logarithmic spiral, along with the sunflower, and the outline of Vermeer's *Lacemaker*:

> At present, the morphologists are not at all certain that the spirals of the sunflower are truly logarithmic spirals. They approach being so, but there are growth phenomena that have made it impossible to measure them with a rigorously scientific precision, and the morphologists do not agree on declaring whether or not they are logarithmic spirals. However, I was able to assure the public at the Sorbonne yesterday that there never has been a more perfect example in nature of logarithmic spirals than those of the curve of the rhinoceros horn. Continuing my study of the sunflower and always selecting and following the more or less logarithmic curves, it was easy for me to distinguish the visible outline of the Lacemaker . . . the Lacemaker is morphologically a rhinoceros horn. (Dalí 1986, 128–29)

So attuned is he to the rhinoceros horn that he seems to see its curve ubiquitously present even in the *Corpus Hypercubus*. He states that the rhinoceros horn is the "essential basis of all chaste and violent aesthetics . . . already found in that first Dalian work of art" (Dalí 1986, 129–30).

Chávez, ignorant of or purposely disregarding Dalí's own interpretation of his favorite painterly symbols, interprets them, if he interprets them at all, as expressing the mysteries of the Catholic faith. The egg, for example, represents the mystery of the Trinity because it is the "fertilizing image of the Word and the Holy Spirit fusing with a maiden's molecules." Martin Rodriguez speculates that in Dalí's painting the egg replaces the father (McCraken 96). Whatever merit lies in Rodriguez's interpretation, one should consider that in Dalí's earlier painting *Leda Atomica* (1949), Gala floats nude above a broken eggshell. In all likelihood, the broken egg in this painting signals fertility and sexuality since this painting is Dalí's version of the myth of Leda and the Swan, in which Zeus rapes Leda.

Before beginning the poem, Chávez provides the reader with an interpretive framework constituted by three superimposed images—transparencies of a sort, visual clues. The three images are those of the Madonna, the Sphinx of Thebes, and the atom. The first image is that of Dalí's painting, *The Madonna of Port Lligat*. At first glance, the image appears as a conventional Renaissance painting, but on closer inspection, the conventions break down. The Virgin does not touch her seat, the Child is suspended in mid-air, and everything is floating. For Chávez, the Virgin and Child do not violate the laws of nature but conform to an astronomical imaginary where all objects move about in space pulled and pushed by gravitational forces: "Reality is violated, as if the laws of terrestrial gravity were suspended; yet, gravity as a whole has not been abolished, for the entire scene reminds one of the gravitational push and pull that keeps the heavenly bodies in place" (Chávez 1956, xv).

For Chávez, undoubtedly, Dalí's Madonna represents the Virgin Mary of Christian tradition. Moreover, Chávez accepts traditional interpretations of certain biblical passages as referring to the Virgin Mary or to Christ. Hence, Chávez applies the attributes of the Virgin Mary to Dalí's Madonna. For example, he interprets Isaiah 7:14, "a virgin shall conceive and bear a son," as applying to the Madonna, and he identifies the heavenly woman in Revelation 12 with her as well.

Curiously, all other references to the Virgin tie in with the image of the Sphinx, the second image, drawn from Greek mythology. Chávez conceives the Sphinx as an intellectual image, metaphor, or allegory "introduced and developed in the classic tradition of poetry" (Chávez 1959, xv). He describes the Sphinx as a "monster with the body of a lion, the face, and breasts of a woman, and the wings of an eagle. Hunched on a flat rock beside the highway, it lays in wait for the unwary traveler, to whom it proposed this simple riddle: 'What is it that walks on four legs in the morning, on two at noon, and on three in the evening?'" (Chávez 1959, xv). Finding a resemblance between the Sphinx of Thebes and the Virgin, the "Sphinx of Christendom," Chávez establishes an analogy between them coupled with a disanalogy, noting that the Virgin is antithetical to the Sphinx. Thus, the Sphinx and the Virgin are Borgesian doubles, each mirrors the other in certain meaningful ways. Chávez, however, focuses one-sidedly on the qualitative difference of the Virgin from the "monster" who strangles. By the way, the word *sphincter* derives from the name Sphinx. A salient difference is that the Sphinx is a composite, whereas the Virgin is a unity. Curiously, he regards the Virgin as real and the Sphinx as mythical. He does not acknowledge that the Virgin is just as mythical as the Sphinx. Therefore, as mythical characters they share more in common than Chávez recognizes. Nonetheless, the Virgin resumes the properties of the Sphinx in her lion's strength and eagle's power of flight, referring to the Madonna's "strange energy and floating quality" in Dalí's painting. At the heart of the analogy, both are images of women and both issue a word. The Sphinx utters a riddle; the Virgin answers with the eternal Logos. "All this because of the Word Incarnate, Who is her Riddle and Himself the Answer, here issuing from her breast instead of her lips" (Chávez 1959, xvii). Overly exuberant, Chávez hyperbolizes the role of the Logos as "the reason for the Dalí masterpiece, the Sphinx allegory, the astro-atomic universe itself" (Chávez 1956, 39). By blithely identifying the Logos with the Christ, he abstracts from the complexity of Logos theology unique to the Johannine literature, particularly the Gospel of John—too complex to go into here.

As for the Sphinx, a little background is in order. Sophocles's tragedy offers the most popular version of the Sphinx, with Oedipus solving the riddle; but Sophocles's narrative never directly presents Oedipus's encounter with the Sphinx, nor states the answer to the riddle. Sophocles alludes to the riddle in certain places, leaving it to the imagination of the reader to piece it together from common knowledge found in Greek folklore. A priest speaking before child suppliants and to Oedipus credits Oedipus for freeing them from the tribute of the cruel singer (Sphinx) by the strength of a god and not because of knowledge. Most familiar riddle goes asks, "What goes on four feet in the morning, two feet at noon, and three feet in the evening?" Traditionally, the answer to the riddle is "Man." Sophocles's tragedy is about Oedipus's search for personal identity. Shepherds provide the clues to Oedipus's identity. Oedipus claims that he answered the riddle by prophetic skill (Sophocles, 385). Tierisias, taunting Oedipus, tells the riddle-solver to solve this riddle: "Do you not excel in answering such riddles" (Sophocles, 440). Interestingly, Chávez does not mention Oedipus in his Ode. To carry through the analogy between the Virgin and the Sphinx to completion, Oedipus would be the Greek counterpart to Christ, but that implies something unacceptable to Chávez's sensibilities.

Chávez's transposition of the "Sphinx of Christendom" (the Virgin) to the Greek Sphinx constitutes the thematic structure of the poem; however, the analogy is weak, and the weakness results from his disingenuous shifting between the Madonna of Dalí's painting and the Virgin of Catholic faith, collapsing the two distinct simulacra into one simulacrum. Referring to the Virgin as "a complete woman" and "a real female human being," he violates the integrity of his comparison because the Madonna of Dalí's painting is an image composed of oil paint on canvas, not a real woman. Moreover, Dalí identifies the modern Madonna with his wife, Gala, and Dalí's Madonna only secondarily expresses a metonymic relationship with the Virgin of the Catholic faith. To reiterate, the Virgin as a character in the Christian myth of the Virgin Birth is no less a mythological figure than the Sphinx.

Turning from myth and religion, Chávez's third image is derived from astronomy and quantum or nuclear physics with special attention to the "interior of the atom"—microcosmic analogue of the cosmos, the glue that holds everything together from the smallest scale imaginable to the astronomical scale of infinite numbers of galaxies whirling throughout the universe. The atom of the eternal divine Logos fuses with the human molecules of the Virgin's body (Chávez 1956, 13).

Chávez stretches the limits of human credulity, speaking about the "atom" of the eternal Logos. If "atom" here is a metaphor, it is hard to see how a metaphor could fuse with literal molecules.

Chávez, in his commentary on line 45, another obvious nod to Dalí, writes that William Tell's unerring aim represents the splitting of the atom. The myth of William Tell, more properly a legend than a myth, is a common motif in Dalí's art. His reference to William Tell suggests that he was familiar with more of Dalí's work than the painting under discussion. Continuing with the motif of the atom, Chávez suggests in lines 77–80 that the unity of the atom resembles the Trinity in the unity of the three figures of the Godhead:

> That even the infinitely opposite Extreme
> Have Proton, mutual Pneum, and still be One?

Chávez's commentary on these lines bears quoting in full: "With the nuclear picture of all Creation still in mind, the poet asks a rhetorical question. He thereby compares the infinite and eternal Trinity with the minutest finite creature: the components of the atom or, if need be further, of the nucleus. Proton suggests the Greek 'firstborn.' Pneum, not a nuclear scientific term like proton, but similar in Greek derivation, means 'spirit' . . . (By a most uncanny coincidence, incidentally, the secret project of the first atomic test and the site of the first nuclear explosion in New Mexico, were called 'Trinity')" (Chávez 1956, 59–60).

By overlapping the images of Dalí's Madonna, the Sphinx, and the atom, Chávez, like Llull and Dalí, conveys the idea of the unity of the "different planes of knowledge and experience in art, science, and theology." Again, Chávez's conception of the unity of different types of knowledge has more in common with Dalí, Llull, and Sebonde than with Duns Scotus, to whom the poem is dedicated. One problem raised by the rhetorical device of three superimposed images is that the relation between them is vague. A temptation exists to interpret these images as three levels of interpretation similar to Origen's levels of scripture. Chávez seems to encourage this type of interpretation. For example, at the level of the nuclear frame, he uses an atomic imagery to express the mystery of the Holy Trinity and Christ's miraculous conception. Christ's conception is a nuclear fusion of a maiden's molecules and the Word. *Nuclear* as used here connotes both the idea atomic energy and the idea of the nucleus of the fertilized ovum of the Virgin Mary symbolized by the egg suspended over the Madonna figure. For Chávez, the egg is a universal symbol of life and resurrection rather than a sexual symbol, but the latter underlies the symbolism of life.

The division of the book into two parts seems to undermine the theme of unity. At the heart of the book is the poem, an ode to the subject matter of Dalí's painting and its concept about the unity of all things; the second part is a commentary on the poem imposing an extraneous rational analysis to an art object. Ironically, the idea of unity is fragmented, resulting in a dualism of reason and spirit. An uneasy tension marks Chávez's easy idea of rational/poetic unity because it excludes the mythical/reality unity that underlies his transposition of the Sphinx/ Virgin images. The division of metaphoric verse from rational commentary fuels the force of the implied dualism. In Chávez's defense, however, the idea for the commentary came from the publisher who, in order to publish a poem in book form, required Chávez to include a commentary (McCracken 2009, 279).

Chávez's allusions to scripture in the poem and his interpretation of the Bible in the commentary invite the appraisal of his Biblical knowledge from the point of view of modern scholarship. Four examples will elucidate his use of scripture, which will then be evaluated by a nondogmatic interpretation: the Immanuel passage in Isaiah 7:14, the Logos doctrine in the prologue to the Gospel of John 1:1–14, the heavenly woman in Revelations 12, and the Song of Mary in Luke 2.

In lines 12 to 16, Chávez likens Dalí's depiction of the window in the Madonna's chest to a portal of time or a mouth issuing the words of Isaiah, the riddle and the answer:

> While in her bosom framed as if within the
> door of Time,
> Or like a pending word in mouth shaped for
> Isaian rhyme,
> There sits her riddle and reply.

Toward the end of the poem, Chávez quotes the first clause of Isaiah 7:14, "Behold, a Virgin shall conceive and bear a Son!" (line 95).

By his own admission, these lines about Isaian rhyme convey the central meaning of the poem, that Christ is the answer to the riddle. Important, too, is the notion that Mary is a portal through whom Christ entered the world. "Isaian rhyme" refers to Isaiah 7:14, a text that Christians have traditionally accepted as a prophecy of the birth of Jesus. Early Christians, seeking to justify their belief that Christ is the promised Messiah, assiduously searched the scriptures of the Hebrew Bible, as well as classical Greek and Latin texts, for proof. Curiously, they mostly cited the Septuagint, a Greek translation of the Hebrew Bible, indicating their preference for the Greek version over the Tanak, the Hebrew version. Their zealousness to prove the

Messiahship of Jesus may have led them to ignore the textual context of certain passages and the historical circumstances of their original setting.

In about 735 BCE, the prophet Isaiah spoke with Ahaz, King of Judea, encouraging him to be loyal to Yahweh in the face of a threat of invasion by a coalition of Ephramite (the northern kingdom of Israel) and Syrian forces in the Syro-Ephramite war. Ahaz had refused to join in an alliance with Syria and Israel to fight off the Assyrians who had subjugated Syria, Israel, and Judea. Because of Ahaz's refusal to join the coalition against the Assyrians, the Syrians and Israelites waged war against Judea. Isaiah prophesied that Syro-Ephramite alliance would not succeed in defeating Judea and gave Ahaz a sign: A young woman "shall conceive, and bear a son, and shall call his name Immanuel [meaning 'God is with us']. Butter and honey shall he eat, that he may know to refuse the evil, and choose the good. For before the child she know to refuse the evil, and choose the good, the land that thou abhorrest shall be forsaken of both her kings" (Isaiah 7:14–16).

The sign is in two parts: first, a young woman shall conceive and bear a son, second, before the child knows the difference between good and evil, the kings of Syria and Israel will be defeated. Two questions immediately present themselves. Who is the young woman? Who is the child?

"Young woman" is an English translation of the Hebrew 'almāh, which connotes a girl of marriageable age, married or single, before the birth of her first child. Of course, some young women of marriageable age are virgins, but others are not. Therefore, to translate 'almāh as virgin, plain and simple, is not justifiable. Nothing in the Hebrew text supports the idea that Isaiah is talking about a virgin. Beginning about 250 BCE, Jews translated the Hebrew Bible into Greek for use among diaspora Jews whose dominant language was Greek. The resulting Greek translation of the Hebrew Bible is the Septuagint, taking its name from the tradition that it was translated by seventy scribes. The writers of the New Testament quoted more frequently from the Septuagint than from the Hebrew text. Early in the history of Christianity, Jews dismissed the authenticity of the Septuagint largely because it was the preferred text of Christians, but particularly because it renders the Hebrew 'almāh into Greek as *parthenos* (virgin), as reflected in Matthew 1:21. An Aramaic Targum, a Jewish commentary of Tanak on Isaiah 7:14, uses the term *girl*, which could support the idea of a virgin, but the Catholic source of the Christian interpretation of "virgin" originates with Jerome (405 CE), who produced the first Latin version of the Bible, the Vulgate. In the Vulgate, Jerome translates the Hebrew 'almāh with the Latin *virgo*, clearly establishing the doctrine of the virginity of Jesus's mother. The Catholic Church adopted Jerome's Vulgate as the official Bible for more than a thousand years.

Thus, the foundation was set for interpreting the woman of Isaiah 7:14 as referring to the Virgin Mary.

Consider that in order for Isaiah's oracle to function as a sign relevant to Ahaz
in light of the Syro-Ephramite War, the young woman in question had to have
been a woman known to Ahaz and Isaiah. Unless Ahaz knew the woman, she
could not function as sign for him. Mary of Nazareth would not exist for more
than six hundred years. How could she function as a sign to King Ahaz?

The second question deals with the identity of the child. Isaiah 7:15–16 predicts
that the Syrian and Ephramite kings would cease to be a threat by the time the
child reached puberty. The child needed to be one known to Ahaz. In all likelihood, the woman in question would have been one of Ahaz's wives and the pre-
dicted child would be none other than Ahaz's son and successor, Hezekiah. A
Christian may object that the name of the child, Immanuel, means "God is with
us" and therefore has to refer to Christ. More likely, the birth of the child was to
serve as a sign that God is on the side of Ahaz and the Kingdom of Judea—God
with us. Moreover, the king of Judea, a direct descendant of David, is identified in
the Bible as God's anointed one or *ha Mashiach* (*Christos* in Greek, Messiah in
English). Hezekiah, a descendant of David, upon ascendancy to the throne of
Judea, would become the anointed one. The purpose of Isaiah's prophecy, then,
was to give Ahaz a sign of God's faithfulness—a recurring Biblical message to
Jews in times of crisis. Hezekiah ruled Judea after the death of his father and
established a reputation for righteousness. According to II Kings 18:1–6, Hezekiah
did what was right in the eyes of the Lord, and destroyed pagan idols in the land.
He trusted in the Lord. Scripture says of him that there was no king like him,
before or after.

Chávez identifies line 14 as the pivotal line of the poem: "Or like a pending
word in mouth shaped for Isaiah rhyme, There sits her riddle and reply" (Chávez,
3). In his commentary, Chávez is clearly referencing John 1:1–14, where Christ is
named the Word (Logos), a Christian hymn serving as a prologue to the Gospel.
In addition, line 89 of Chávez's poem mixes the Logos conception of Christ with
the Virgin Birth narratives in Matthew and Luke, disrespecting the integrity of
John's Gospel, which never acknowledges the myth of the Virgin Birth:

> Saw in a wailing Nova how the Word that
> Fashioned all,
> By fusing with a maiden's molecules, geared infinite to nuclear. (Chávez, 27)

In his commentary, Chávez describes the second person of the Trinity as the "real
Nova, not only in astronomy and biology" suggesting that the Logos is the

infrastructure of the physical universe (Chávez, 63). The Logos, by fusing with the
nuclear particles in the Virgin's womb, implies the atomic structure of the Logos
that pervades at the quantum level the very fabric of the universe. A metaphysical
conundrum follows from the idea that the eternal enters into time to become a
temporal being. By definition, the eternal is timeless. If the eternal entered time,
through fusion with the maiden's molecultes, then the eternal is temporal. Whatever is temporal is subject to temporal succession. If something is subject to temporal succession, it is composed of temporal parts. If something is composed of
temporal parts, then it is not eternal. Therefore, the Logos is both eternal and not
eternal. That is a contradiction.

The contradiction does not originate with Chávez but with the Nicene Creed.
Chávez's commentary reflects the Catholic dogma of hypostatic union:

> The Word, the first and only begotten Son of the Eternal Father, by the power
> of the Holy Spirit, has assumed onto Himself a human nature; more wonder-
> ful than the fusion of elements in the sun is this hypostatic union of the
> Second Person of the Eternal Triune God with the atomic particles quickened
> for this purpose by His power in the Virgin's womb. (Chávez, 63)

"Hypostatic union" connotes the substantial unity between God the Father and
the Son of God enunciated in the Nicene Creed (325 CE). Although this doctrine
became the orthodox party line, theologians contested its orthodoxy in the fourth
and fifth centuries. Chávez deftly shifts the emphasis from the relation between
the Father and Son to the relation between the Logos and particle physics.

In Chávez's vision, the Virgin Mary is a portal through which the infinite, by
means of the Spirit, unites with the nuclear, producing the embryo that develops
into the infant Christ. How can the infinite God assume finite form? How can the
universal become a particular? Chávez does not address these metaphysical questions, assuming that the beliefs he is dealing with are mysteries of faith, paradoxes
beyond human understanding.

In another instance, Chávez continues to follow traditional Catholic dogma in
identifying the woman clothed with the sun in Revelation 12 as the Virgin Mary.
Charitably, one could argue that this makes sense from a Christian point of view.
However, this point of view is highly selective. Other alternative readings more
consistent with Biblical language are possible. First, that woman appears as a won-
drous sign in heaven, not on earth. That the setting is in heaven should be the first
clue to a proper interpretation. Clothed with the sun, the moon as her footstool,
she wears a crown of twelve stars. Keep in mind that Revelation contains over five
hundred citations from and allusions to the Hebrew Bible, many from the books

of Daniel and Ezekiel. Therefore, in all likelihood, the twelve stars probably symbolize either the twelve tribes of Israel or the Christian Church. Early Christian writers such as the author of the epistle of James use the term "twelve tribes of Israel" in reference to the Christian church (James 1:1). According to Revelation, the woman gave birth to a son who will rule all the nations with an iron scepter. In Jewish prophecy, the cosmic Messiah will rule all nations with an iron scepter. If this refers to Christ, it does not make sense, since Christ never ruled all the nations, with or without and iron scepter. A Christian may object that the prophecy is about the coming of Christ to rule the nations in some remote future. This interpretation is plausible, but it contains the serious flaw that if it is about the remote future it is not relevant to the author's original audience of persecuted Christians living in Asia Minor at the end of the first century. The dragon waited eagerly to devour the son, but God snatched him up to his throne immediately following birth. Snatched up to the throne may allude to the resurrection, except that it takes place immediately after birth. In any case, the enraged dragon made war against the rest of her offspring, those who obey God's commandment and the testimony of Jesus—Christians. It is highly unlikely that the woman clothed with the sun is identical to Mary.

Returning to the Sphinx's riddle, Chávez offers Christ as the Virgin/Dalí's Madonna's answer. In other words, Christianity is the answer to paganism's question. Chávez constructed his words cleverly to parallel in Gospel terms the language of the traditional response to the riddle, "What walks on four legs in the morning, two at noon, and three at night?"

> Oh, blessed little pattering in Bethlehem!
> Oh, sacred walking to and from Jerusalem?
> Oh, dragging cross to Calvary! (lines 104–106)

Jesus in his infancy crawls on all fours, in adulthood walks on two feet, and on the Via Dolorosa, Jesus drags his cross. With these words, Chávez could close his poem, but he does not. While still keeping the focus on Christ as the center of gravity of Dalí's painting, Chávez ends his ode with a double allusion to Dalí's *Madonna of Port Lligat* and the Song of Mary or *Magnificat* found in the Luke 2:

> Both magnified and magnifying in her portaled breast
> The central Infant, watches how His playing brings
> More births in bread through lovelier alchemy
> To fill the hungry with good things. (lines 110–13)

Chávez gives these words a Catholic sacramental interpretation by identifying the Eucharist as that which fills the hungry with good things. Wittingly or not, Chávez spiritualizes a text with an undeniable materialist content. The hungry mentioned in Luke are not communicants at mass but the economically impoverished who do not get enough to eat. The "good things" imply the things that the poor lack—nutritious food, decent housing, livable wages, and meaningful jobs. Chávez ostensibly makes Mary the focus of his poem writing, "For she is the door, and in her the Infinite united with the nuclear finite; henceforth, and for this reason (ex hoc), all generations will call her blessed" (Chávez 1956, 71). On the other hand, in perfect agreement with Dalí's own declarations, Chávez asserts that the infant Jesus is the center of gravity in Dalí's painting and in his own ode:

> For all her glory and magnificence Mary is not the heart of the poem, but the Infant Jesus, But the real Core and Purpose of all things made is the Incarnate Word, the Infinite One whose act of Creation was, and is, child's play. As He sustains Creation in being through the continual rebirth of things in energy and matter, He causes further and lovelier transubstantiations in the Eucharist, as hinted in His Mother's *Magnificat*: "He hath filled the hungry with good things." (Chávez, 71)

Unfortunately, Chávez's mystical vision obfuscates the materialist content of the Song of Mary and probably for this reason, he leaves out the second clause of Luke 1:53. Stated in its entirety, it reads, "He hath filled the hungry with good things; and the rich he hath sent empty away." The second clause is antithetical to the first and presupposes the economic content of the first clause. By spiritualizing the text, Chávez strips it of its social justice content. Class division in first-century Palestine follows a complicated hierarchy characteristic of Mediterranean societies, but basically separates the people into two groups—the hungry (the poor) and the rich. According to the Gospel, God sides with the poor, filling them with good things, but he sends away the rich. "Good things" does not refer to the Eucharist because in the church, the rich partake of the communion along with the poor.

Moreover, there is an intertextual connection with Hannah's prayer, most likely the source of the *Magnificat*. The relevant clause in Hannah's prayer in I Samuel 2:5 reads, "they that were hungry ceased" to hunger. That Hannah is speaking about the materially poor is clear from the synonymous parallelism in 2:8: "He raiseth up the poor out of the dust, and lifteth up the beggar from the dunghill." Chávez missed an opportunity to address questions of social justice. Given that Chávez resigned from the church because of the social injustice it levelled at Hispanics, it is hard to understand why he spiritualized the text. An exclusive focus on the spiritual implications of Christian doctrine tends to overlook pressing earthly matters.

Dalí's *Madonna of Port Lligat* inspired Chávez at a deep spiritual level, so that the image is more than a jumping-off point for Chávez's religious ruminations on the Virgin and infant Christ. However, the real source of the inspiration was the subject matter and not the content of Dalí's painting. Had Chávez considered the painting in light of Dalí's relationship with Gala, Chávez would have realized that Dalí's painting represents the apotheosis of Gala as the divine virgin mother. At first glance, a viewer sees a representation of the Virgin and the Christ Child. Dalí well aware that viewers would associate his painting with the traditional Catholic images purposely disguised a double image—that of Gala in the guise of the Virgin—in accord with his paranoid critical method. The infant, too, functions as a double image: the infant manifestly represents the child Jesus but latently symbolizes Dalí as having been birthed or reborn by his divine mother, Gala. Both Dalí in his painting and Chávez in his ode exemplify the principle that representations of Christ are projections of human self-understanding.

Chávez's ode to Dalí's painting, *The Madonna of Port Lligat,* reflects traditional Catholic Christology, but modifies the latter slightly by appropriating Dalí's nuclear mysticism, affirming the dialectics of the spirituality of matter and the materialization of spirit. By asserting the claim that Christ represents the unity of spirituality and materiality, Chávez, however, is merely reiterating Chalcedonian Christianity. Christianity in the early centuries was anything but monolithic. Theologians, bishops, priests, and laypeople hotly debated and literally fought over the correct interpretation about the true nature and identity of the person of Christ. Ebionite Christians denied the divinity of Christ. The Docetics, at the opposite extreme from the Ebionites, denied the reality of Christ's human body, holding that all matter is inherently evil, and spirit good. Therefore, God, who is spirit, could not have taken on human flesh without denigrating the integrity of God's goodness. Thus, the physical incarnation never occurred. Christ only appeared human; what others saw as a human individual was only a phantasm. The Apollinarians, followers of Apollinaris, split the difference, holding that only Christ's body was human: his mind, however, was divine. In any case, like the Docetics, they denied the integrity of Christ's humanity. Nestorianism, the doctrine of Nestorius (450 CE), tried to have it both ways; for them Christ was both a human person and a divine person without a true unity. The Monophysites believed that Jesus' human nature was absorbed into the divine nature of Christ. The orthodox view defended at the Council of Chalcedon (451 CE) won out, upholding the doctrine that Jesus Christ is one person with two natures, human and divine, united organically and morally in a hypostatic union. Formally, Chávez appears to defend Chalcedonian Christology in "The Virgin of Port Lligat," sublating Dalí's unorthodox vision. In terms of content, he seems to defend Dalí's metaphysical monism. José Clemente Orozco's Christ, in the next chapter, takes an antithetical approach, depicting a Christ who denounces traditional Christianity.

CHAPTER THREE

José Clemente Orozco

Christ Prometheus

I
n the last panel of the fourteen large murals painted by José Clemente Orozco
at Baker Library at Dartmouth College, Hanover, New Hampshire (1932–
1934), entitled *Modern Migration of Spirit* (figure 3.1), an angry, apocalyptic,
eschatological Christ defiantly raises his clenched left fist into the air while tightly
clinging with his right hand to the long wooden handle of a steel ax. Flayed skin
on his thighs recalls the ghastly religious images of the apostle Nathaniel, better
known as St. Bartholomew. Behind Christ rises an imposing mereological pile of
the ruins of silenced weapons of death and destruction, the machinery of war, and
desecrated symbols of the world's religions. Prominently placed in the foreground
lies fallen the ambiguous symbol of the ax-hewn cross of organized Christianity.
Christ's ethereal Byzantine face looks out of wide-open, crazy eyes at the viewer,
fixed at a dimensionless point of infinite space from where the spectator beholds a
bizarre but familiar figure from the past, both ancient and modern, stiff, wooden,
frozen in time, eternally motionless, yet vibrant with a nervous energy.

Departing from traditional Spanish and Mexican portrayals of Christ as the
suffering Son of God, Orozco's disturbing vision of an angry Christ conveys a
compelling warning to the modern world. Orozco's Dartmouth Christ symbolizes
Orozco's central motivating idea expressive of his own emotional core, with which
he transgresses tradition and unsettles complacent believers. Orozco's Christ
recalls Prometheus of Greek myth—rebel, hero, creator—but in this case the rebel
rises not so much against deity but against the credulous masses of humanity, who
are easily led to violence and war, and who crave the fantastic, superficial, materi-
alistic and utopian substitutes for the authentic life. Orozco's driving idea is the
dynamic dialectical tension between the ideal heroic human individual and mass
humanity. His distressing spiritual vision began in Colegio San Ildefonso, Mexico
City; left a memorable imprint on the walls of Pomona College, California;
expressed humanistic impressions on the fifth floor of the New School for Social
Research, New York City; and culminated in a profound ideational representation

FIGURE 3.1   José Clemente Orozco, *Modern Migration of Spirit*, 1934. Hood Museum of Art, © Artist Rights Society, New York/SOMAAP, Mexico City, 2017.

at Baker Library, Dartmouth College, New Hampshire. In this chapter, I will argue that Orozco's Christ recapitulates the ancient Greek Promethean ideal analogously presented in the Aztec deity Quetzalcoatl.

Franz Kafka and José Clemente Orozco, expressionists respectively in literature and in painting, were both born in the year 1883. Kafka wrote his most famous works between 1912 and 1914, about ten years before Orozco painted his first murals at the Colegio San Ildefonso in Mexico City. Both artists strove for emotional effect, expressed the angst of the early twentieth century, and conveyed the idea of the loss of meaning in modern society. Orozco was born in Ciudad Guzmán,

Jalisco, Mexico. Two years later, the family moved to Guadalajara, and then, in 1890, to Mexico City. He studied at the Escuela Normal de Maestros and between 1897 and 1903, and took classes at the National Preparatory School and the Escuela de Agricultura de San Jacinto. In 1906, Orozco enthusiastically began art training at the San Carlos Academy for Fine Arts. As a child walking to and from school, he peered curiously into the dusty windows of the popular printmaker José Guadalupe Posada, watching the master work on illustrations for the printing press of Vanegas Arroyo. Seeing the artist at work, Orozco felt the flames of his own artistic aspirations ignited.

Later, while a student at the agricultural school, Orozco experimented carelessly with explosives one day, costing him his left hand and wrist, a devastating loss for a would-be artist. That same year his father died, freeing Orozco to pursue his artistic ambitions despite the loss of his left hand. Enrolled at the San Carlos Academy for Fine Arts, he learned his craft from one of Mexico's leading artists, Dr. Atl (Dr. Gerardo Murillo). After travelling widely throughout Europe, Dr. Atl returned to Mexico to become one of its most influential teachers infecting his students with his enthusiasm for the Italian Renaissance, especially for the monumental masculine figures of Michelangelo. Orozco, in his autobiography, recalled what it was like being a student at San Carlos under Dr. Atl:

> He had a studio there (at the Academy), and he used to visit us in the painting rooms and night classes. While we were copying he would entertain us, speaking in his easy, insinuating, enthusiastic tone of his travels in Europe and his stay in Rome. When he spoke of the Sistine Chapel and of Leonardo his voice took fire. The great murals! The immense frescoes of the Renaissance, incredible things, as mysterious as the pyramids of the Pharaohs, the product of a technique lost these four hundred years. He was drawing muscular giants in the violent attitudes of the Sistine. We were copying models required to resemble the guilty on Doomsday! (Orozco 1962, 16)

Dr. Atl encouraged his students at the San Carlos Art Academy to face the fact of the colonial situation they were in as artists and to commit to rediscovering their own identity and values as Mexican artists. Orozco laconically observed that until Dr. Atl, Mexican art students were trained to emulate the French, since Mexican art was deemed inferior. In an attempt to discover Mexican identity, Orozco went to poor barrios to paint Mexicans of the lower classes, where he believed that the essence of Mexican identity survived with minimal contamination from foreign influence, "Why must we be eternally on our knees before the Kants and the

Hugos? All praise to the masters indeed, but we too could produce a Kant or a Hugo" (Orozco 1962, 21). Mexico has produced Hugos, but not a Kant yet. Orozco expressed sentiments similar to those of Unamuno, who boldly proclaimed that Spain does not need Kant: "One greater than Kant is here, Teresa de Ávila." With these words, Unamuno takes a swipe at the limitations of rational thought and exalts Spanish mysticism as a higher form of knowledge. Echoing the ideas of Vasconcelos's *La raza cósmica*, Orozco rhetorically asks, "Was it not from a mixture of two races that the Titans sprang?" (Orozco 1962, 21).

The first exhibition of the academy artists began in September 1910 in commemoration of the centennial, only to close down prematurely because of the outbreak of the Mexican Revolution on November 20, 1910. Francisco Madero, the oppositional candidate, a liberal, emerged victorious as the leader of the anti-re-electionists, who sought to unseat the dictator Porfirio Díaz. Unlike Emiliano Zapata and Francisco Villa, Madero believed in political change, not social reform, revealing his social class status and his ignorance of the majority of people's basic needs and wants: "The Mexican people do not want bread. They want liberty" (Elliot 1980, 6). Madero published the *Plan of San Luis Potosí*, calling for mass civil uprisings on November 20. Díaz's thugs, the *rurales*, however, put down many peasant uprisings that followed. The Mexican Revolution had begun in earnest.

In 1911, Díaz resigned, and Madero succeeded to the presidency in October. Díaz's departure left a power vacuum and consequently a struggle among Mexican revolutionary leaders, who differed in their ends. For example, Madero rejected Emiliano Zapata's demand for land reform. As a result, Zapata withdrew his support for Madero. General Pascual also withdrew support from Madero and marched on Mexico City. Victoriano Huerta Pascual helped defeat Madero, who died at the hands of assassins. Huerta succeeded to the presidency, only to face opposition by Venustiano Carranza with the support of Pancho Villa and Álvaro Obregón. Zapata also opposed Huerta. In July 1914, Huerta resigned from the presidency, partly under pressure from the United States. Carranza lost the support of Villa and Zapata, who became his staunch rivals. Although Eulalio Gutiérrez was formally elected president, the United States intervened, giving Veracruz to Carranza as a provisional capital. In 1915, Obregón led Carranza's forces against Villa, decimating his cavalry with machine guns supplied by the United States. The United States officially recognized Carranza's presidency. Vindictive, Villa attacked Columbus, New Mexico. General Pershing pursued him into Mexico against Carranza's wishes in a bid to kill or capture the elusive Villa. In 1917, Carranza called a convention of constitutionalists that resulted in the 1917

Constitution. Two years later, in a trap, Carranza's agents assassinated Zapata. In 1920, Obregón assassinated Carranza, seizing the presidency and unofficially ending the Revolution. Adolfo de la Huerta led a short-lived uprising against Obregón. In 1924, Obregon handed over power to Plutarco Calles, who ruled dictatorially for ten years.

Implementing social reform, Obregón appointed José Vasconcelos to head the Ministry of Education and built one thousand schools and two thousand libraries. As Minister of Education, Vasconcelos commissioned Diego Rivera, David Alfaro Siqueiros, Orozco, and others to paint the murals at the Colegio de San Ildefonso in 1923.

Up to two million people died in the violence of the Mexican Revolution. No class or group of people was immune from killing, maiming, and loss. Miners, railroad workers, peasants, clergy, merchants, accountants, government workers, ranchers, rich and poor, men and women, old and young, turned against each other as harbingers and victims of death. For what did people fight and die?

People fought for abstract ideals and concrete hopes. Some fought for liberalism and democratic freedoms, others fought for personal liberty; some fought for bread, others for land reform. Some fought for the constitution of 1857 or 1917; anticonstitutionalists opposed them. Some fought for socialism or communism, conservatives sought to maintain the old order of privilege for elites, and others wanted to bring down the old order and set up something new. Whatever the ideal, reality met the seeker with chaos, destruction, death, amputations, beheadings, hangings, rape, and loss of family members, homes, and jobs. All experienced despair. The Mexican Revolution conditioned Orozco's outlook, shaping his pessimistic attitude, forming his skepticism about religion, determining his cynicism about political ideals, and molding his expressionistic aesthetic vision already evident in his early cartoons, pencil drawings, and ink washes.

Political cartooning and lithographic cartoons enjoyed a long history in Mexico prior to Orozco. Cartoonists illustrated penny sheets eagerly consumed by people regardless of class. Orozco began drawing political cartoons in 1911. He produced cartoons for the radical newspapers *El Imparcial, El Hijo del Ahuizote,* and *La Vanguardia.* In the 1920s, he drew many political cartoons for *El Machete,* a publication of the Syndicate of Painters and Sculptors. Why did an academically trained artist like Orozco draw political cartoons? Did he draw political cartoons out of conviction or out of economic need and opportunity? Orozco, famously apolitical, states in his autobiography that artists should not have political convictions of any kind, arguing that artists with political convictions are not artists (Orozco 1962, 30). Orozco, contrary to reports in American newspapers,

adamantly denied playing any active role in the revolution: "I played no part in
the Revolution, I came to no harm, and I ran no danger at all. To me the Revolution was the gayest and most diverting of carnivals, that is, of what I take carnivals
to be, for I have never seen one. The great leaders I knew only by sight, from seeing
them parade through the streets at the head of their troops, accompanied by their
staff officers" (Orozco 1962, 40).

After joining a students' strike at San Carlos Academy, Orozco opened his own
studio in Mexico City and worked on the *House of Tears* series based on local
brothels. After visiting the artist, José Juan Tablada noted that the drawings and
watercolors of the House of Tears series are about women. "Woman is the perpetual theme of all these works . . . Young women meet and kiss endearingly, furtive
looks and affected gestures rehearse nascent perfidies, weapons are being tried and
sharpened for the coming duels of passion" (Charlot 1972, 246–47).

Dr. Atl moved to Veracruz following Venustiano Carranza, a rival of Victoriano Huerta who deposed Madero. Orozco followed Dr. Atl to Veracruz, drawing
cartoons for the *carrancista* newspaper *La Vanguardia*. At the time, Diego Rivera
was still in Europe. Orozco managed to participate in two exhibitions in 1916
before his first departure to the United States—a collective exhibition in San Carlos, Mexico City, then a first one-man exhibition at the Librería Biblos in Mexico
City.

When Carranza ascended to the presidency, Orozco, finding the art scene
repressive, made his first visit to the United States in 1917, traveling to San Francisco and New York. His first impression of the United States was resoundingly
negative. US customs officials at Laredo confiscated his work, destroying sixty
drawings for the sake of preserving the purity of American culture:

> I was given to understand that it was against the law to bring immoral
> drawings into the United States. The pictures were far from immoral; there
> was nothing shameless about them. There were not even any nudes, but the
> officials were firm in the conviction that they were protecting the purity and
> innocence of North America from stain, or else that domestic concupiscence
> was in sufficient supply, without any need to be augmented from abroad. At
> first I was too dumbfounded to utter a word, but then when I did protest
> furiously it was to no avail, and I sadly continued on my way to San Fran-
> cisco. (Orozco 1962, 60)

Jean Charlot, artist and friend, describes Orozco's years in the United States as "an
orgy of cold and hunger and incomprehension" (Charlot 1974, 11). While living in

San Francisco, Orozco took humble technical jobs, including one tinting portrait photographs and movie posters for theaters.

When Orozco returned to Mexico City in 1920, he built a studio in Coyoacán, exhibited with the Acción y Arte group, and continued to produce drawings and sketches, focusing on schoolgirls and prostitutes. Álvaro Obregón succeeded Carranza to the presidency after Carranza's assassination and indirectly promoted the mural movement in Mexico in 1920 by appointing José Vasconcelos to the offices of president of the university and minister of education. Diego Rivera and David Alfaro Siquieros, committed communists, returned from Europe at the behest of Vasconcelos to participate in the mural project at the Escuela Nacional Preparatoria (ENP; formerly Colegio San Ildefonso) in 1923. Murals existed in Mexico in the pre-Columbian period and resurfaced at the turn of the century. Arguably, however, Rivera, Siquieros, and Orozco invented modern Mexican mural painting. Dawn Ades contends that the muralists aimed at the "eradication of bourgeois art (easel painting), and pointed to the native Indian tradition as their model for the socialist ideal of an open, public art: 'a fighting educative art for all'" (Ades 1999, 153). Orozco, however, did not oppose easel painting, arguing that it was impossible to repudiate easel painting because easel painting stakes a rightful place in art and is not inherently opposed to mural painting. Orozco produced many easel paintings, which he called mobile art.

While Orozco did not repudiate easel painting, he spoke disparagingly about the popular themes that Vasconcelos promoted: "Anyone can paint, the stupider the better. Indigenous art should be revived and exported. Popular art should flourish. Mexican nationalism should be a predominant theme. Art should be at the service of the working class in class struggle. Artists should be political activists wrangling with sociology and history" (Orozco 1962, 82). Orozco despised Vasconcelos for promoting the depiction of indigenous and nationalistic themes in mural art (Orozco 1962, 86).

Orozco cofounded the Syndicate of Technical Workers, Painters, and Sculptors with Siqueiros and Rivera. Siqueiros wrote a manifesto acceptable to Orozco, Rivera, and the others. Their "Aesthetic Manifesto" (1922) vowed to repudiate bourgeois, individualistic, European art norms in favor of the artistic expression of native aesthetic. The main points included socializing art, rejection of easel art, production of monumental art for public consumption, and the integration of struggle with beauty (Orozco 1962, 92). The emphasis on workers' art bothered Orozco, for he felt that that after a hard day, workers would not want to come home to see pictures of more toiling workers.

The issue of Mexican identity caused considerable problems and interminable debates among intellectuals and artists, who generally conflated Indians with the working class. Fundamentally, the issue boiled down to the question of whether Mexicans are Spanish, Indian, or some mixture of the two. Racism prevailed, favoring the Spanish element. Vasconcelos, for example, even though admitting to a little Indian blood, nevertheless entitled his autobiography, *Ulises criollo* (*criollo* refers to a Mexican of Spanish descent) and not *Ulises mestizo* (mestizo refers to a Mexican of mixed Spanish and Amerindian heritages). An auxiliary problem questioned whether there is one Mexico or two. Consensus proved elusive. Orozco seemed exasperated about the whole problem: "We go on classifying ourselves as Indians, Creoles, and mestizos, following bloodlines only, as if we were discussing race horses, and the effect of the classification is to divide us into implacable partisan groups—the Hispanists and the Indigenists who war to the death" (Orozco 1962, 104). Orozco longed for the cessation of all talk about race.

The concept of revolutionary art as much as that of indigenous, popular, or nationalistic art also troubled Orozco who asked the question: Can a painting arouse revolutionary fervor in people's brains? Orozco protested against art serving political or other ideological purposes, for doing so reduced it to the narrative level of anecdotal art (Orozco 1962, 98). Art for the collectivity, he argued, is ambiguous, for it is unclear whether the artist delivers content to the collective or the collective that supplies themes for the artist. Are the masses the subjective agency represented by the artist, or are the masses incapable of being anything other than the object of art? Moreover, Orozco pointed out that there is a multiplicity of collectivities. Orozco wondered to what collectivity the artist is related. Gloria Anzaldúa in her modern Chicana classic, *Borderlands/La Frontera*, asks a similar question: "To which collectivity does the dark woman belong?" Rivera, Siquieros, and Orozco are known collectively as *los tres grandes* (the three great ones), but unlike the other two, Orozco refused to commit himself to an ideology or a political party.

After student unrest (Orozco's pagan themes struck a discordant note with the Catholics) and Vasconcelos's resignation interrupted his work at the ENP, Orozco accepted a commission by Francisco Sergio Iturbide to paint a mural in the Casa de los Azulejos. His painting, *Omnisciencia* (1925), presaged the theme, form, and architectural-compositional principles later employed in the US mural *Prometheus* at Pomona College. Both paintings express a creation motif, the symbolic gift of fire, and larger-than-life heroic figures, revealing the influence of his former teacher Dr. Atl. David Scott, an Orozco scholar, gives the following description: "Hands offer the gift of fire and of matter in the upper register, while in the main composition a woman kneels between standing male and female nudes, which in turn seem to be newly formed by suggested giant figures. The creation theme, the allegory of the gift of fire or knowledge, the giants, the slightly academic approach to the anatomy—all look forward to the Prometheus" (Scott 2001, "Orozco's Prometheus," 20).

Supposedly, Masonic or theosophical iconography reveals itself in the title that "refers to the end of the Masonic ignition; to a universal consciousness, free of passions, and useful for the domination of the world" (Mello 2001, 49).

In 1926, the Cristero Rebellion erupted as a Catholic uprising against Calles's attempts to enforce anticlerical measures. Reactionary Catholics led by militant priests turned their anger on the public school, a symbol of Calles's secular government. Cristeros burned schools, murdered public school teachers, and rallied under their battle cry, "¡Viva Cristo Rey!" (Long live Christ the King!). The struggle raged on, mostly in western Mexico, resulting in about eighty thousand deaths. Orozco left Mexico for the United States in August 1927 and remained there until 1934.

Living in New York, Orozco felt cold and lonely, but he found zealous supporters in the art patrons Alma Reed and Eva Sikelianos, widow of the Greek poet Angelos Sikelianos, who facilitated his initiation into the Delphic Society, a Greek cultural society committed to promoting universal goodwill and peace by organizing the intellectual and artistic global elite. Orozco glowingly describes a particularly memorable experience he had with them: "The other night there was a gathering at her house and Mme Sikelianos, in Greek costume and Greek sandals, danced a part of Prometheus, singing the words in Greek. Wonderful!" (Orozco 1974, 66).

With the support of the Delphic Society, Orozco's works appeared in a group exhibition at the Art Center, New York, and a one-man show of drawings of the Mexican Revolution at the Marie Sterner Gallery, New York (1928). There followed shows of oils and drawings at the New Student's League, Philadelphia, at the Art Students League in New York, and an exhibition of drawings at Ferme la Nuit Gallery, Paris, and an exhibition at Delphic Studios, New York.

New York's art scene afforded Orozco opportunities to see the work of the European masters up close. Orozco frequented exhibitions in galleries and art museums, seeing with his own eyes the works of Picasso, Renoir, Matisse, Toulouse-Lautrec, Velásquez, El Greco, Goya, de Chirico, and Degas. He found Picasso and Renoir unforgettable. Henry Matisse's colors struck him as something novel. Viewing Matisse and Derain, and modern art in general, he felt nostalgia for Mexican art, contrasting the French artists as people who live in gardens and frequent salons with himself and his compatriots, who were cursed and starving.

Spanish painters particularly inspired him. He wrote exuberantly of El Greco to his friend, artist Jean Charlot, "El Greco is a God" (Orozco 1974, 38). He marvels at the mastery of Velásquez and extolls Goya's paintings as though invoking in him the mysticism of nature's sublimity comparing it to the sublimity "one feels in the presence of a storm, a star, or any other spectacle of nature" (Orozco 1974, 39). Juan Tablada, a Mexican living in New York, wrote an article proclaiming Orozco the "Mexican Goya," an honorific that surprisingly displeased him.

Whatever his initial feelings about Degas, his sentiments changed by the time he declared, "Degas has begun to bore me, I don't want to see any more Degas for any reason" (Orozco 1974, 43). He was unimpressed by Giorgio de Chirico, so admired by Salvador Dalí, finding his exhibit "daring but nothing."

Given his feelings about Degas, it should come as no surprise that he dismissed Toulouse-Lautrec. "What idiot said that Toulouse-Lautrec was a painter?—or even a magazine illustrator" (Orozco 1974, 43). Maybe Orozco recognized something of himself in Toulouse-Lautrec's work. Orozco's drawings of schoolgirls and prostitutes (1913–1916) bear a striking resemblance to Lautrec's drawings and sketches. Octavio Paz, the acclaimed Mexican writer, Orozco would be surprised to learn, recognizes the influence of Toulouse-Lautrec on Orozco, claiming, "In a quite different direction, he also assimilated that of Toulouse Lautrec" (Paz 1993, 174). Unsurprisingly, Orozco saw in Georges Rouault a spiritual kinsman seriously inquiring of Jean Charlot whether Rouault was acquainted with Mexican culture: "Tell me: did Rouault come in contact with Mexican things, like the *santos* in the churches, the flogged Christ of Holy Week, folk penny sheets, or *pulquería* murals?" (Charlot 1972, 301). Seurat's work appeared truly religious to Orozco, but not in the negative way that he usually deprecates religion: "if there were a need (and there is not) for religious painting, it would be—Seurat—and not the ugly monkeys they put on altars. But both religious painting and altars and religion are superfluous in this confounded world" (Orozco 1974, 43). Given the religious, spiritual, mystical, and transcendent quality of many of his works, Orozco appears insincere on this score. Orozco spoke deprecatingly about American art in contrast with European art, feeling puzzled that American art would be exhibited alongside Cezanne, Monet, and Picasso. "The real American artists are the ones who make the machines" (Orozco 1974, 32).

Seemingly envious of Diego Rivera, he often refused to name him, referring to him only as "that man." In a letter to Jean Charlot, he calls Rivera the "potentate" and resentfully claims that Mexican painters, including himself, are not his disciples. He described a recent showing of Rivera's drawings and paintings as a "really ridiculous show" in spite of the high praise heaped on it (Orozco 1974, 34). After all, Rivera made Mexican art popular. About a showing of Mexican art at the Art Center, Orozco recalls bitterly, "the only purpose of the show is to sell trinkets of 'Mexican folk art.' . . . To talk about Indians, revolution, Mexican renaissance, folk arts, retables, is to talk about Rivera, the 'con man'" (Orozco 1974, 37). He wrote to Jean Charlot, expressing hope that the latter would come to New York to do something about the "damnable" Mexican movement, "which in the end is going to ruin us all" (Orozco 1974, 55).

Busy with his own commissions, Orozco left New York and traveled to California to paint the fresco mural *Prometheus* at Pomona College, California. In 1931 Orozco returned to New York, where he painted the New School murals, and afterwards he made his way to New England to begin his murals *Epic of American Civilization* on the walls of Baker Library at Dartmouth College, Hanover, New Hampshire (1932). Interrupting his work at Dartmouth temporarily, he traveled to Europe, making a three-month tour of famous art museums in Italy and Spain. Returning to New Hampshire, he finally completed the Dartmouth murals by February 1934.

After Dartmouth, Orozco returned to Mexico, where he painted the mural *Catharsis* at the Palacio de Bellas Artes. Governor of Jalisco Evarado Topete, invited Orozco to paint murals at the university's Assembly Hall in Guadalajara. At Guadalajara, he painted murals at the government palace and the Hospicio Cabañas. In the cupola at the Hospicio Cabañas, Orozco painted his famous mural *Man on Fire*. Luis Cardoza y Aragón may be perceptive when he writes, "Those who do not know Orozco at Guadalajara do not know Orozco" (Rochfort 1980, 86). Orozco kept his distance from Rivera and Siquieros, whom he saw as overly optimistic socialists and humanists clinging to the dubious belief in the human struggle to attain justice and freedom. Rivera and Siquieros were both members of the Mexican Communist Party.

In 1940, Orozco returned to New York to paint the six panels of *The Dive Bomber and the Tank*, a mobile mural, at the Modern Museum of Art, the same year a KGB agent murdered Leon Trotsky who had been staying with Rivera and Frida Kahlo in Coyoacán, Mexico City. Interestingly, many suspected that David Siquieros, a Stalinist, participated in a previous assassination attempt on Leon Trotsky. Between 1941 and 1948, Orozco kept busy painting murals, portraits, making engravings and drawings. In 1948 and 1949, he painted murals at Chapultepec Castle in Mexico City and the vault of the government palace in Guadalajara. The modern world lost one of its greatest artists when Orozco died September 7, 1949, in Mexico City.

MURALS AT THE COLEGIO SAN
ILDEFONSO IN MEXICO CITY

Orozco's first murals, painted on the Great Patio of the Escuela Nacional Prepara-toria (ENP), formerly the Colegio San Ildefonso (1923–1926), foreshadow the murals he would paint in the United States. The first panel on the ground floor, to the spectator's left, entitled *The Rich Banquet While the Workers Fight* (1923) depicts caricatures of drunken rich people at a party, while the scene below depicts brawl-ing workers. An inebriated woman jubilantly raises a glass of wine while a jolly drunk embracing her gives her a lascivious look. A second inebriated man laughs hilariously, pointing down to the pathetic workers brawling below. On the table, a fallen bottle of wine spills its intoxicating contents into a bowl of fruit on the table. Below the degenerate rich people, a worker wearing suspenders lands a punch on another worker, who is collapsing to the ground. Behind the central figure stands a worker wielding a hammer, threatening to rain down blows on the middle worker. The workers, like the rich, are caricatures. Orozco mocks the rich and the workers with equanimity, showing the defects and vulnerabilities of each, seeming not to take sides in the class struggle. He succeeds in spite of himself, dramatizing in a cartoonish way the fact of social inequality.

The adjacent mural, called *The Trinity of the Revolution* (figure 3.2), shows three pitiful but typical figures of the Mexican Revolution—peasant, soldier, and worker. On the spectator's left, a peasant on his knees, desperately grasping his hands in prayer, hides his face. The hands clasped in prayer recall Dürer's famous drawing of praying hands, but Orozco's renders them more powerfully and emo-tionally because of the expressionist style that characterizes his art. On the other side of the panel, a worker whose arms meekly hang down, his hands amputated at the wrists, looks over his right shoulder to the soldier standing behind and in between the peasant and the worker. With his powerful arms, the soldier grasps a rifle ready for a fight, yet the red banner of revolution blown by the wind drapes his face, preventing him from seeing what lies ahead. Blinded by their ideals, rev-olutionaries cannot see where they are really going.

The next mural, titled *The Strike* (figure 3.3), portrays a group of three workers holding a red banner at waist level standing in front of a closed door, seemingly unsure of whether to hang the banner or not. At the top center of the panel floats the head of Christ, the only surviving remnant from the mural *Christ Destroying the Cross*, painted in 1923–1924. Conservative students had defaced that mural, leaving Orozco no choice but to paint over it. For unknown reasons, he left intact the head of Christ. The symbolism of the painting is ambiguous and appears to present

FIGURE 3.2   José Clemente Orozco, *The Trinity of the Revolution*, 1926. Wall painting.
Escuela Nacional Preparatoria San Ildefonso, © Artist Rights Society, New York/
SOMAAP, Mexico City, 2017. Photo Credit: Schalkwijk/Art Resource, New York.

workers with a forced choice of either the way of Christ or the way of socialism. A
rival interpretation holds that revolutionaries wrongly identified socialism with
Christianity. Fernández, a principal interpreter of Orozco's work, sees the mural in
precisely these terms: "As the painter went along, he continually encountered with
increasing confidence his own style and in *The Strike* he underlined the central conflict of our time—Christ and the red banner" (Fernández 1956, 39).

FIGURE 3.3   José Clemente Orozco, *The Strike*, 1926. Mural. Escuela Nacional Preparatoria San Ildefonso, © Artist Rights Society, New York/SOMAAP, Mexico City, 2017.
Photo Credit: Schalkwijk/Art Resource, New York.

One of Orozco's favorite paintings, *The Trench*, evokes the Christological symbols of the Crucifixion and the Trinity (figure 3.4). Among three bare-chested
men, dejected revolutionaries, the central figure, inclined at a forty-five-degree
angle, stretches out his arms, hinting at the Crucifixion. On his knees, a forlorn
figure despairingly buries his head in his bent left arm. Seen from behind, a third
shirtless, barefoot revolutionary lies pitifully on top of the first figure. Oddly,
according to Elliott, *The Trench* suggests Orozco's skepticism about the meaningfulness of the death of Christ and that of the revolutionary (1980, 25). Skepticism
may be the right word if Elliott means that it is doubtful we can know the significance of their deaths. Cynicism may be a better term for Orozco's general attitude
toward overarching meaningfulness expressed in these murals.

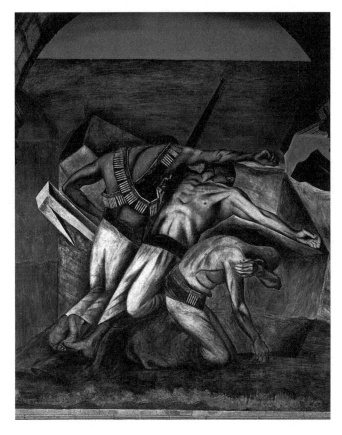

FIGURE 3.4   José Clemente Orozco, *The Trench*, 1926. Mural. Escuela Nacional
Preparatoria San Ildefonso, © Artist Rights Society, New York/SOMAAP, Mexico City,
2017. Photo Credit: Schalkwijk/Art Resource, New York.

To the right of *The Trench*, the mural *Destruction of the Old Order* offers a frontal
view of two barefoot soldiers or peasants looking over their shoulders at ruins of
destroyed buildings reminiscent of classical style depicted in cubist form. A figure
on the left raises his hand, open and waist high as though in pitiful supplication,
expressing puzzlement as though asking himself, "Now what?" The somber figures
face the destruction and chaos of civilization, looking backwards, not forwards.
Revolution and religion are inherently utopian, rejecting the present order of things
for something better. Consequently, both revolution and religion contain in their
respective bosoms an incredible capacity to create and destroy. Orozco's murals
recall one-sidedly the chaos, corruption, destruction, and hopeless idealism of
the Mexican Revolution. By contrast, the North American murals display the

dialectical dynamic interplay between both creative and destructive forces, cynicism, and optimism.

The last panel on the ground floor, called *Maternity*, is the only surviving panel from 1923. One has to wonder why Orozco did not paint over this Botticelli-like picture standing in stark contrast with the darker murals. At the center of the picture, a nude young woman with blonde hair lifts a baby to her lips for a kiss. Another nude woman sits on the ground at her feet holding a bunch of grapes over her mouth. Four angelic women—angels, muses, or goddesses—float in the air around the Madonna figure. Perhaps Orozco intended to associate revolutionary hopes with mythology.

How conservatives mistook the image to be a deviant depiction of the Virgin puzzles a secular mind. A Catholic women's group protested the mural as blasphemous, demanding that Orozco dismantle it. Orozco recalled the event:

> Ladies of the Red or Green Cross, I don't quite remember which, needed the
> main patio of the school for a charity bazaar; but instead of politely asking me
> to suspend my work for a few days, they haughtily ordered me to withdraw,
> had my scaffolding dismantled on the spot, and hung ornaments for the for
> the bazaar directly over the pictures in process. They were loud voiced in their
> disapproval and their disgust. In particular, the nude figure of a woman with
> a child displeased them; they believed that it was a Virgin. However, I had no
> intention of painting a virgin, I was painting a mother. (1962, 116)

With an ancient Greek theme, Orozco expresses a universal ideal, transcending the provincialism of nationalistic art and the particularism of Mexican Catholic religious art, in contrast to the particularity of the revolutionary panels.

Not recognizing the mythical universal ideal, thinking traditionally, conservative students, Catholic women's groups, and critics reacted angrily to Orozco's murals. "Hostility to the murals, particularly among the relatively conservative students of the ENP, led to direct action, and the regular casual defacement the painters had contended with became more serious, damage, especially to Orozco's work" (Ades 1989, 160). Salvador Novo criticized Orozco's murals as "repulsive pictures, aiming to awake in the spectator, instead of esthetic emotion, an anarchistic fury if he was penniless, or if wealthy, to make his knees buckle with fright" (Charlot 1972, 250). Orozco's murals and the hostility they provoked reveal the two major contrasting and opposing ideals at the core of the Mexican conflict—a conservative traditional ideal and a progressive seeking a new social order. In the end, social reality quashes the airy hopes of abstract ideals. In the Pomona murals,

Orozco shifts the focus of the conflict from one of political ideals to the anthropological and sociological conflict between mass behavior and heroic action, to the transition from the old religions and mythologies to a secular idea.

PROMETHEUS

José Clement Orozco's *Prometheus* mural (figure 3.5) painted at Pomona College, California, in 1930, is the first Mexican mural painted in the United States. Orozco's association with Alma Reed and Eva Sikelianos probably influenced his choice of a Greek theme. José Pijoán, adjunct faculty at Pomona College, initiated the project, and Jorge Juan Crespo de la Serna, Los Angeles art instructor and art critic, helped recruit Orozco for the project and assisted in the mural painting. José Pijoán providentially suggested the Prometheus theme that Orozco was prepared to embrace so enthusiastically.

Prometheus is the creator-hero of humankind in ancient Greek mythology. Zeus punished Prometheus for stealing fire and giving it to humankind and sentenced him to a corner of Hades where he was chained to a rock forever, where an eagle would eat his liver after it grew back every day. Prometheus makes an appearance in Hesiod's *Theogony* and *Work and Days*. Aeschylus memorializes the story of Prometheus in three plays, *Prometheus Bound*, *Prometheus Unbound*, and *Prometheus the Fire-Bringer*. Mary Wollstonecraft Shelly revives in her own fashion the shadow of Prometheus in her book, *Frankenstein: The Modern Prometheus*. Prometheus symbolizes the rebellious hero antagonistic to divine will, and at the same time human autonomy and human overreaching. For good reason, Karl Marx named Prometheus the first saint in the philosophical calendar. Orozco painted the mural in an alcove above a fireplace in Frary Hall, then the men's cafeteria. In the central panel, the masculine Titan with his bare hands tears Heaven open, raining down rays of fire. Fire symbolizes knowledge, and knowledge, like fire, is a double-edged sword, capable of creation or destruction, or better yet, creative destruction. Below and around the Michaelangelesque Titan stand the masses, a monolithic, generic humanity doing what humans do. Some face him, suggesting acceptance or wonder, others face away, indicating rejection. As knowledge dawns on humanity, some are indifferent: lovers embrace in a deep kiss, a killer wields a sharp knife, ready to strike a doomed opponent. Regardless of consequences, Prometheus, as a great sacrifice, delivers the fire of knowledge to an ungrateful crowd. Nonetheless, Prometheus and the masses are polar opposites unified by a sacred totality.

Orozco, interviewed in a Pomona College student publication, *Student Life*

FIGURE 3.5   José Clemente Orozco, *Prometheus*, 1930. Pomona College Museum of Art, © Artist Rights Society, New York/SOMAAP, Mexico City, 2017.

(May 17, 1930) said that the masses are simply the crowd and contain no symbolism in his mural. To the unsettled interviewer, he says, "You are trying to take the crowd apart and analyze it. This is unnecessary; you miss the meaning. The crowd is just a crowd as you see anywhere. The crowds are always in motion—I have tried to make them dynamic. They move, they do things. Look at any crowd; it is made up of many people. All of them are active." The unity of Prometheus and the crowd constitutes the dynamic content of the mural and hang inextricably together. Orozco downplayed the symbolism in the scene: Prometheus and the crowd stress the eternal yet everyday human context of the masses (Hurlburt 1989, 28).

The crowd serves as a dissonant counterpoint against the rising melodic line of the hero. Lacking nationalistic, ethnic, and racial features, Orozco's crowd qualitatively differs from Diego Rivera's crowd, made up of distinct individuals brimming with personality. Rivera carefully defines the unique features of each individual in the crowd, oftentimes recognizable historical people. Though Orozco denied the symbolism of the crowd, Mello is probably correct in pointing out the symbolism of the masses: "The masses beside Prometheus are neither popular nor national: they do not represent social life, but rather, have a significance that is once again, closer to Symbolism" (Mello 2001, 55).

Orozco projects his heroic self-understanding on Prometheus as David Scott rightfully noted when he recognized a resemblance between the isolation and suffering of Orozco and Prometheus. Scott also notes the similarity between Prometheus's flaming hands and the explosion that cost Orozco his left hand and wrist in his teens (Scott 2001, 15).

On the left recessed wall, Zeus, Hero, and Io gaze in disbelief as the rebel Prometheus brings the era of the gods to an ignoble end (figure 3.6). The recessed wall to the right shows centaurs in agony. One, a female centaur, wrapped in the death grip of a large serpent, pitifully reaches out in vain for her infant, seized by horror (figure 3.7).

FIGURE 3.6   José Clemente Orozco, *Zeus, Hera, and Io* or *Destruction of Mythology*, 1930. Pomona College Museum of Art, © Artist Rights Society, New York/ SOMAAP, Mexico City, 2017.

FIGURE 3.7   José Clemente Orozco, *Centaurs Strangled by Serpent* or *Centaurs in Agony* or *Strangulation of Mythology*, 1930. Pomona College Museum of Art, © Artist Rights Society, New York/ SOMAAP, Mexico City, 2017.

Above the alcove on the ceiling, overlapping rectangles projecting flames express an abstract conception of deity (figure 3.7). Orozco's last easel painting, *Metaphysical Landscape* (1948), echoes the Pomona abstraction, featuring a large dark rectangle menacingly descending from the heavens, breaking through cloudy skies above a barren landscape. To avoid anthropomorphism, Orozco turned to geometric forms to represent the metaphysical while breaking from the Renaissance tradition of using triangles and circles to represent deity. Orozco's preference for rectangles may be due to the use of rectangles in Greek geometry in illustrating the Golden Section, a principle Orozco would utilize in the New School murals.

Some critics reject the ultramodernism reflected in the work, others pessimistically see in the Prometheus figure "a monstrous disfiguration"; still others perceive the specter of communism driving away the college's conservative supporters. Racist attitudes confront Orozco at Pomona, New School, and Dartmouth. In any case, Orozco's mural created a culture shock (Hurlburt 1989, 41). Students and faculty generally supported the mural. Orozco's murals at the New School in New York stirred similar controversy.

NEW SCHOOL

Between the feverish Prometheus mural and the energetic Dartmouth murals, Orozco painted the less enthusiastic New School murals in little more than forty-six days. Except for the six portable panels of Orozco's *Dive Bomber and Tank* commissioned by the Metropolitan Museum of Art, the New School murals represent the first and only surviving Orozco murals in New York. The New School murals featured portraits of Lenin and Stalin even before Rivera's controversial mural at Rockefeller Center prominently displayed Lenin's portrait, which an outraged Rockefeller ordered dismantled. While critics may find the political content of the New School murals inconsistent with Orozco's shying away from politics, in reality the thematic content of the murals unquestionably express the political concerns and utopian ideals of Alma Reed's and Eva Silkenios's Delphic Society—universal peace and international brotherhood. There is no narrative sequence to the murals, unlike the Dartmouth murals. The panels featuring Carrillo Puerto, Lenin, and Gandhi display a posterlike quality suitable for *Time Magazine*'s "Man of the Year" cover.

Orozco painted the murals on the fifth floor of the school built in 1939 on West Twelfth Street. Entering the room, the first panel one sees is entitled *The Table of Universal Brotherhood*. It features a rectangular table, around which sit a group of men representing many global racial types. Eleven male figures sit expressionless,

FIGURE 3.8   José Clemente Orozco, *Abstract Composition* or *Godhead*, 1930. Pomona College Museum of Art, © Artist Rights Society, New York/SOMAAP, Mexico City, 2017.

passive, and motionless. On the table, a nondescript book lies open, symbolizing knowledge, reason, and the intellect—in short, global literacy. The faces of the men sitting around the table are portraits of members of the Delphic Society or persons who sometimes attended its meetings. At the head of the table sit a Mexican, an African American, and a Jew, representing the "most despised races." At the time, Orozco rankled critics situating a black man at the head of the table. From left to right there is a Mandarin Chinese; Lloyd Goodrich, art critic; Leonard Charles Noppen, Dutch American poet; a Tartar; a Sikh; a Mexican peon; an African American; Rubin, a Jewish artist from Palestine; an African; Paul Richard, a French philosopher; and a Cantonese coolie (Miliotes 2002, 121). The glaring absence of women around the table stands out as a remarkable anomaly given the strong influence of the women of the Delphic Society on Orozco, especially his promoter, Alma Reed. Women, however, appear in the panel *Future Homecoming of the Worker of the New Day*, and in the Gandhi panel, which features Sarojini Naidu, a Delphic Society associate, who sits behind Gandhi.

An exterior wall contains the panel *Allegory of Science, Labor, and Art*, which depicts three men working in side-by-side panels, seriously engaged in their respective activities that represent major types of work in modern society. A laborer, at the center, works between a scientist and an artist. Both the scientist and the artist employ triangles, a tool common to science and art; but the artist's triangle connects with a rainbow, suggesting inspiration.

On the opposite wall facing the *Table of Universal Brotherhood*, the mural *Future Homecoming of the Worker* also known as the *Homecoming of the Worker of the New Day* shows weary workers of the future arriving home to the warm embrace of their families. A mother with her children, perhaps recalling Orozco's own wife and children, sit behind a table set with bowls of fruit, representing prosperity, and a small stack of books, symbolizing knowledge and literacy for the masses. Warm but anxious looks on the women and worn-down faces on the men reveal Orozco's worry that even in the future utopian society, work is still alienating. Workers carrying pickaxes suggest miners, exhausted, but strong and determined. Orozco, consciously or unconsciously, envisions the future existence of hard labor and a continuation of a system of specialized division of labor but not necessarily exploitation. There is no utopia.

On the west wall, the mural *Struggle in the Occident* depicts the bitter struggle for peace and goodwill in socialism and communism. Felipe Carrillo Puerto and Vladimir Lenin personify the socialist struggle in the western world. Orozco probably includes Puerto's portrait out of deference to Alma Reed. He told her at one point, "You are always going to feel very much at home here, Almita. You will be among your friends; it is just another ashram" (Reed, 208). Carrillo Puerto, a socialist Mexican reformer and governor of Yucatán state who was slain in 1924, was Alma Reed's fiancé. At the right of his portrait stands the pyramid of Chichén Itzá from Puerto's home state. Below the portrait and the pyramid, Orozco depicts a group of Mayan peasants representing the masses. On the right side of the panel, Lenin's portrait looks over a parade of armed soldiers, leaders march defiantly in front. Stalin stands out prominently placed in the foreground and in the front rank. Several patrons of the mural project withdrew their support because of the depiction of the African American at the head of the table of goodwill, and the portraits of Lenin and Stalin.

The mural on the east wall, *Struggle of the Orient*, represents the struggle of African and Asiatic workers. Both white-collar workers and slaves wear manacles. On the left, one bold rebellious slave rises up, ready to overthrow the established order. Gandhi quietly sitting, bravely faces the British and Indian forces, soldiers with gas masks, armed with bayoneted rifles. Behind Gandhi sits his associate, Delphic Society member Sarojini Naidu. At work in both murals, the *Struggle in the Occident* and *Struggle of the Orient* is the dialectical principle of the elite heroic figures and the masses.

At the New School, Orozco employed the compositional principles of Jay Hambidge's theory of dynamic symmetry. Widely followed by artists, artisans, and decorators in the 1920s and 1930s, the basic compositional idea of Hambidge's dynamic theory represents a classical path to beauty. Hambidge's book *Dynamic Symmetry* exploits the golden section, whose compositional principle informed the design of the Parthenon, Apollo's Temple, Zeus's Temple, and the decoration of Greek and Egyptian vases. Plato's *Theaetetus* demonstrates the golden ratios derived from squares and diagonals. According to Eudoxius, the golden section is a ratio of 1.611. The principle of dynamic symmetry, as opposed to static symmetry, allows for movement, growth, and development, producing rhythm and harmony and creating beauty (Orozco 1962, 145–46). Partly out of curiosity, partly out of pressure from Jay Hambidge's wife, Orozco employed the theory of dynamic symmetry in the structural composition of his murals.

Orozco felt his creativity constrained by the rigidity inherent in Hambidge's compositional principle. In his discomfort with rules dictating art, Orozco echoed the sentiments of his Mexican compatriot Antonio Caso, a philosophy professor who denounced contemporary art for taking geometry as the basis for compositional form. Caso said that art should arise from an inner subjective aesthetic intuition: "Using geometry as a basis for compositional form reflects calculative thinking not the intuition of beauty. The defect of contemporary art consists in taking impersonal geometric forms that give guidance to action as adequate expression of the mystery of nature. It doesn't intuit, rather it calculates; and between the artist and her own work the law of geometry intervenes that drowns, because it obfuscates, the individual creative genius" (Caso 1971, 165).

Feeling that the geometrization of art was too mechanical, Orozco rejected the notion of calculative rationality and the application of mechanical principles in the work of artists, at least ideally. He bucked at the idea that art could flow naturally from the technical application of ruler and compass: "Still, as it always happens, the principles were ill interpreted or turned into an academic rule. People imagined that at last the secret of Greek beauty had been uncovered, that it was at the service of anyone in possession of a compass or a foot rule who could add or divide. It was strange to see artists begin a picture or a carving like an accountant striking a balance at a ban, by making a long series of calculations" (Orozco 1962, 149). Consequently, he gave up Hambidge's principles of dynamic symmetry after he took on New School techniques, although he continued to apply some of its basic ideas: "After doing the pictures in the New School I abandoned the over rigorous and

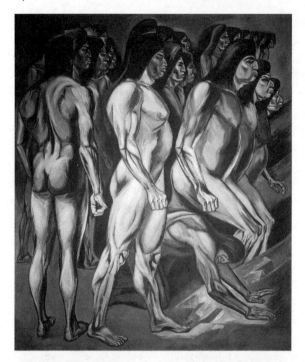

FIGURE 3.9   José Clemente Orozco, *The Epic of American Civilization: Ancient Migration* (Panel 1), 1932–1934. Fresco. Overall: 120 × 105 in. (304.8 × 266.7 cm). Hood Museum of Art, © Artist Rights Society, New York/SOMAAP, Mexico City, 2017.

FIGURE 3.10   José Clemente Orozco, *The Epic of American Civilization: The Arrival of Quetzalcoatl* (Panel 5), 1932–1934. Fresco. Overall: 120 × 205 in. (304.8 × 520.7 cm). Hood Museum of Art, © Artist Rights Society, New York/SOMAAP, Mexico City, 2017.

scientific methods of dynamic symmetry, but I kept what was fundamental and inevitable in it and with this I shaped new ways of working. I had the explanation of many former errors and I saw new roads opening up" (Orozco 1962, 149–50).

DARTMOUTH COLLEGE BAKER LIBRARY MURALS

At Dartmouth, Orozco largely abandoned the compositional principles of dynamic symmetry, but without leaving behind the fundamental technique of beginning a project with an informal geometrical outline: "At Baker Library Orozco liberated his composition from the confines of Dynamic Symmetry, employing only a broad armature he termed a 'geometric skeleton,' on which he painted directly" (Hurlburt 1989, 77). Unlike the New School murals, the Dartmouth murals do not express the optimistic themes of universal goodwill and social progress so dear to the Delphic Society. The Dartmouth murals show Orozco returning to the pessimistic, cynical, and somewhat apocalyptic dystopian vision that inspired the Colegio San Ildefonso and Pomona murals.

Eleazer Wheelock, a missionary intent on "civilizing" Native Americans, founded Dartmouth, the ninth oldest college in the United States. His idea of civilizing were a bit odd, for as Orozco puts it, Wheelock "came among them with a grammar, a Bible, a drum, and more than five thousand quarts of whiskey. To the sound of his drum, the Indians assembled, drank his whiskey, and learned the idiom of the New Testament. Today there are no more Indians left to be educated after this admirable plan" (Hurlburt 1989, 59).

At Dartmouth, Orozco embarked on a project to capture the essence of the epic of American civilization. Instead of beginning with Native Americans of the North American northeast, Orozco, a postcolonialist, starts with the Aztecs, and along the way, he contrasts Europeans and Amerindians, and then turns to the differences between Mexican civilization and Anglo-American civilization. In this way, Orozco reminds US Americans that Mexicans are Americans, too. His goal, as he puts it, is to express an idea and not a story:

> In every painting, as in any other work of art, there is always an IDEA, never a story. The ideas are the point of departure, the first cause of the plastic construction, and it is present all the time as energy-creating matter . . . But the important point regarding the frescoes of Baker Library is not only the quality of the idea that initiates and organizes the whole structure, it is also the fact that it is an AMERICAN idea developed into American forms, American feeling, and, as a consequence, into American style. (Elliott 1980, 59)

In spite of his intentions, however, the outcome looks like a narrative sequence. Orozco first came to Dartmouth on May 2, 1932, by invitation to paint a demonstration fresco for the art students, *Man Released from the Mechanistic*. In a Dartmouth College news release (May 25, 1932), Orozco explains that the Dartmouth murals depict two cultural currents colliding in the Western hemisphere, giving rise to the idea of a unitary America: "The American continental races are now becoming aware of their own personality as it emerges from the two cultural currents, the indigenous and the European. The great American myth of Quetzalcoatl is a living one, embracing both elements and pointing clearly by its prophetic nature, to the responsibility share equally by the two Americas of creating here an authentic American civilization" (Hurlburt 1980, 55).

Dawn Ades, historian of Spanish and Latin American art, articulates an alternative view, emphasizing the retrogressive aspect in Orozco's idea of the progress of American history, keenly observing that "in the Dartmouth murals Orozco shows the progression of American history but then turns the modern era back, satirically, as a grotesque mirror image of the past" (Ades 1989, 170).

The long north wall bears the majority of the panels, divided into two sections. The first half begins on the western wall depicting the ancient Indian part of the epic; the arrival and departure of Quetzalcoatl occupy principal panels leading to the reserve desk. Sergei Eisenstein wishes that Orozco had used his frescoes to wage war on the old world, heralding a new world—that Orozco would have replaced "the beard of the mythical Quetzalcoatl with that of the combative Marx" (Eisenstein 1980, 69). Cortez's ominous arrival with the cross inaugurates the modern age of mechanism, preparing thematically for the successive panels on the eastern half of the wall. American and Mexican civilizations exemplify the Latinism/Anglo-Saxon antithesis. Ending the series of the *Epic of American Civilization* is the violent image of Christ standing in front of the ruins of civilization, having chopped down the cross.

The cycle begins on the west end wall perpendicular to the north-south wall with a panel appropriately titled *Ancient Migration* (figure 3.9) depicting Aztec-Mexica people migrating to their unknown but fixed destination as prophesied by their priest-king Huitzilopochtli. The next mural on the right, titled *Ancient Human Sacrifice*, represents the old order of human sacrifice carried out in the belief that in a relation of mutual reciprocity to the ancient deities, humans owed the gods a blood debt. Hope first appears in the American continent in the form of the Meso-American Prometheus, Quetzalcoatl, the feathered serpent god who gave arts to humans in the panel called *The Arrival of Quetzalcoatl* (figure 3.10).

Aztec children were taught about the ancient kingdom of Tollan (Place of

Reeds) ruled by the priest king Topiltzin Quetzalcoatl (Our Young Prince the Feathered Serpent) a priest of the god Quetzalcoatl. Thanks to the divine benefactor Quetzalcoatl, the Toltecs of Tollan enjoyed agricultural abundance, technological and artistic brilliance. Of the priest-king Topiltzin Quetzalcoatl, it is said, "Truly with him it began, truly from him it flowed out, from Quetzalcoatl—all art and knowledge" Also known as Ce Acatl, the Topiltzin Quetzalcoatl of song, poetry, and art, like Christ, the Buddha, and Lao Tzu, was born miraculously. Trained to become both a priest and a warrior, Topiltzin replaced the sacrifice of human beings with that of quail, butterflies, and rabbits, provoking the wrath of Tezcatlipoca, Lord of the Smoking Mirrors, whose priests drove Topiltzin into exile by tricking him into becoming so drunk that he violated a taboo. Prophecies told that he would return in the year Ce Acatl or One Reed (Carrasco 1990, 44).

Auspiciously, Cortez arrived in Mexico in the Aztec calendar year Ce Acatl or One Reed. Of course, the odds of that were one out of fifty-two, since Ce Acatl occurs every fifty-second year according to the coordination of the Aztec lunar and solar calendars. Although the Toltec empire fell in the eleventh century for unknown reason, elements of their civilization lived on in the culture of the Aztecs (Carrasco 1990, 45).

At Dartmouth, the artist continues the motifs from his earlier work—the heroic self-sacrifice of Prometheus exemplified by Quetzalcoatl, the dialectic of elites and masses, the overthrow of old orders, and utopian hopes for a new civilization. As in past times when people reject, kill, martyr, crucify, and exile the great prophets and founders of religions all over the world, so the people drive away Quetzalcoatl. Dejected but determined, Quetzalcoatl, according to myth, leaves Mexico on a raft of serpents eastward (figure 3.11). Following the panel of Quetzalcoatl's departure, a smaller panel represents the prophecy foretold of Quetzalcoatl's return.

Cortez and the Cross (figure 3.12) ironically depicts the fulfillment of Quetzalcoatl's prophecy in the eyes of Moctezuma II and his priests. The ominous armor-clad figure of Cortez prefigures the invasion of European civilization, mechanism, and technology. While Orozco disavows mechanization in the form of art, he revels in using the machine as a symbol of mechanization and dehumanization.

Fire, too, recurs in Orozco's murals to ambiguously symbolize knowledge and destruction. In the 1925 mural *Omnisciencia*, rays of fire radiate from the sky to a monumental earth mother. In *Man on Fire*, painted inside the copula of Hospicio Cabañas, Guadalajara (1939), a burning man falls precipitously into a deep, foreboding abyss. At Pomona, Prometheus steals fire from the gods, and in *Gods of the Modern World* (Dartmouth), fire rages in the background behind skeletal figures

FIGURE 3.11   José Clemente Orozco, *The Epic of American Civilization: The Departure of Quetzalcoatl* (Panel 12), 1932–1934. Fresco. Hood Museum of Art, © Artist Rights Society, New York/SOMAAP, Mexico City, 2017.

FIGURE 3.12   José Clemente Orozco, *The Epic of American Civilization*: *Cortez and the Cross* (Panel 13), 1932–1934. Fresco. Hood Museum of Art, © Artist Rights Society, New York/SOMAAP, Mexico City, 1917.

in academic garb. In the *Cortez and the Cross*, burning ships in the background symbolize Cortez's indomitable will to press on, leaving his soldiers without possibility of retreat. Turning back is not an option literally or figuratively. Cortez's arrival links ancient indigenous civilization with the nascent civilization of industry and mechanism in the New World (figure 3.12).

Between the Cortez panel and the last panel, *Modern Migration of Spirit*, in order, are the murals *Machine*, *Anglo-America*, *Hispano-America*, *Gods of the Modern World*, and *Modern Human Sacrifice*. *Mechanism* links the Spanish Conquest with Anglo-American civilization, symbolizing industry, technology, and the de-humanization of the human spirit. In *Anglo-America*, a towering schoolmarm stands over a group of expressionless cookie-cutter children. A barn and a one-room schoolhouse stand in the background. In the middle ground, a group of men and women stand around an apparently empty open space as though gathered around a grave. Pragmatism, formalism, rationalism, and science are the dominant traits of Anglo-America. Mass conformity belies the abstract ideal of individualism. Law, order, and instrumental rationality sap life of its vitality and rob society of its soul. *Hispano-America*, by contrast, shows a chaotic, violent Mexico. A Zapata-like revolutionary occupies the center of the panel, vertically dividing the composition. Ruined pillars of classic civilization, reminiscent of the Colegio San Ildefonso mural *Destruction of the Old Order*, lie silently in the background. Uniformed and garishly decorated military officers, political leaders wearing top hats and mask, and bankers fallen over a bag of gold coins round out the composition. A military general raises a knife to strike either the revolutionary or another general, either is an option. In contrast to the lifeless orderliness of *Anglo-America*, *Hispano-America* is ruled by chaos, death, destruction, corruption, social injustice, war, revolution, and inequality. Blind lust for money and the will to power dominates the cultural ethos of elites in Orozco's Mexico.

The last panel on the western half of the wall, *Gods of the Modern World*, shows a female skeleton lying on its back on top of a pile of books, giving birth to a baby skeleton wearing a commencement cap. With a stern gaze, a group of skeletal academics dressed in cap and gown oversee the travail of birth; behind them, a wall of fire engulfs the world. At the east end wall, the panel *Modern Human Sacrifice* depicts the tomb of an unknown soldier. The skeletal remains of a dead soldier, still wearing his boots, lying atop a stone slab, is draped in flags and wreaths as a band plays to the left. This mural directly faces the opposite wall, which is adorned with the mural *Ancient Human Sacrifice*.

The final panel (figure 3.1) depicts an angry Christ after having chopped down his cross. *Modern Migration of Spirit* recalls and recapitulates the symbolism of the heroic rebel of Prometheus in Orozco's first North American mural at Pomona and the panel of Quetzalcoatl at Dartmouth. Between Prometheus and Christ, the Mesoamerican Quetzalcoatl arrives and departs. Together the three noble figures call forth the idea of a triumvirate of avatars, each an individual manifestation of the same single grand form—divinity humanized. In between the Pomona and Dartmouth murals, the New School panels contain no Titans, superhuman heroes, or God-men—only humanity in its diverse guises—expressing the idea of a divinized humanity or humanized divinity diffused throughout the globe, from East to West.

The panel on the opposite wall, directly facing *Modern Migration of Spirit*, the mural *Ancient Migration*, exhibits grim-faced, determined Aztec warriors steadily and irrevocably marching to the sounds of an unheard drumbeat toward an unknown but preordained, prophesied destination. Both panels intimate new beginnings. *Modern Migration of Spirit*, unlike *Ancient Migration*, boldly depicts creative destruction. Destruction of the old ways makes room for the new, unseen, and undreamed of human world—a second chance for humanity.

This second chance, however, is no real chance, for things are bound to repeat, as in Nietzsche's eternal recurrence. Orozco's vision is boldly and thoroughly pessimistic about humanity's potential to get it right. Recall Robert Frost's gloomy prediction in the following words:

> Some say the world will end in fire,
> Some say in ice.
> From what I've tasted of desire
> I hold with those who favor fire. (Frost 1920, 67)

CONCLUSION

Orozco interpreters rightly hold that his main theme is the wrenching disparity between lofty ideals and messy reality. Rochfort, for example, succinctly expresses this point of view: "Orozco was captivated and absorbed by what he saw as the stark reality of human existence, of man's apparent inability to realize his most noble aspirations or to live with others in freedom and liberty. Orozco believed passionately in the sanctity of freedom but when he looked around him, in spite of the 'progress' of the 20th century, he saw oppression and slavery" (Rochfort 1980, 74). No doubt the collision and subsequent collapse of abstract ideals against the concrete wall of a recalcitrant reality in all of its grim and dirty detail finds expression in many of Orozco's works. Living through the Mexican Revolution, Orozco formed a cynical attitude about human ideals, their disutility, impracticality, ideological character, and impossibility of realization.

Though it is true that he expressed the idea that reality undermines the utopian fantasies of moral and political ideals, his greatest contribution comes from the idea that the dialectical tension between the heroic rebel and the inert masses exemplifies concretely the general clash between reality and ideality. Prometheus, Quetzalcoatl, and Christ represent the ideal human, humanity's full potentiality instantiated in the form of a rebellious hero. From a Mexican perspective, Orozco looks back to the Greeks, then turns to Mexico's own mythological past, and culminates with a futurist eschatological Christ, utopian and antiutopian at the same time.

Prometheus, Quetzalcoatl, and Christ instantiate not only the hero but the rebel, whose rebellion is not the atheistic denial of God, but the brash defiance of God, the gods hallowed by tradition. Prometheus rebelled against Zeus, Quetzalcoatl defied Tetzcatlipoca, and Christ denounced the legalistic religion of perfect conformity to law and order. Prometheus, Quetzalcoatl, and Christ represent the spirit of freedom seeking to break the bonds of dependence upon heteronomous powers, striving for autonomy, fighting to overcome human alienation and to create a truly human world. Flesh resists the spirit; darkness futilely tries to repress the light. Flesh is mass humanity, resisting the heroic by taking refuge in the line of least resistance. Orozco's affirmation of an elite/mass dialect, assertion of the superiority of universal art over national art, and his preference for expressionism over realism support the interpretation of Christ Prometheus, the rebel hero.

The Mass/Elite Dialectic

The terms *mass* or *masses* are ambiguous and yield associated ideas like the *people, mob, hoi polloi, folk, crowd,* or *proletariat*. Terms like *people* and *proletariat* carry positive connotations, attributing historical agency to the masses, as in "of the people, by the people and for the people" or as in the Marxist notion that the proletariat is the historical agent of class struggle and social transformation. On the negative side, the masses are rabble, a crowd, or a mob. In a neutral sense, the masses are a statistical majority, suggesting uniformity or at least a perceived or imagined shared resemblance as against the minority. Along these lines, mass behavior refers to the quotidian, ordinary, everyday style of life. In this way of speaking, certain determinisms are implied. Mass media targets these determinisms at work in human beings.

In the same year that Orozco painted his mural at Pomona, José Ortega y Gasset published his most famous work, *The Revolt of the Masses*, which laments the rise of the masses as the paramount problem facing modern public life. Given the traits of mass behavior, the masses cannot guide private life or rule society, yet they are in the ascendant in modern democratic and liberal society. Prior to modern times, the elite minorities gave direction and guidance to cultural life. Presently, the masses are hurling themselves into all spheres and levels of cultural and social life. A painful contradiction between the elites and the masses marks modern life. Elites possess the requisite intellectual, artistic, moral, and political capabilities for leading public life, but the masses lack special capabilities, qualities, and distinctions, preventing them from leading. They demand greater power and access to offices and opportunities for social leadership. Ortega y Gasset observes that the key difference is that elites make more of themselves and demand the maximum from themselves and others. The masses, by contrast, settle for the minimum from themselves. Ortega y Gasset suggests class distinctions, but his analysis transcends class. He holds, rightly, that elite or select individuals may occupy any class position. What dismays him is the rising predominance of the average person, the mass man, and the waning influence of the elite individual that worried Nietzsche. Like Nietzsche, Ortega y Gasset feared the prospect that the possible rule of the masses portends the reign of mediocrity: "The characteristic of the hour is that the commonplace mind, knowing itself to be commonplace, has the assurance to proclaim the rights of the commonplace and to impose them wherever it will" (Ortega y Gasset 1957, 11–18).

The elite/mass problem concerned not only conservatives like Ortega y Gasset, but Marxists, too. Vladimir I. Lenin wrote *What is To Be Done?* (1905) largely to criticize the revisionism of Eduard Bernstein, the German Social Democratic theoretician, and to oppose Russian economistic thinking that sought only trade union consciousness, not revolutionary action. At the core of the book is the question of the relationship between the revolutionary party and the spontaneity of the masses, or the relationship between revolutionary consciousness and the spontaneity of the masses. "Spontaneity of the masses" refers to the possibility of workers to rally and mobilize for trade unionism but not for social revolution. Lenin argues that since the masses follow the path of least resistance, and because the masses act as masses, they are incapable of revolutionary actions. They desire and seek simple solutions and immediate goals. Inertia dominates mass behavior. The masses, according to Lenin, prefer a kopeck to a social revolution. For Lenin, revolutionary consciousness is not limited to social class status. Not class status but immunity to mass tendencies is a necessary condition for revolutionary consciousness, the ability to resist passivity, simplicity, and immediacy. Change kopeck to dollar and Lenin could be speaking about American workers in the twenty-first century (Lenin 1905).

From the 1920s through the 1930s, Marxists racked their brains trying to explain why the working class failed to congeal as a revolutionary agent and why capitalism did not break down. The scientific Marxism of the Second International put its faith in the objective structures of capitalism, believing that its downfall was inevitable due to its inherent logic. György Lukács and Karl Korsch shifted the emphasis to the subjective nature of class-consciousness. They rejected deterministic theories of Marxism, stressing the voluntaristic aspect of human action. They concluded that workers and peasants failed to become revolutionary because they lacked class-consciousness. Since the lack of class-consciousness among workers posed an intractable problem for Marxists, some of them, such as Max Horkheimer and Theodore Adorno, turned from economic concerns to ideology critique.

Theologically, the phenomenon of the masses raises similar thorny issues. Søren Kierkegaard, for instance, in his 1846 essay "The Present Age," castigated Denmark Christendom for promoting a leveling of society through the formalization of Christianity. Kierkegaard denounced the public as a crowd curious about everything but committed to nothing; a public eager to devour trivia, equally shy about serious reflection.

Juan Luis Segundo, an Uruguayan theologian, identifies three determiners of mass behavior—passivity, simplicity, and immediacy. Passivity concedes decision-making power to others. This determiner is universal; all human beings in many areas of their lives leave it to others to make decisions about what is prohibited, permissible, obligatory, and so on. There are areas of life, knowledge, and action that we leave to specialists or experts. Simplicity is an essential characteristic of the masses, demonstrated in the need for clearly defined values. Immediacy, another hallmark of mass attitudes and behaviors, refers to the need for immediate gratification. These determinations suggest to Segundo that there is a law of nature at work, which he sums up in one word—entropy.

Mass phenomena, quantitatively or qualitatively, acts analogously to the distribution of energy throughout the universe. In other words, the price we pay to excel in some areas of our life is the routinization of the rest of our activities. Confronting problems the masses pose to the church, Segundo asks the following questions: Is the church a mass phenomenon or an elite institution? Do we conceptualize the universality of Christianity in numerical terms or in qualitative terms? Segundo's inquiry leads him to conclude that the masses, led by the law of least resistance, seek simple and immediate solutions to problems. Right on point, Segundo affirms the possibility of mass tendencies in any individual at whatever station in life. Segundo adapts Lenin's framing of the question of the masses to the church's thinking about the masses: "Was the original Christian message aimed at masses as such, so that it must be thought out and propagated in those terms; or was it rather aimed at minorities who were destined to play an essential role in the transformation and liberation of the masses?" (Candelaria 1990, 89). Since inertia dominates mass behavior, and because the passive Christian masses will seek simplicity and immediacy in their ideals and values, consequently, the Christian ideal is beyond the reach of the masses. Segundo concludes that Christianity is not the easy and quick solution to life's daily problems that the masses take it to be. Only a heroic far-sighted believer can bear the knowledge that the realization of one's hopes and labor will probably outstrip the believer's longevity (Candelaria 1990, 92).

In summary, in the quantitative sense, the masses refer to multitudes, great numbers of people, the hoi polloi, the crowd as such. In the qualitative sense, mass man refers to a common human trait vulnerable to passivity, simplicity, and immediacy. In both cases the mass or masses is a dialectical concept whose antithesis is a minority/elite capable of specialized, extraordinary conduct.

Universal Art/Nationalist Art

A second reason supporting the centrality of the theme of the mass/elite dialectic is Orozco's condescending attitude toward nationalist, indigenous, and folk art. An elitist, Orozco deplored the tendency to confuse the particularity of national folk art with higher painting that aspires to universality. Nationalist and folk art draws on contingent local traditions rooted in a particular history subject to change. By contrast, universal art is timeless and not relative to culture, thus the values expressed transcend time and place (Orozco 1923, 88–89). Hence, Orozco applies the label "nationalism" to folk art but not to great painting. Orozco does not despise folk art in itself; he opposes the confusion of the particularity of community, tribe, or nation with the universality of humanity, calling such mislabeling a "serious error."

"Each race will be able to make, and will have to make, its intellectual and emotional contribution to the universal tradition but will never be able to impose on it the local and transitory modalities of the minor arts" (Orozco 1974, 89–90). Orozco despised the tourist depiction of Mexico because it generalizes from the attributes of the lower and rural classes to stereotype Mexican nationality. For instance, the tourist takes the *charro* (Mexican cowboy) to typify the Mexican, *lo mexicano*: "Personally, I detest representing in my works the odious and degenerate type of the common people that is generally taken as a 'picturesque' subject to please the tourist or profit at his expense. . . . Why do the most trite and most ridiculous attributes of one social class have to belong to a whole country?" (Orozco 1974, 90).

Reflecting his academy training and elitist attitude, Orozco claims that only the universal ought to occupy the artist: humanity, emotion, and the ideal representation of bodies. He prides himself on the fact that in his 1916 exhibition, there are no sombreros or huaraches. In Orozco's words, "A painting should not be a commentary but the thing itself: not a reflection but light itself; not an interpretation but a thing to be interpreted" (Orozco 1974, 91). Thus, in a text prepared for a catalogue of his retrospective works in 1947 at the Palacio de Bellas Artes, Mexico, Orozco reiterates his disdain for the content of Mexican mural painting: virgins, angels, martyrs, hells, heaven, the Holy Sepulcher, all of Christian iconography, revolutionary symbols, and the signs of democracy.

Expressionism/Realism

A third reason for supporting the claim that the theme of the dialectical tension between the hero and the masses subsumes the idea of the clash between ideal and reality is that Orozco chose to work in an expressionist style rather than in the realist style preferred by Diego Rivera. Expressionism is the art style best suited to conveying the dialectical pathos existing between ideal and real humanity, the heroic, and plebian. Expressionist theory holds that art connects feeling and the role of emotion in art. Expressionism suits an artist's intention to convey the vitality of psychological states through a work of art. Artists transform inchoate feelings and project them as images painted on canvas, objectify mental states into intelligible forms of wood, clay, and stone. Realism, by contrast, assumes a one-to-one correspondence between the elements of a picture and those that make up the state of affairs that is the subject matter of realist art. Realism conveys an idea but largely through cognitive and rational means. This premise makes up in plausibility and relevance what it lacks in adequacy. Expressionism alone does not suffice to show that Orozco's Christ is a type of Prometheus, but expressionism would be most suited to the idea and feeling conveyed by Orozco.

Octavio Paz, an astute and prolific Mexican art critic, situates Orozco in the expressionist movement, albeit, at the same time, claiming that Orozco transgresses against expressionism. "His work takes place within the Expressionist current of our century, but it is impossible to understand it if one does not realize that it defines itself by being nothing less than a transgression of Expressionism. Orozco's painting hallows the very thing he denies: his transgression of Expressionism is an Expressionist act" (Paz 1993, 172). David Scott, art historian, also recognizes Orozco's *Prometheus*, in particular, as exemplifying expressionism: "The

Prometheus at Pomona College was the first major 'modern' fresco in this country and thus epochal in the history of the medium. It revealed a new concept of mural painting, a greatly heightened direct and personal expression. It challenged accepted conventions, which decreed that wall decoration should be flat and graceful, pleasant, decorous, and impersonal. In the Prometheus, Expressionism achieved a monumental scale" (Scott 2001, 13).

Quotes like these by historians and art critics could be repeated ad nauseam, but these few suffice to show that Orozco's style was expressionist. Expressionism as a modern art movement shares a spiritual kinship with Dadaism, abstractionism, and surrealism. Max Beckmann, Otto Dix, Georg Grosz, Ernst Kirchner, and Franz Mark left their indelible marks on Orozco's aesthetic style, whether or not Orozco consciously or intentionally recognized them. El Greco, to all intents and purposes, was an expressionist painter before his time. His *View of Toledo* strikes the modern viewer as a classic example of expressionism. Francisco Goya's wartime drawings and paintings resemble the expressionist style. Octavio Paz identifies Matthias Grünewald as a precursor to the expressionist style of Orozco: "The affinities between this German painter of the sixteenth century and the Mexican artist of the twentieth century are the result of a spiritual kinship: across the centuries and across cultures, both shared a belief in the supernatural value of blood and sacrifice. Both succumbed to the fascination of the dual figure of the executioner and the victim, united not by psychological but by magico-religious ties" (Paz 1993, 173).

Paz may have in mind the Crucifixion scene from Grünewald's *Isenheim Altarpiece* (1515), which portrays a pockmarked, agonizing, ugly Christ condemning the inherent evil of the material body. Dalí, repulsed by Grünewald's ugly Christ, painted *Christ of St. John of the Cross* in order to demonstrate the beauty of Christ's mystical body. True, Orozco rarely tried to capture the essence of beauty in his work. His Byzantine Christ, with flayed skin, instantiates the motif of the *Cristo feo* (ugly Christ), similar in some respects to Grünewald's *Crucifixion*.

For Orozco, Christ is an elitist, a Promethean hero, a Hebrew Quetzalcoatl, Albert Camus's rebel, Nietzsche's superman, the ideal human, the antithesis to the masses. Against what does Orozco's Christ rebel? At first glance, the answer would be institutional religion and the machinery and glorification of war. This may be a partial answer. Prometheus rebelled against Zeus, but his myth expresses a revolt against heteronomy. To think that Christ rebels against God strains the credulity of anyone familiar with the New Testament. Not that Orozco defends the existence of the Christian deity; rather, he shines the spotlight on Christ's rebellion against humanity as a mass phenomenon, exalting abstract ideals, institutionalizing them in religious institutions, and propagating and defending them with the technology and mechanism of war, death, and destruction. Orozco's skepticism and cynicism, born of the Mexican Revolution, make skepticism and cynicism lively options.

On the other hand, Orozco's equal condemnation of all ideologies risks leaving the status quo intact, a position favored by ruling classes. Neutrality is a façade in that neutrality disguises an attitude of social withdrawal, leaving everything as is. Pretentiousness characterizes this point of view, as if one takes an otherworldly transcendent position untouched by the dirty ontology of earthly existence. The chaos of the Mexican Revolution spawned a political and ideological black hole that sucked out the marrow of all contending political ideals and conflicting ideologies until they were irrelevant, hence Orozco's cynicism and nihilism. In the next chapter, Miguel de Unamuno expresses a like-minded cynicism.

CHAPTER FOUR

Miguel de Unamuno

The Quixotic Christ

M iguel de Unamuno y Jugo was born in Bilbao, Spain, September 29, 1864, the third of six children. In 1874, when he was ten years old, the bombardment of the Basque city of Bilbao seared his memory, indelibly burning into his young mind the fear of death and the belief that death means utter annihilation. Fortunately, his father bequeathed to Miguel his library of a few hundred books, where he read philosophy and learned about the Ancient Greek philosophers, such as Plato and Aristotle, and the modern European philosophers René Descartes, Immanuel Kant, and Georg Wilhelm Friedrich Hegel. In particular, he studied the Catholic philosopher Jaime Balmes (1810–1848). Unamuno studied at the School of Philosophy and Letters at the University of Madrid, an institution strongly influenced by the Krausist Giner de los Ríos. Intellectually curious and proficient in languages, Unamuno learned German to study Hegel, and Danish to study Kierkegaard. Awarded a licentiate in 1883, a year later he earned a doctorate based on his thesis, *Critical Study of the Problem of the Origins and Prehistory of the Basque Race*. He returned to Bilbao and remained there for seven years giving private lessons, teaching part time, and writing for the local papers. On July 13, 1891, Unamuno accepted a post at the old and venerable University of Salamanca as a professor of Greek language. Earlier that year he had married Concepción Lizarraga, who gave him nine children. The death of a child in 1897 precipitated a deep spiritual crisis about the reality of death and its portentous power to annihilate, leaving an indelible impression on all his future writings. His faith tested, Unamuno discovered the impotence of his traditional religious beliefs in the face of tragedy, science, and reason.

After the defeat of Spain by the United States, Spanish literary figures sought national regeneration. Unamuno stands first among these intellectuals known as the Generation of 1898, including Azorín, Ramón del Valle-Inclán, Pío Baroja, and Antonio Machado. Although Unamuno earned a reputation as an outspoken critic, he became rector of the University of Salamanca in 1900 and kept the post until 1914. In 1920, he accepted the post of vice rector until General Primo de Rivera exiled him to the Canary Islands in 1924. With the help of concerned friends, he escaped to France and eventually made his way to the border, becoming a resident of the border town Hendaye, not returning to Spain until February 1930. Appointed rector again in 1931, the republican government ousted him in 1936. He died later that year on December 31.

Miguel de Unamuno complains that scientifically minded philosophers limit the world and life to the intellectual, the rational, and the analytic ignoring reason's subordination to the vital needs of the heart and will. St. Teresa of Ávila, St. John of the Cross, Miguel de Cervantes, Hernando Cortez, Bartolomé de las Casas, and Unamuno exhibit the characteristics the latter regards as definitive of the Spanish soul: passion, mysticism, idealism, individualism, and a practical orientation. According to Unamuno, in contrast to the Spanish orientation, rationalistic science and philosophy reduce life and the world to a logical system. For Unamuno, the mechanistic and rationalistic understanding of the world is the work of "idle men." Unlike rationalistic and mechanistic philosophies, Spanish philosophy offers a theory of the world and existence that gives moral orientation to human action, provides "a sense of life," and forms a tragic sentiment.

Undaunted by the objection that Spain has not produced an Immanuel Kant, he proudly boasts that it, nonetheless, has produced a St. Teresa of Ávila: "St. Theresa is worth any . . . *Critique of Pure Reason*" (Unamuno 1954, 323). For Unamuno, Spanish philosophy is not technical, but arises from the blood, soil, and the religious soul of Spaniards, exemplified by the Spanish Christ, don Quixote. Taking Unamuno's description seriously, we conclude that Spanish thought, and derivatively, Latin American thought, is quixotic, anti-intellectualist, otherworldly, idealist, voluntarist, and vitalistic. An uneasy tension, therefore, lies at the heart of quixotic thinking and feeling, a tension caused by the push and pull of rational and irrational psychological and social forces giving rise to the tragic sense of life that brands the Spanish Catholic outlook: "What I call the tragic sense of life in men and peoples is at any rate our tragic sense of life that of Spaniards and the Spanish people, as it is reflected in my consciousness, which is a Spanish consciousness, made in Spain. And this tragic sense of life is essentially the Catholic sense of it, for Catholicism, and above all popular Catholicism, is tragic" (Unamuno 1954, 295). For Unamuno, all thinking about the world, every philosophy, reflects basic precognitive psychological and emotional attitudes toward life. Spanish philosophy is tragic because it reflects the tragic sentiment of life, the "science of the tragedy of life."

Don Quixote expresses the tragic sense of life also exemplified by the adventurous spirit of the conquistadors, the militant faith of the counter reformers, the zealous commitment of Loyola, the mysticism of St. John of the Cross, and the ecstasies of St. Teresa. *Spiritual* and *spirit* are such vague and nebulous terms easily associated with religion, mysticism, spiritualism, and so on. By "spirit," Unamuno means life. *Life* may not be more definable than *spirit*, but it connotes something more concrete, tangible, and sensual than the word *spirit*. In the lust for God, glory, and gold, not necessarily in that order, speculative quixotic philosophy and practical quixotism are equally irrational, and, to some extent, forms of madness (spirituality?). Christ and Quixote are doubles, mirror images of each other. As Unamuno puts it, Christ on the cross is a divine tragedy; Quixote is a human tragedy. In either case, pitting faith against reason is the stuff of tragedy: "To put faith above reason is tragic, but to place reason above faith is comedy" (Unamuno 1954, 214). Rhythms of everyday life undulate between the tragic and the comic, readily transparent in Unamuno's nivolas, a little less so in writings like his essay "Mi religión."

"MI RELIGIÓN"

"Mi religión" (1913) was written in response to a Chilean friend who asked Unamuno to clarify his position on religion. Unamuno's essay reveals the religious nature of his own personal agony. Acutely aware that his readers are confused about his religious identity, Unamuno recalls a moment in his youth when he inscribed a note in the margin of a book debunking the idea of God as superfluous. Confiding in the reader, he admits that he remains of the same mind about the God of the philosophers:

> In my early youth, when first I began to be puzzled by these eternal problems, I read in a book, the author of which I have no wish to recall, this sentence: 'God is the great X placed over the ultimate barrier of human knowledge; in the measure in which science advances the barrier recedes.' And I wrote in the margin, 'On this side of the barrier, everything is explained without Him; on the further side, nothing is explained, either with Him or without Him; God therefore is superfluous.' And so far as concerns the God-Idea, the God of the proofs, I continue to be of the same opinion. (Unamuno 1954, 160–61)

A little clarification is in order. To deny the God of the philosophers is not the same as denying the God of Spanish Catholicism. The God of Western philosophy is an abstraction, while the Spanish God is a tragic figure.

Writing to his friend Jiménez Ilundain, he states that he is neither an atheist nor a pantheist. According to Margaret Rudd, Unamuno's English biographer, Unamuno consistently maintained that he was a Christian. The Catholic Church, accusing Unamuno of heresy and proscribing his writings, did not share Rudd's view. Part of the confusion regarding Unamuno's faith is due to his enigmatic and passionate writing style. Dialectics, logic, paradox, ambiguity, uncertainty, and contradiction make his writings obscure. Chameleonlike, he changes positions and shifts outlooks, strategically adapting the complexities of his thinking to varying social and political circumstances. A strategic dialectician, Unamuno could argue against any position for the sake of unsettling people comfortably settled in their neat and unassailable dogmas. In any event, Unamuno disdained certainty, dogmatism, and smug authoritarianism and stoutly opposed the self-assured, whatever their faith persuasion. Unfortunately, Unamuno refuses to give a clear-cut answer to his erstwhile nervous enquirer. Attuned to the hidden motives of those anxiously seeking clear-cut, black and white answers, he declines to satisfy their curiosity, the curiosity of the insecure looking for a confirmation of their own psychological but doubtful certainties. Unamuno was convinced that people who raise questions about other people's religious beliefs are really searching for an easy solution to their own vexing questions.

Dodging the question, Unamuno impatiently warns the reader against spiritual sloth. Spiritual sloth is a vice in its own right, but its danger lies in its power to drag the unsuspecting into the abyss of an uncritical dogmatism. Dogmatism, in Unamuno's idiosyncratic dictionary, is a disease of the mind to which the intellectually lazy are vulnerable. Thankfully, there is a cure for dogmatism—a healthy dose of skepticism. Unamuno's skepticism goes beyond Cartesian methodological skepticism searching for a firm footing; Unamunian skepticism does not aim for epistemological certainty, but is committed to an ongoing open process of questioning for the sake of inquiry. Intellectually satisfying solutions may be long in the making or may never arrive; in the meantime, Unamuno insists, life has to be lived: "And it is also necessary not to lose sight of the fact that in order to live our life we rarely need wait for definitive scientific solutions. Men have lived and continue to live on the basis of very frail hypotheses and explanations and even without any at all" (Unamuno 1965, 211).

Unamuno's pragmatism echoes William James's views articulated in "The Will to Believe," which was written in response to W. K. Clifford's argument for evidentiary beliefs as a moral duty or an ethics of belief. Clifford had argued that people are obligated to withhold belief in God until scientific evidence is forthcoming. Until that day, belief in God is unethical. James took issue with Clifford, arguing that where there are no rational grounds for judging between two live, forced, and momentous hypotheses, our "passionate" nature is justified in making a decision without sufficient evidence. Unamuno, probably taking James too far, argued that no rational evidence supports our belief in God; yet, life has to be lived. Life is a struggle; faith, therefore, is like a wrestling match with God, a recursive Sisyphean climb toward an inaccessible summit:

> My religion is to seek the truth in life and life in the truth, even though I know I will not find it while I live. My religion is to struggle incessantly and tirelessly with the mystery; my religion is to wrestle with God from the break of dawn until the fall of night, as they say Jacob wrestled with Him. I cannot compromise with the concept of the Inconceivable, or with the notion that 'you will not get beyond this point.' I reject the eternal ignorabimus, the we-shall-not-know. In any case, I want to climb the inaccessible. (Unamuno 1965, 211)

Like the mystics before him, Unamuno describes God using the language of the *vía negativa* (negation route). Since language falls short of describing God, the human mind can only speak about God as a "mystery" and must take recourse to negative descriptors like "the inconceivable," and "the inaccessible." Turning to God, from a rational point of view, he confronts *la nada* (nothingness). However, faith struggles to transcend the limits of reason. Faith's true nature is agonistic—a struggling—not agnostic.

Transcending the limits of reason, religion asks questions reason cannot deliver: "As regards religion there is scarcely a single point I have resolved rationally, and since I have not, I cannot communicate any of these points logically, for only what is rational is logical and transmissible" (Unamuno 1965, 211). Religion operates in the non-rational domain of human experience, the affective region of the human psyche. Consequently, Unamuno's Christian faith is something felt rather than something believed, "I do have, in my affections, in my heart, in my feeling, a strong tendency toward Christianity, without abiding by any special dogmas of this or that Christian confession" (Unamuno 1965, 212). Unamuno does not identify himself as a Catholic or a Protestant, for he eschews orthodoxy, dogma, creedalism, and sectarianism. Reluctantly identifying himself as a nonsectarian Christian, he possesses little patience for orthodox thinking and for narrow-minded dogmatists who are intolerant of each other. He rejects both the rational theistic proofs for the existence of God and the atheistic arguments for God's nonexistence. God does not magically occur in the conclusion of a syllogism, for

God is the object of the desires, longings, and yearnings of the heart. Reformulating Descartes's *cogito ergo sum*, "I desire God; therefore, God exists." By dint of determination, the heart longs to bring God into existence by the sheer force of longing. Desire produces the fruit of religion.

Unamuno leaves readers with the vague impression that the agony itself, the struggle to believe, suffices as the true end and final aim of the Christian religion. However, it is more than a vague impression. Unamuno straightforwardly asserts, "And I will spend my life wrestling with the mystery, even though there is no hope of penetrating it, for the struggle itself is my sustenance and my consolation" (Unamuno 1965, 218). When the heart is restless for truth, but truth is not forthcoming, either resignation to life without God or willing acceptance of the agonic unending struggle for unattainable truth become the only options. For Unamuno resignation is unthinkable; the only real option is ceaseless struggle in the hope of an unconceivable victory. Reason may not support Unamuno's religious beliefs, but he refuses to resign, believing that subjective comprehension of the truth— "what I feel is truth"—is all that counts. His classic book, *On the Tragic Sense of Life of Men and Peoples* elaborates and develops more fully the ideas sketched out in "Mi religión."

ON THE TRAGIC SENSE OF LIFE OF MEN AND PEOPLES

Unamuno's inspired literary classic, *Del sentimiento trágico de la vida en los hombres y en los pueblos* (On the tragic sense of life of men and peoples), published in 1913, originated as a philosophical work as early as 1899. In a letter to Jiménez Ilundain (May 24, 1899), Unamuno writes that he first began working on *The Tragic Sense of Life* in 1899 (one year before he studied Kierkegaard). Intending it to be a work on philosophy, he tentatively entitled it *Diálogos filosóficos* (Philosophical dialogues). As the work progressed intermittently over the course of thirteen years, it increasingly focused on the central theme of Unamuno's intellectual and emotional concern—the conflict between faith and reason. In fact, he toyed with the idea of changing the title to either *Religion and Science* or *Reason and Faith*. In a 1902 letter to Santiago Valenti (March 11, 1902), he confides that the agonic theme, which became the core of *The Tragic Sense of Life*, sprang from the conviction that religion and science are, ultimately, irreconcilable. Even though he affirmed the Kantian antimetaphysic that God is no more than a postulate of practical reason, by 1905, Unamuno gave the work-in-progress a mystical title, *Tratado del amor de Dios* (Treatise on the love of God). Taking an antirationalist perspective, he lightheartedly conceded that logical arguments may be able to arrive at the idea of God, but logic is powerless to deliver the living God. Reference to the final title, *Del sentimiento trágico de la vida en los hombres y en los pueblos*, occurs for the first time in a 1911 letter to his friend Ilundain. In this letter, he describes the philosophy expressed in the work as a "philosophy of uncertainty and desperation"—an apt description of Unamuno's own thought (Malvido Miguel 1977, 247–58).

Clearly, the tragic sense of life in Unamunian terms looms large not as an abstract theoretical problem, but as a vital problem of resolving the paralyzing tension created by the inherent antagonism between religious feelings and rational beliefs. Consequently, for Unamuno, a narrowly rational or intellectualist construal of thought fails to do justice to the causal role of passion, instinct, desire, temperament, and character in the formation of action-guiding beliefs. Ideally, while evaluating arguments, philosophers should suspend consideration of circumstances and temperaments, because considerations of such matters in the search for truth constitute a fallacy—the genetic fallacy—for what really matters to philosophy are the arguments, not the lives, of the philosophers. A risk, however, accompanies the rational work of the philosopher, namely, the risk of abstracting philosophy from the everyday concerns of the human condition. However theoretically minded or rational people take themselves to be, and whether they accept it or not, people are men and women of flesh and bones, of passion, and reason. It is the whole person who thinks and not just the intellect alone: "Philosophy is a product of the humanity of each philosopher, and each philosopher is a man of flesh and bone who addresses himself to other men of flesh and bone like himself. And, let him do what he will, he philosophizes not with the reason only, but with the will, with the feelings, with the flesh and with the bones, with the whole soul and the whole body. It is the man who philosophizes" (Unamuno 1954, 48). Unamuno points to Immanuel Kant as an example of a philosopher who tried to square his religious feelings with his rational theory. Kant philosophized as a man, and as a man required religion. Ethical consideration presented him the opportunity he needed to allow God entry in a practical way into an overarching rational system that excluded God, immortality of the soul, and free will. In effect, Kant created a religious or eschatological basis for ethics. Kant postulates the immortality of the soul as a requirement of pure practical reason. He argues that the attainment of the highest good is necessarily an object or the object of a will determined by moral law and that a condition for attaining the highest good is the "complete fitness of dispositions to moral law." This complete fitness he identifies as holiness, perfection not attainable in this life. So "unending progress" is required as a practical necessity. Of course, unending progress presupposes the immortality of the soul: "this infinite progress is possible, however, only under the presupposition of an infinitely enduring existence and personality of the same rational being; this is called the immortality of the soul." Briefly put, the demand to be moral cannot be satisfied during our earthly life. Therefore, if we are to be morally perfect, then we must live indefinitely beyond the death of the body. Belief in the possibility of moral life requires that we posit the immortality of the soul as a regulative idea. What began as a severe epistemological critique of metaphysics that slammed the door in the face of beliefs about immortality, turns, in the end, to slightly open the door.

Benedict Spinoza, too, according to Unamuno, denied the rationality of belief in personal immortality, and yet, paradoxically, maintained the eternal intellectual love of God as the highest blessedness attainable by the human mind. In *Ethics*, Part 5, proposition 23, Spinoza writes that the mind is not destroyed along with the body; rather, after the death of the body, something of the mind remains, which is eternal. We feel and experience, claims Spinoza, that we are immortal. We desire to know things under the form of eternity (a kind of higher knowledge) such as God and that God is the immanent cause of all things, even the cause of our conception of God. The attainment of the knowledge of God is the highest contentment for the mind and constitutes a blessedness or highest pleasure of the mind, the eternal intellectual love of God (Part 5.33). Applying Spinoza's conatus propositions exclusively to human beings, we can reasonably interpret Spinoza to be claiming that every human being inherently strives consciously to preserve his or her own existence indefinitely. Acting hastily, Unamuno runs away with the somewhat shaky interpretation that the conatus supports the belief in personal immortality.

"Endeavor," a translation of the Latin term *conatus*, can also be freely translated as "impulse" or "effort." Harry Austryn Wolfson, in his erudite study of Spinoza's *Ethics*, documents the many ways in which the concept of the conatus has been employed in the history of Western thought as the principle of self-preservation. The stoics, St. Augustine, Thomas Aquinas, Duns Scotus, Dante, and Hobbes recognized the principle of self-preservation as a fundamental law of nature and used terms synonymous with conatus like "wish," "will," "desire," "appetite," "cupidity," and even "natural love." Spinoza intensifies the term by speaking of it not only as a principle of action but as the very essence of human nature. In Part 3, proposition 7, Spinoza identifies conatus as the actual essence of a thing, meaning the identity and individuality of a thing and not simply the ideal conception of it. Since human beings are conceived as modifications of the attributes of God and God is self-caused, *causa sui*—that is, God, too, is motivated by the principle of self-preservation—it necessarily follows that human endeavor for self-preservation stems from God's own power. "And inasmuch as the conatus for self-preservation follows from the necessity of the eternal power of God itself, this conatus does not involve finite but indefinite time." By "thing" in propositions 6 to 8, Spinoza means bodies, modes of the attribute of extension. In proposition 9 Spinoza applies the conatus to the human mind. For Spinoza, whatever happens in the attribute of extension is paralleled by a similar event in the attribute of thought. From a Spinozistic standpoint, things can be viewed as aspects of the external world or as aspects of the mind. Related to the mind, conatus means *voluntas* (will), but related to the body, conatus means *appetitus* (desire or appetite). Spinoza seems to be saying that the striving for self-preservation follows necessarily from the eternal nature of God, for individual things, including people, are only "modes whereby the attributes of God are expressed in a given determinate manner."

For Unamuno, the principle of self-preservation is a fundamental law of human nature that explains and predicts human behavior. His interpretation of Spinoza holds that the conatus or endeavor of self-preservation is not limited to earthly existence. True, Spinoza holds that the conatus involves no definite time; however, in Part II of the Ethics, "Of the Nature and Origin of the Mind," Spinoza defines duration as the indefinite continuance of an existing thing. Spinoza reasons that from the nature of a thing or its efficient cause, its duration cannot be given a fixed determination. In other words, consideration of the qualities of an existing thing cannot lead to a determination of the quantitative magnitude of its duration. Indeed, for Spinoza the duration of the endeavor, the conatus, to preserve life is indefinite simpliciter. To preserve life is to preserve consciousness.

Why does consciousness exist? In the *Metaphysics*, Aristotle delineated four types of causes: material, formal, efficient, and final. Final cause answers the question of purposiveness, for the sake of what. Aristotle argued, in the *Nicomachean Ethics*, that the final cause or purpose of human life is happiness. Alternatively, Unamuno considers that the final cause of consciousness is the endeavor to perpetuate consciousness. Consciousness exists for the sake of preserving consciousness. The endeavor to preserve consciousness is the very essence and nature of being a concrete man or woman of flesh and bone: "This means that your essence, reader, mine, that of the man Spinoza, that of the man Butler, of the man Kant, and of every man who is a man, is nothing but the endeavor, the effort, which he makes to continue to be a man, not to die" (Unamuno 1954, 7).

Unamunian anthropology describes the fundamental human attitude toward life or the finality of consciousness expressed in the longing for personal immortality; yet, and here's the rub, this desire conflicts with the laws of logic, reason, and science. In essence, reason's denial of this fundamental longing constitutes the tragic sense of life: "There is something which, for lack of a better name, we will call the tragic sense of life which carries with it a whole conception of life itself and of the universe, a whole philosophy more or less formulated, more or less conscious . . . And this sense does not so much flow from ideas as determine them . . . these ideas react upon it and confirm it" (Unamuno 1954, 17).

Subjectivity in a broad sense is the starting point of Unamuno's quixotic philosophy. On closer examination, the point of departure for reflection is the tragic sense of life resulting from the inner struggle between life and reason. The tragic sense of life is constituted by the tragic and agonic conflict between the iron-clad refusal of reason to warrant belief in personal immortality and the stubborn clinging to an irrational hope in eternal life: "Now we remain in this vehement suspicion that the fear of death, the hunger of personal immortality, the conatus that drives us to preserve indefinitely in our own being, and that is, according to that tragic Jew (Benedict Spinoza) our fundamental essence, is the affective basis of all knowing and the intimate point of departure for all human philosophy, forged by one man for all men" (Unamuno 1954, 36).

The gnawing question at the heart of *The Tragic Sense of Life* agonizes over the point of the conatus, self-preservation, and the perpetuation of consciousness. In Spanish the question is *¿para qué?* (what for?). What's the purpose—¿para qué?— of philosophy? Why philosophize at all? Unamuno's angle concerns the relevance of philosophy for life. What's the point of doing philosophy unless it matters for living? Theoretical philosophy possesses no value for Unamuno. Only practical philosophy counts, for practical philosophy is about living, and the ¿para qué? or reason for practical philosophy is life: "The philosopher philosophizes for something more than for the sake of philosophizing . . . the philosopher is a man before he is a philosopher, he needs live before he can philosophize, and, in fact, he philosophizes in order to live" (Unamuno 1954, 26). At best, Unamuno establishes that there exists a fundamental human longing to preserve existence, to perpetuate consciousness. Is there anything more to it than a wishful fantasy? Is there anything in the world of nature or artifact that gives any objective reason for thinking that belief in immortality is justified?

Presumably, if there is a divine reality, a possible world in which immortality is a feature of the entities who populate it, would not there exist signals of transcendence, footprints of the divine, or traces of this possible world, discernible within the limits of the actual world? Following through with this intuition, Unamuno indicates certain aspects of human experience that seem to offer glimpses of another world lying beyond the changing, transitory world of earthly existence. Love is one such signal of transcendence. Love expressing a thirst for the eternal suggests to Unamuno an underlying pessimistic view of the transitory world, a feeling of the vanity of earthly existence. Hope of personal immortality rooted in the fear of death constitutes another signal of transcendence. For Unamuno, however, the fear of death is really the fear of the annihilation of consciousness, la nada. Arguably, the longing for personal immortality arises from both the feeling of the vanity of earthly existence and the fear of la nada. The rhetorical figure of the suicide could strike a blow against Unamuno's tenet of the universality of the belief in personal immortality. However, the suicide confirms the longing for the eternal and the vanity of earthly existence. Signed works of art, too, testify to the longing for immortality. No rational proof, however, can ground arguments for or against the immortality of the soul or the existence of God.

Unamuno longed for immortality and thus projected his longing upon Christ, imagining Christ as an immortalizer. Christ's death unlocks the mystery of immortality: "The discovery of death is that which reveals God to us, and the death of the perfect man, Christ, was the supreme revelation of death, being the death of the man who ought not to have died yet did die" (Unamuno 1954, 63). That Christ is the man that ought not to have died holds a clue for overcoming reason's objection to the belief in immortality.

St. Paul made belief in bodily resurrection the foundation, the sine qua non, of Christian faith. In I Corinthians 15:17–19, St. Paul writes, "if Christ be not raised [. . .] we [Christians] are of all men most miserable." After St. Paul, if Unamuno's historical theology is correct, the responsibility of safeguarding "faith in the immortality of the individual soul" fell on the shoulders of the fourth-century Alexandrine Church father Athanasius, defender of the orthodox Christological doctrines enshrined in the Nicene Creed. Arguably, Athenagoras, a second-century theologian, in his *De Resurrectione*, preceded Athanasius in securing the doctrine of the resurrection of the soul. In any case, Emperor Constantine, unraveled by the fear of the instability of the Roman Empire, convened the Council of Nicea in 325 CE largely in an effort to settle the religious disputes about the nature of the relationship between Christ and the Father. Ostensibly, theological disputes threatened to destroy the socio-political unity of the empire. The Christological doctrines of Arius, known as Arianism, held that Jesus was not consubstantial with God the Father. In the archaic language of early Christian theology, Arius held that Jesus possesses a similar substance but does not share the same substance with the Father. In short, Arianism denied that Jesus was fully God and thereby compromised the integrity of Christ's divinity. Jesus is like God but not God. Athanasius defended the orthodox view that Jesus shared the same substance with the Father.

Arius proclaimed the doctrine that there was a time when Christ was not. Athanasius countered Arius by writing a book called *De Incarnatione Verbi Dei* (On the Incarnation of the Word of God), in which he explains why God became man. (Centuries later, St. Anselm of Canterbury addressed the same question in his book, *Cur Deus Homo* [Why Did God Become Man?], offering an ingenious theological hypothesis known as the Satisfaction Theory of the Atonement, mirroring the honor system of feudal Europe). In the *Incarnatione*, Athanasius links the story of salvation with the story of creation. According to Athanasius, God created human beings in his likeness, the *imago dei*, in order to share his divinity with his creatures. However, human beings sinned and became corruptible; that is, human beings became mortal. Human nature originally reflected the divine nature, but the divine element in human nature was lost. In order to restore human beings to their divine status, Christ died for our sins. Why did Christ have to die to redeem humanity? Surely, an omnipotent God could have saved humankind in some other way. God, for example, could have called human beings to repentance or God could have forgiven humans by divine fiat. However, that, says Athanasius, would only stop sin, not the process of corruption: "For this purpose, then, the incorporeal and incorruptible and immaterial Word of God entered our world." Being immortal, God could not die; yet God in Christ took on our mortal body and exchanged his death for that of all human beings so that we all might live. Christ died as our substitute. Christ's incarnation and death made possible our own recreation in the likeness of the immortal Word of God; consequently, we are able to share in Christ's immortality and in his divinity: "Naturally also, through this union of the immortal Son of God with our human nature, all men were clothed with incorruption in the promise of the resurrection." Athanasius, thus, identifies Jesus Christ as God himself: "these things show that Christ on the cross was God . . . Christ is revealed as God and Son of God" (Athanasius 1944, 13). One consequence of the Athanasian doctrine, identifying the substance of Christ with the substance of God the Father, is the risk of compromising the integrity of the humanity of Jesus, a point not lost on Syrian Christianity, which emphasized the humanity of Christ.

What Unamuno loved about the Catholic Christ of Athanasius and the Nicene Creed is their affirmation of a strictly religious Christ: "The Athanasian or Nicene Christ, who is the Catholic Christ, is not the cosmological nor even strictly, the ethical Christ, he is eternalizing, the deifying, the religious Christ." Athanasius's Christ is not the philosophical Logos mediating the chasm between the realm of grace and the realm of nature, but God become man "in order that He might better deify us." Athanasius, as far as Unamuno is concerned, rightly conceived salvation as the restoration of the gift of immortality to a fallen humanity. Athanasius "devoured by the hunger of immortality" projected the image of Christ as a grand immortalizer (Unamuno 1954, 64).

On closer inspection, Unamuno too eagerly recognizes only a religious Christ in the Nicene Creed and in Athanasius. One can readily see the cornerstone of the Athanasius/Nicene Creed is the shared substance doctrine that expresses a philosophical concept about identity—that two named entities share the same identity, the same substance. The shared substance doctrine is not religious but ontological. Unamuno is seeing what he wants to see. Along the same lines, he minimizes the historical Jesus.

By the nineteenth century, with advances in science and the historical critical method in scriptural exegesis, Protestant theologians tried to uncover the historical Jesus, the man of flesh and bone hidden beneath the layers of theological tradition and mythology. They worried that the church's emphasis on the Christ of faith risked losing sight of the historical Jesus, a concern revived by Latin American liberation theologians in the twentieth century. Unamuno attacks Adolf Harnack, a Protestant historical theologian, for his emphasis on the historical Jesus. Harnack accused Athanasius of Docetism, the doctrine that denies the integrity of Jesus's human nature, a doctrine rejected by the Council of Chalcedon (451 CE). According to Harnack, the Athanasian defense of the substantial identity between God and Jesus Christ obliterates the historical Jesus. Harnack rejected the Christology of the church because it abstracts from the Jesus of the Gospels and uses philosophy to systematize doctrines of Christ not found in the Gospels. Specifically, Harnack attacked the Logos doctrine of the fourth-century Christian theologians, in particular Athanasius's attempt to show the consubstantiality of the son of man with God the Father. The Logos doctrine holds that Christ is God's own reason and that through Christ God created the world. The Logos doctrine appealed to the Greek Christians because the Jewish notion of *Messiah* (anointed one) was foreign to them and at the same time, from a Christian point of view, the image of Christ as a Greek hero appeared too heathen. The ambiguity of the doctrine of redemption, when tied closely to Logos Christianity, raises the question: Did Christ die to redeem humanity from sin or from death? As Harnack points out, by the third century the dominant interpretation came to be that Christ died to redeem us from death (Harnack 1986, 231–33).

This interpretation of redemption, according to Harnack, while having starting points in the Gospels and St. Paul, nonetheless, is in accord with Greek philosophy and foreign to the New Testament. The third- and fourth-century Alexandrine theologians conceived redemption "as redemption from death and therewith as elevation to the divine life, that is to say, deification." Consequently, "mortality is in itself reckoned as the greatest evil, and as the cause of all evil, while the greatest of blessings is to live forever." Divine power, in this line of thought, possesses qualities that allow it to enter into mortal human life. Therefore, God in Christ entered human life and become man: "It is not, however, the hero, but God Himself alone, who possesses the divine, that is to say, eternal life, and so possesses it as to permit of his giving it to others. The Logos, then, must be God Himself, and He must have actually become man." Harnack argues that these considerations enabled Athanasius to formulate the Logos doctrine that Christ was the same nature as the Father (Harnack 1986, 237).

Harnack opposes the Logos doctrine of consubstantiality because it is "sub-Christian" and "too slippery" to attach ethics to it; moreover, the Athanasian doctrine, Harnack insists, has no connection to the Jesus of the Gospels. Harnack rejects the formulaic intellectualism that tries to systematize philosophically the Jesus of the Gospels. Abstract rational interpretations of the Gospels are hard to square with the stories of real flesh and blood people facing real fears and dangers, such as the Syrophoenician woman and the centurion at Capernaum.

Contrary to Harnack, Athanasius did not conceive of redemption solely in terms of salvation from death but also in terms of salvation from sin as aptly demonstrated by Gustaf Aulén in his classic work, *Christus Victor*: "But such an interpretation would not be just either to Athanasius or to the other Greek Fathers. Athanasius does, in fact, regard sin as not merely the cause of the corruption from which men need to be saved, but as being identical with it." Athanasius makes it clear that corruption and death hold sway over humankind "for transgressing the commandment" and "their sinning surpassed all limits" and thus "they involved themselves in death and corruption" (Aulén 1969, 43–44).

Against Harnack's claim that Athanasius "obliterated" the historical Jesus, Unamuno defends Athanasius, arguing that what really matters to faith is not the historical *Jesus* but the historical *Christ*, the Christ contemporaneous with the believer, the present Christ, the existentialist Christ, the mystical Christ not subject to the scalpel of biblical criticism. The Jesus of history that biblical scholars such as Harnack have been busily trying to uncover beneath the layers mythology, redaction, and theological accretion in the Gospel stories belongs to the past and does not walk among the living: "Among Protestants, this historical Jesus is subjected to the scalpel of criticism, while the Catholic Christ lives, the really historical Christ, he who lives throughout the centuries guaranteeing the faith in personal immorality and personal salvation" (Unamuno 1954, 65).

Preoccupied with the Jesus of history, Harnack considered talk about divine substances as irrational or contra-rational. Unamuno, by contrast, celebrates the contra-rational that Harnack rejects: "In truth, it [Athanasius's doctrine of consubstantiality] drew closer to life, which is contra-rational and opposed to clear thinking." Unamuno asks, what is contra-rational in the doctrine of the consubstantiality? The doctrine of consubstantiality holds that God the Father and Christ the Son are identical. God is an infinite being and Jesus Christ, a finite being—a paradox for Kierkegaard. The doctrine of consubstantiality is self-contradictory, and, therefore, contra-rational. Contradictions are not rational; they entail a false value. The doctrine of consubstantiality is a value judgment, not a descriptive statement of what is the case. Assuming the fact/value distinction, Unamuno holds that judgments of value are "never rationalizable—they are anti-rational." It follows that the affirmation of the consubstantiality of the Son and the Father is a judgment of value. Athanasius' Christ, then, is not the historical Jesus the object of interest for rational, historical, and critical biblical scholarship, but the religious Christ or the Christ of faith. The Jesus of history matters for scholars; the historical Christ matters for life (Unamuno 1954, 65).

To be clear, Unamuno's "historical Christ" has little to do with the Jesus of history and everything to do with the believer's religious imaginary and with the collective mythical imaginary of church dogma as if the two converge as one. In light of Unamuno's existentialism and pragmatism, Christ is alive to the extent that the subjective appropriation of Christ makes a difference to human experience. By representing Christ as the living word and not the dead letter, Unamuno targets what he sees as the sterility of Protestant Biblical criticism and a rational approach to religious studies in general. Unamuno, like Duns Scotus, recognizes a great gulf between faith and reason.

Tragic consequences, Unamuno writes, occur when one attempts to reconcile faith with reason. One such tragic consequence, scholastic theology, resulted when faith sought the aid of reason. Theologians such as Athanasius appealed to Aristotelian philosophy to give dogma a rational basis. Thomism exemplifies this enterprise. Faith, however, according to Unamuno, is nothing less than the struggle of life against reason, echoing Tertullian's sentiments expressed in his widely misunderstood anti-intellectual credo, *credo quia absurdum* (I believe in that which is absurd). Tertullian never said the words "credo quia absurdum." Rather, he said, "The Son of God died; this is by all means to be believed, because it makes no sense. And he was buried and rose again; this fact is certain, because it is impossible" (Pelikan 1999, 63–64). The impossibility of the Resurrection makes faith appear absurd. Faith refuses to lay down in defeat, but rises up in struggle against rational skepticism. Yet, in the struggle, Unamuno finds the possibility of a principle of life: "What I wish to establish is that uncertainty, doubt, perpetual wrestling with the mystery of our final destiny, mental despair, and the lack of any solid and stable dogmatic foundation, may be the basis of an ethic" (Unamuno 1954, 128).

Don Quixote exemplifies for Unamuno the tragic sense of life and the agony of Christianity. Don Quixote personifies instinct, the will to believe, uncertainty, doubt, striving, the nonrational, faith—in short, life itself. Unamuno describes Quixote "as the eternal exemplar of every man whose soul is the battleground of reason and irrational desire. Our Lord Don Quixote is the prototype of the vitalist whose faith is based upon uncertainty" (Unamuno 1954, 120). Unamuno likens the quixotic believer to a man who sets sail on a crude, hastily constructed raft. When the raft begins to sink, the man remains unfazed, struggling to keep it afloat. This man, this quixotic believer, "thinks that he acts not because he deems his principle of action to be true, but in order to make it true, in order to prove its truth, in order to create his own spiritual world" (Unamuno 1954, 262).

Accepting the conflict between reason and the longing to believe may be the basis of ethics. Despair can be a wellspring of human, profoundly human, action, effort, solidarity, and, even, progress: "We are about to enter—if it be that you wish to accompany me—upon a field of contradictions between feeling and reasoning, and we shall have to avail ourselves of the one as well as of the other" (Unamuno 1954, 130). In other words, act as if the belief in immortality were true.

This neo-Kantian principle finds poignant expression in Étienne Pivert de Senancour's *Obermann*, one of Unamuno's sources. Senancour reformulates the Kantian categorical imperative in Letter XC (1804): "Man is perishable. That may be; but let us perish resisting, and if it is nothingness that awaits us, do not let us so act that it shall be a just fate" (Unamuno 1954, 263). Unamuno makes *Obermann*'s imperative his own ethical criterion of action, "And if it is nothingness that awaits us, let us so act that it would be an unjust act" (Unamuno 1954, 263). Spinning the idea, several different versions result: Act as if you could make yourself irreplaceable; strive to make others feel that we ought not to have died: "Our greatest endeavor must be to make ourselves irreplaceable; to make the theoretical fact . . . the fact that each one of us is unique and irreplaceable, that no one else can fill the gap that will be left when we die, a practical truth. . . . And, to act in such a way as to make our annihilation an injustice. . . . that we ought not to have died is something that is within the reach of all" (Unamuno 1954, 269). Mephistopheles, Unamuno reminds the reader, states that every existing thing deserves annihilation. Channeling Kierkegaard, Unamuno affirms the contrary, stating that those who desire eternity most passionately deserve it the most: "All men deserve to be saved, but . . . he above all deserves immortality who desires it passionately and even in the face of reason" (Unamuno 1954, 265). Merit and deservingness reward the passionate. Actions, to some extent or other, may stem from passions, but our passions are not our actions. Feeling passionate is a necessary but not sufficient condition. Actions, in the end, are what merit eternity: "Act so that annihilation of consciousness would be an unjust fate." This negative formulation is the corollary of the more positively stated: Act as if you merit eternity. The sacrifice of Christ exemplifies the altruistic ideal implied by this maxim: "And the Christ who gave himself for his brothers in humanity with an absolute self-abnegation is the pattern for our action to shape itself on" (Unamuno 1913, 269).

THE AGONY OF CHRISTIANITY

Living in exile, Unamuno wrote *The Agony of Christianity*, continuing the passionate analysis of finitude of *The Tragic Sense of Life*. In *The Agony of Christianity*, he shifts themes to emphasize the Kierkegaardian incompatibility between personal Christianity and social Christianity. Having criticized the repressive military dictatorship of General Primo de Rivera, Unamuno was exiled to the island of Fuerteventura in the Canary Islands on March 10, 1924. Within a few months, assisted by friends, he escaped to France. In Paris, L. Couchoud commissioned Unamuno to write a monograph for Couchoud's series entitled *Christianisme*. Couchoud, familiar with *The Tragic Sense of Life*, suggested the title *The Agony of Christianity*. Jean Cassou translated the book into French before its publication in Spanish in 1930, after Unamuno's return from exile (Nozick 1974, 4). In the 1930 prologue to the Spanish edition of *La agonía del cristianismo*, Unamuno confides that when writing the book in Paris, he was "in a strange state of mind, prey to a veritable spiritual fever, to a nightmare of waiting." Attending services at a Greek Orthodox church, he noticed a bust of Christ with the inscription: "I am the way, the truth, and the Life." Meditating upon the recurring theme that truth kills illusions but life maintains them, he recalled Dostoevsky's words: "If I have to choose between Christ and the truth, I choose Christ" (Unamuno 1974, 243–4).

Agony is ambiguous, signifying two ideas. First, agony connotes a mental state of suffering, anxiety, despair—Kierkegaard's sickness unto death. Second, Unamuno's own use of the term retrieves the etymological sense of the original Greek—"struggle." He attributed the "flattering success" of *The Agony of Christianity* to the recuperation of the original sense of agony as struggle. By derivation, an agonist is one who struggles, not one who suffers: "And because of that reaffirmation, people will not mistake an 'agonizer' for a dying or a moribund person. One can die without agony and one can live—live for many, many years—with agony and on the strength of it. A true agonizer is an agonist, sometimes a protagonist, other times an antagonist" (Unamuno 1974, 246).

Conventionally, *agony* connotes the death throes of a dying person. Unamuno agonizes to disabuse us of this popular misconception. *Agony* means struggle, specifically, the struggle of life against death. He who lives in the throes of life, struggles against life itself, lives in agony, agonizes. In *The Tragic Sense of Life*, Unamuno empathizes with St. Teresa of Ávila's agony pathetically expressed in her soulish words, "Muero porque no muero" (I am dying because I do not die). Unamuno fondly quotes Teresa's emotional expression because it faithfully captures his own agony: "What I am about to narrate here, my reader, is my own agony, my struggle for Christianity, the agony of Christianity in me, its death and resurrection at each moment of my inner life" (Unamuno 1954, 5).

The centerpiece of Unamuno's *The Agony of Christianity* is a chapter entitled "The Faith of Pascal," originally appearing as an essay Unamuno wrote for the occasion of the tercentenary of Blaise Pascal's birth, June 19, 1623. For Unamuno, learning from Pascal the man is more important than learning from the thoughts of Pascal. Moreover, since the only Pascal he can write about is the Pascal that he has assimilated and internalized, he can only write about Pascal as Unamuno felt about him. Pascal agonized about faith because faith does not square with reason. Faith and reason to Pascal seemed incommensurable. Pascal, the believer, according to Unamuno, sought refuge from reason: "It suffices to read Pascal with an unprejudiced mind to sense that he did not believe through reason; he was never able even when he so desired, to believe with his reason; he was never convinced of what he had persuaded himself to believe. And that was his personal tragedy. He sought his salvation through the skepticism he favored against the inner dogmatism he suffered" (Unamuno 1974, 77). According to Unamuno, Pascal the scientist, the mathematician, had no need for God, but Pascal the man needed the security that faith in God could provide him from the fear of nothingness. Pascal did not attempt, like Aquinas, a synthesis of faith and reason, nor did he follow the way of the mystics and only grab the religious horn of the dilemma. Instead, according to Unamuno, he suffered the consequences of living with the contradiction. Living with the contradiction constitutes the essence of tragedy. Moreover, if Unamuno is right, tragedy afflicts all modern believers. Ultimately, Unamuno finds Pascal's wager unsatisfying because, in the end, Pascal is rationally motivated to give reasons for believing in God. Pascal disappointed Unamuno, for after conceding that we cannot give reasons to prove God's existence, Pascal, in effect, rationalizes belief in God. Ironically, Unamuno's solution to the conflict between faith and reason echoes Pascal.

Out of the interstice between reason and faith, multiple possibilities lie before the human will. Reason cannot support our religious beliefs or our ethics because our ethics is grounded on our religious beliefs. Acknowledgement of the fact/value distinction requires decisionism in ethics. Decisionism, however, is not a compromise between rational skepticism and the passion to religious belief but a necessary result. Life has to be lived and reason cannot tell us how to live it. Unamuno chooses to act as if he can make his belief true, which in practical terms means that he must act as if to make himself irreplaceable and that implies a perfectionist ethic. In the view of the Platonic scholastic philosophers, the more perfect a thing is, the more real it is. Perfect ideals are the only realities in this philosophy. In the end, Unamuno is a scholastic philosopher of the Platonist school, for he insists that to eternalize yourself, to make yourself immortal, you must strive toward perfection and goad others likewise. To contemporary eyes, the ethics of the impossible ideal remains a quixotic ethics and therefore an irrational philosophy.

ST. MANUEL THE GOOD, MARTYR

Written in 1930 and published the following year, *St. Manuel the Good, Martyr* opens with a familiar quote from Paul's first letter to the church at Corinth, a busy Greek seaport: "If in this life only we have hope in Christ, we are of all men most miserable" (I Cor. 15:19). Unable to demonstrate rationally the existence of immortality and unwilling to abandon religious hope, Unamuno resorts to a decisionistic solution. He counsels the unbelieving faithful to live by the maxim, "Act as if you deserve immortality." St. Manuel the Good embodies Unamuno's maxim to act as if he believes for the sake of his faithful parishioners. This character "stands as a final and major statement of all of Unamuno's antinomies" (Nozick 1971, 166).

Set in an isolated, unpretentious, archaic, almost medieval village of Valverde de Lucerna, in the diocese of Renada, the story opens with the bishop of the diocese in the process of the beatification of the deceased village priest, don Manuel. Angela Carballino, in her fifties, former friend and disciple of don Manuel since childhood, narrates religiously if not confessionally, the story of don Manuel and his mystical and magical effects on her and the village. She regards him as her spiritual father but describes him as a matriarchal man. Her own father, deceased in her childhood, left her books. She recalls that when she was ten years old, don Manuel was a tall, slender man with penetrating, deep, blue eyes. He enchanted everyone, her memory joyfully recalls.

She recalls her childhood, when her brother Lazarus, away in America, arranged for her stay a convent since there was no secular academy for girls. He desired her refinement, not religion. Mainly, he sent her away so that she would not turn out to be like the other village girls.

As she tells the story, returning to her village at age fifteen, she discovers that village life revolves around don Manuel, the center of gravity. At some point, she learns that don Manuel became a priest so that he could support his widowed sister and her children. Although his brilliance attracted opportunities for social advancement, he turned them down to be the priest of a remote village between a lake and a mountain. On reading this, the reader's credulity is tested. If don Manuel's objective purpose was the support of his sister and her children, then reasonably he should have accepted one of the more lucrative opportunities instead of a lonely post in a backwater village.

In any case, Angela tells how don Manuel busied himself, constantly attending to the daily challenges of earthly existence that troubled the villagers. Nothing escaped his concern. He even insisted that the villagers wear clean clothes. He provided the poor with clean shirts. Of all the local folk, he directed his attention particularly to the village idiot Blasillo, the priest's double.

Above all his features, don Manuel's glory lay with his voice, for it was divine, divine in the sense that when he quoted Jesus's words from the pulpit, parishioners felt as though God were speaking directly to them from the depths of God's own soul. On one memorable Good Friday mass, he cried the words of Jesus, "My God, My God, why hast thou forsaken me?" Everyone in the church shuddered as though they heard Christ's voice calling out from the crucifix. Curiously, Blasillo, in imitation, echoed the priest's words with a similar effect.

All the villagers went to mass just to see the transfiguration of don Manuel's physical presence. When the priest led the church in a recitation of the creed, they spoke with one voice, but when they got to the last part about the resurrection, his voice fell silent, unnoticed by the church.

Angela perceived something hiding behind his ceaseless activity for others. Was he fleeing from idleness, leisure, and thinking? If not busy, he occupied himself trying to find something to do for the villagers. She persuaded herself that in all this busyness there existed sadness, hidden from others. In time, he priest admitted to her his fear of solitude.

She frequented the confessional, revealing intellectual doubts of her faith. Once, the priest admonished her to believe the dogmas of the Holy Mother Church and to stop listening to the devil. Answering her question whether hell really existed, he told her to believe in Heaven, enigmatically pointing to the mountain, the lake, and the sky. He counselled her to believe in everything taught by the church. At this, she noticed sadness in his eyes.

Her brother Lazarus returned from America before her twenty-fourth birthday. His anticlerical outlook perceived the village as a feudal medieval "obscurantist theocracy." His progressive ideas and secular denunciations moved no one. Lazarus brought books for Angela, encouraging her to read. The priest had instructed her to read worthy books, by which he meant novels, saying that they describe reality better than nonfiction. Unamuno, similar to Salvador Dalí and Jorge Luis Borges, blurred the lines between reality and fiction, doubting that any factual description of reality can actually approach the reality described.

As Angela's and Lazarus's mother lay dying, don Manuel whispered in Lazarus's ear to vow to her that he, Lazarus, would pray for her. Lazarus promised his dying mother. Expressing her desire to see God, she heard don Manuel say that God is all around us. At first glance, it seems that the priest is echoing the pantheism of the Dutch philosopher Benedict Spinoza, for by enchanting the world, the priest is disenchanting the supernatural.

Lazarus's promise to his mother transformed him. He began to follow don Manuel, attend mass, and accompany him on his rounds. On the day of Lazarus's communion, don Manuel's hands trembled, dropping the wafer; Lazarus quickly picked it up and put in his own mouth. When alone with her brother, Angela embraced him, rejoicing in his conversion. Within moments, she shuddered at the terrible news that Lazarus revealed to her. Don Manuel had told Lazarus to feign religious belief and to conceal his true skepticism. The villagers must be encouraged to believe their illusions, because the truth (there is no God and no Resurrection) would be unbearable to them.

From that moment on, she was afraid to be alone with don Manuel. Yet, she came again to don Manuel, hoping that he would assuage her doubts. He consoled her, as always, to keep on believing and to suppress her doubts because the main thing is to live. Angela mustered the courage to ask him if he believed. Diffidently, he responded, "I believe." No sooner did the words leave his lips than doubt plagued his mind and he confessed that he did not know what he believed, only that life needs to be lived. Perplexed Angela again saw a deep sadness in him.

Talking with the priest, Lazarus mentioned the good social work of the Catholic syndicates. Don Manuel, suspicious of institutional Christianity, surprised Lazarus by replying that religion does not exist to resolve economic or political conflicts. In the face of the illusion of eternal life, don Manuel advised Lazarus to focus on the interiority of faith and to preach resignation in the face of worldly events: "Let men think and act as they will, let them console themselves for having been born, let them live as happily as possible in the illusion that all this has purpose . . . Preach resignation" (Unamuno 1976, 165).

Don Manuel goes on to describe his own life as a kind of altruistic suicide so that the people can live. He also helps the poor die well and in helping them, he discovers the real cause of their "sickness unto death" the "abyss of their life-weariness." "Sickness unto death" is Kierkegaard's term for generalized anxiety, an anxiety that comes from a powerful and personal sense of mortality and the awful burden of freedom and responsibility that accompanies it. The priest implores Lazarus to live life as a suicide, working for the people that they may dream their lives. Chiding Lazarus for zealously denouncing the superstitions of the people, don Manuel counsels, "It's better for them to believe everything, even things that contradict one another, than to believe nothing" (Unamuno 1965, 104). José Carlos Mariategui, the Peruvian Marxist, wrote in his essay, "The Religious Factor," that people need a myth to keep on living. For don Manuel, people need consolation for having been born only to die. It is illusory to think that life has purpose. Let the people resign themselves to their fate and accept their lot in life.

As time passed, Angela noticed the weakening of don Manuel's spirit. Whenever he spoke about the other world, he paused uncomfortably. At communion, he whispered to Lazarus, "There is no other life but this, no life more eternal . . . let them dream it eternal . . . let it be eternal for a few years" (Unamuno 1965, 106).

At church Angela, turning to the statue of the Mater Dolorosa cried out, "Pray for us sinners!" Reflectively she asked, "What is sin?" Don Manuel replied quoting the Calderón play *Life is a Dream*: "The greatest sin of man is to have been born" (Unamuno 1965, 107).

In the final moments of his death, don Manuel told Lazarus and Angela to let the people believe what he himself could not believe, and to take comfort in that. Bidding them farewell, he said, "until we never meet again, for this dream of life is coming to an end." (Unamuno 1976, 169). Giving his final blessing to the village gathered at the church, he prayed the Paternoster, the Ave Maria, and the Salve. Arriving at the final verses of the Creed, he grew silent before the words about the resurrection of the flesh. His eyes closed for the last time. Blasillo died the same moment.

Speaking to Angela, Lazarus reveals that don Manuel had once said to him that there are truths that one must keep to oneself, adding that even Christ died without believing in another life. Her brother's death left her disconsolate.

At this point the narrative ends, but the self-conscious narrator, Angela, reflects on life, death, and loneliness. She thinks don Manuel and her brother died believing they did not believe, all the while not really believing their belief. She hopes that in their dying moments God removed the veil from their eyes. She admits that she does not know what is true or what is false.

Unamuno adds an epilogue to the story, stating that it does not matter whether the villagers would have been able to understand, had don Manuel and Lazarus revealed to them the truth. For the villagers, what counts are not words but works.

Several features about Unamuno's Christ require highlighting in closing this discussion. First, there is an inconsistency in Unamuno's notion of the historical Christ. Of this notion, one must divorce it from the Jesus of Nazareth, the historical man of flesh and bone, and dissociate it from the Jesus of the Gospels. Unamuno's historical Christ is not the result of the Protestant scholar's scalpel. Unamuno would not find any interest in the Jesus in Jesus seminars. The historical Christ is the Christ of tradition, culture, and nation. For Unamuno, the historical Christ is the Spanish Christ. However, and this is where the inconsistency appears, the Spanish Christ is a bloody corpse, a dead Christ. Unamuno's Christ is the living Christ, so Unamuno feels revulsion at the thought of the Spanish Christ. To salvage the living Christ, the historical Christ, finds the true Spanish Christ not in the crucifix, but in Quixote, the errant idealist who lived as if he could immortalize himself.

Second, St. Manuel the Good, like Quixote, lived as if he could immortalize himself in the lives and memories of the villagers. The village priest, a type of Christ, fuels the villagers' dreams of immortality, and feeds them the pablum of church doctrine to give them a living hope, a reason for enduring all the while doubting the substance of that hope. The atheist's mistake is in thinking that God's nonexistence matters. What matters is whether life can be lived in a way that merits immortality. In the end, Christ symbolizes the human yearning for life.

Third, Unamuno counsels the believer in a state of doubt. Reasonable and reflective persons sometimes doubt their most intensive convictions and their most extensive commitments. The slothful believer, by contrast, probably does not experience serious doubt for lack of probing with the light of reason all the diverse aspects of his or her beliefs from all the cognitively accessible angles. Reason exacerbates doubt. What is the doubting believer to do when frightened by the prospect of giving up faith? Unamuno's unequivocal answer, pragmatic it may be, is to live as if religious hopes will be redeemed eschatologically. Even if the redemption never materializes, people can rest their hopes on the belief that their lives merit eternity. For this reason, Unamuno prefers the dying agonistic Christ, not the crucified Christ of the Spanish imaginary. Not everyone hopes for immortality like Unamuno did. The next figure, the Argentinean writer Jorge Luis Borges, desired not immortality but annihilation.

CHAPTER FIVE

Jorge Luis Borges

The Fictional Christ

Jorge Luis Borges, the famous Argentinean writer, although a skeptic, immersed himself in theology. He read scripture, studied the world's religions, and familiarized himself with the history of Christian thought. He wrote two fantastic stories about Christ—"The Gospel According to Mark" and "Three Versions of Judas." The recalcitrance of reality to the grasp of human knowledge, the absurdity of the human condition, and the slipperiness of language underlie Borges's discourse about Christ, proving that theologies about Christ are nothing more than games that grown children take too seriously. Accordingly, Borges treats Christ as a fictional figure.

In his 1937 essay "Raymond Llull's Thinking Machine," Borges gives us a clue to interpreting his unconventional views on religion and theology. Ramon Llull (1232–1315), philosopher and patron saint of computer geeks and one of Dalí's scholastic hero, hoped to convert Muslims to the Christian faith, and to this end, he set about to refute Averroes, the great Arabic philosopher. At the risk of repetition, it is a good idea to recall from the chapter on Fray Angélico Chávez that scholastic philosophers engaged in the great cooperative venture of the age, reconciling faith and reason. Duns Scotus convinced many that faith and reason are antithetical, while Llull advanced the claim that reason could prove the mysteries of supernatural truths. Llull, patron saint of computer science, constructed a device consisting of concentric circles or wheels which, when turned, combined subjects and predicates, providing answers to possible objections raised by Muslims and skeptics. Whatever the merits of Llull's thinking machine, Jorge Luis Borges points out that Llull's thinking machine cannot think.

Borges skeptically points out that the machine does not work any more than the magic lantern or the perpetual motion machine. Theology's fairy dust may bring consolation for human anxiety, but theology (and philosophy) only offers fantasies about the ways the world might be: "The perpetual motion machines depicted in sketches that confer their mystery upon the pages of the most effusive encyclopedias don't work either, nor do the metaphysical and theological theories that customarily declare who we are and what manner of thing the world is" (Borges 1999, 155).

LIFE AND WRITINGS

Jorge Luis Borges was born on August 24, 1899, in Buenos Aires, Argentina, in the Italian suburb of Palermo, to Jorge Guillermo Borges, a lawyer and psychology teacher, and Leonor Acevedo de Borges. Borges's paternal grandmother, Francis Haslam, an Englishwoman, made English a familiar language for the Borges family. His father, a would-be writer, instilled in his son the desire to write. Blindness overtook the father, eventually Jorge, too, would lose his sight. His father taught him philosophy, simultaneously enlightening and perplexing the young Borges with Zeno's paradoxes.

Borges's father wanted to make up for the low quality of education in Buenos Aires public schools and taught the young Borges himself. His teachings about Zeno's paradoxes in particular awakened in the youth an avid interest in the puzzle of motion and the riddle of time. Reminiscing about this aspect of his father, Borges writes, "he explained to me the paradoxes of Zeno, Achilles and the Tortoise, you remember, the arrows, the fact that movement was impossible because there was always a point in between and so on" (Monegal 1978, 101).

Zeno of Elea (490–430 BCE), disciple of Parmenides, argued against the reality of change and motion, and hence time, using logical absurdities. Zeno's arrow paradox argues that an arrow cannot move in a place in which it is not, nor can an arrow move at a place at which it is. At any instant, a flying arrow occupies a definite length of space; it is at rest. Therefore, the arrow is not in motion. Our knowledge of Zeno comes primarily from Aristotle's *Physics*, where Aristotle interprets Zeno's third argument against motion as meaning that "the arrow is stopped while it is moving" implies that time is "composed of 'nows'" (Aristotle 2006, 18). Early exposure to Zeno's paradoxes left Borges with the lifelong conviction that philosophy and theology provide no definitive answers or satisfying solutions to questions about the world.

Seeking a cure for his eye disease, the older Borges moved his family in 1914 to Geneva, where Jorge Luis would live for four years, acquiring fluency in Latin, German, and French. At College Calvin, Borges read symbolist literature, studying the likes of Carlyle, Schopenhauer, and Walt Whitman. From Geneva, the family moved to Spain, ending up in Madrid, where Borges came under the influence of poet Rafael Cansino-Asséns and the literary movement known as the ultraists, a group that promoted Europeanization instead of renovating Spain's golden age.

In 1921, the family returned to Buenos Aires, where Borges fell under the influence of Macedonio Fernández, poet and philosopher, strongly influenced by Schopenhauer and the British empiricists. In 1923, Borges began his career as a writer, publishing his first collection of poems, *Fervor de Buenos Aires*. The family travelled again briefly to Switzerland for the elder Borges's eye treatment. Returning to Buenos Aires in 1924, Borges discovered that he had acquired the reputation of a poet and began writing prolifically, contributing especially to the magazine *Martin Fierro*. In 1925, he met Victoria Campo, who promoted Borges through her literary magazine, *Sur*. Borges's short flirtation with politics ended when a military junta overthrew Hipólito Yrigoyen, whom Borges supported. Succumbing to his father's illness, blindness began to set in and the younger Borges underwent the first of a series of operations in 1927.

Undaunted by his eye disease, if not provoked by it, Borges devoted himself to writing and published a collection of essays, *Discussion*, and articles in the magazine *Megáfono*. His first short story, "Streetcorner Man," appeared under a pseudonym. In another short story, "A Universal History of Infamy" he began experimenting with a style and storytelling technique that reinvented characters from other works, mixing fact and fiction, reality and unreality—the first seeds of Borgesian writing. In 1935 he wrote his first "Borgesian" story, "The Approach to al-Mu'tasim," purporting to be a review of a fictional novel. The next year he published a collection of philosophical ruminations on time and eternity, *A History of Eternity*.

Economic depression and the senior Borges's dependence on Borges's mother pressured the young Borges to take a job at the Miguel Cané Library where he remained for nine long, unhappy years. "The Library of Babel" (1941) allegorized his experience as a librarian. He famously describes his fictional library as "a sphere whose exact centre is any one of its hexagons and whose circumference is inaccessible."

In 1938, Borges suffered two personal tragedies. First, his father died, and on Christmas Eve Borges suffered an accident that nearly ended his life. He memorialized this accident in his popular short story "The South." While running up the stairs, he wounded his head on a casement and contracted blood poisoning. After an operation, he recovered slowly in the hospital for a month. He feared that he had lost his ability to write and his creativity. To test his abilities as a writer he tried his hand at a short story, "Pierre Menard, Author of Don Quixote." Pierre Menard, the protagonist and narrator, sets out to write, not copy, Cervantes's

Quixote exactly, word for word, becoming Cervantes in the process. Borges uses this occasion to demonstrate that all writing is inefficacious because all writing is imitation. The importance of a book, stresses Borges, is not the writing of it but the reading of it:

> The genesis of a work in historic time and in the life of an author is the most contingent and most insignificant moment of its duration. . . . The time of a book is not the limited time of its writing, but the limitless time of reading and memory. The meaning of books is in front of them and not behind them; it is in us; a book is not ready-made meaning, a revelation we have to suffer; it is a reserve of forms that are waiting to have some meaning; it is the 'imminence of a revelation that is not yet produced' and that everyone of us has to produce for himself. (Monegal 1964, 331)

Following this story with "Tlön, Uqbar, Orbis Tertius" (1940), Borges created a fictional encyclopedia article about an imaginary planet, Tlön, where philosophy is played as a game in which amazement, not truth, is the prize. One of the schools in Tlön has reached the point of denying the reality of time. For, if the present is undefined, then the future has no other reality than as a present hope, the past is no more than present memory. Borges called "Tlön" his most ambitious story, a story for criticizing theories about reality. It is "Tlön" where Bioy Casares discovers in an encyclopedia originating in Uqbar, a part of Asia Minor, the statement that "copulation and mirrors are abominable, because they increase the number of men." Borges corrects Bioy Casares, pointing out that the encyclopedia states that "Mirrors and fatherhood are abominable because they multiply and disseminate that universe" (Borges 1998, 68). Borges plays with the hypothesis that if idealism is correct and we see the world not as it is but as it appears to us, then the apparent world is unreal. Contemplating the unreality of the apparent world, Borges wondered how it was possible to trust anything that brings that unreality into existence.

To illustrate Borges's storytelling, a brief look at one of his most famous stories and one of his personal favorites, "The Secret Miracle" (1944) will suffice for grasping a little of that Borgesian style, tone, timbre, and uncanny, surrealistic philosophical insight. The story is about the interplay of subjective and objective notions of time occurring in the mind and the last days of a Jewish author facing execution by the Nazis. The night before the Nazi invasion of Prague on March 14, 1939, the protagonist, Jaromir Hladik, a Jewish author and scholar preoccupied with the nature of time, dreams that he is playing a game of chess. Suddenly all clocks sound simultaneously, signaling the time to make his next move. Unfortunately, he cannot remember the rules of chess, startling him awake from his dream. Five days later, on March 19, the Nazis arrest Hladik because he is Jewish. Nazis sentence him to die by firing squad on March 29 at 9:00 a.m.

Every night after his arrest, he has the same dream or variations of the same dream about the firing squad and his execution—"each simulacrum lasted a few seconds." Wrangling with ideas that could help him change his fate, he arrives at the wishful metaphysical conclusion that if he can only imagine the details of a particular circumstance, he can prevent its occurrence: "he strove to hold fast somehow to the fugitive substance of time." As the fateful day approached, he feels that "time was precipitating itself toward the dawn of the twenty-ninth." Nonetheless, he takes comfort in the now, the present moment, and feeling that as long as he is alive he is immortal (Borges 1962, 144–45).

On the eve of his scheduled execution, he consoles himself by pondering his book on time, *Vindication of Eternity*, whose first part examines the history of the theories of time; the second part makes an argument refuting the reality of time similar to Francis Bradley's. According to the narrator of "The Secret Miracle," Bradley argues that a single repetition of an event is a counterexample disproving the existence of time; noting, however, that Bradley's arguments are as fallacious as other theories.

Contemplating his fate, the condemned man's anxious thoughts fall on his unfinished tragicomedy, "Enemies." Overwhelmed by a consuming desire to complete the work, he cries out to God, pleading for another year of life: "In order to bring this drama, which may serve to justify me, to justify you, I need one more year. Grant me that year, You, to whom belong the centuries and all time" (Borges 1998, 160).

At 9:01 a.m. the next morning, the moment of his execution, at the sergeant's command, "The physical universe came to a stop" (Borges 1998, 161). Between the sergeant's command and the actual deathblow delivered by the striking volleys, a mere second of measurable time elapses, but an entire year of subjective time passes. Physically paralyzed, his body comes to a stop and objective time ceases; his mind, however, is free to observe, to contemplate, reflect, and, most importantly, to compose hexameters, for an entire year until the final moment arrives. He dies on March 29, at 9:02 (Borges 1998, 162).

The storyline in "The Secret Miracle" offers the flavor of the Borgesian story found, for example, in the short stories published collectively in 1941 as *The Garden of Forking Paths*, later added to *Artifices*, also a collection of short stories, jointly published as *Ficciones* in 1944. Typical of the Borgesian story is an uncanny mix of fact and fantasy playing with philosophical conundrums about the nature of reality, time, and the self, not for the purpose of analyzing and evaluating arguments, but for showing the unreal and fictional nature of philosophy.

Working at the Michael Cane Library gave Borges time and opportunity to read and he read voraciously authors like Gibbon, Bloy, Claudel, Shaw, Kafka, and Dante. Kafka was an early favorite and the subject of many writings Borges produced for the popular women's magazine *El Hogar*. In 1937, he wrote a review of a new translation of Kafka's *The Trial* demonstrating his familiarity with Kafka's work (See "Kafka and His Precursors" in *Other Inquisitions*, 1952). He also translated some of Kafka's stories for a collection published as *La metamorfosis* (1938). This work predates Borges's "Pierre Menard, Author of the Quixote" and his travail at the Michael Cane Library.

In 1940, he wrote the rest of the stories that became *El jardín de senderos que se bifurcan*. Ocampo's magazine *Sur* published "Las ruinas circulares" and "La lotería en Babilonia" in 1941. Juan Perón, whom Borges criticized, was on the ascendancy in the 1940s. As vice president, Perón abolished political parties and restricted the press. Appealing to the masses of working class people, *las cabezas negras* (black heads), Perón secured the conditions favorable for an autocracy. The liberation of Paris in 1944 spurred Borges to write in *Sur* of a feeling of "physical happiness" that the end of Nazism was in sight. The last story of this period, "Three Versions of Judas," is a Christological fantasy published in *Sur* that explores a scholar's search to understand the nature of Christ's sacrifice and the role of Judas Iscariot. Along theological lines, Borges wrote "The Phoenix Sect" nine years later. Borges wrote no more fiction until 1970, when he published *El informe de Brodie*, which contains his second Christological fantasy, "The Gospel According to Mark."

In 1946, president-elect Juan Perón, out of spite, appointed Borges to the position of "Inspector of Poultry and Rabbits in the Public Markets," which Borges immediately rejected. Leaving the library position, Borges took temporary assignments as a lecturer on American and British literature. In 1949, he published another collection of short stories, *The Aleph*. Collections of essays followed, including *Other Inquisitions* (1952) and *Revolución Libertadora* (1955) The same year a more liberal-minded military junta appointed Borges to the prestigious position of the Director of the National Library. By this time, he was almost completely blind. In the next year, he took a position as professor of English and American Literature at the University of Buenos Aires and the same year he won the National prize for literature. Turning to poetry in 1960, he published *El hacedor*, titled *Dreamtigers* in English, a collection of prose and poems. Curiously, Borges did not gain international attention until 1961, when he won the International Publisher's

Prize. The translation of *Ficciones* into many languages launched his global fame, leading to travel in the United States and lectures in New York, San Francisco, Austin, and others. In 1963, he traveled to Europe and in 1967 spent a year at Harvard as a visiting professor. By 1970, he returned to writing the Borgesian short story thanks to Norman Thomas Di Giovanni who, having arrived in Argentina in 1968, convinced Borges to recover his storytelling powers from the heyday of the 1940s (Woodall 1996, 225). The result was *Doctor Brodie's Report*, consisting of eleven short stories about different aspects of Argentinean life. In 1975, the same year his beloved mother died, another collection of short stories, *The Book of Sand*, came out. Afterward, he travelled abroad frequently accompanied by Maria Kodama. He died on June 14, 1986.

THREE VERSIONS OF JUDAS

Reading Borges's "Chinese Encyclopedia," Michel Foucault chuckled. In the introduction to *The Order of Things: An Archaeology of the Human Sciences*, Foucault reveals that this passage inspired the writing of his book *The Order of Things*: "This book first arose out of a passage in Borges, out of the laughter that shattered, as I read the passage, all the familiar landmarks of my thought—our thought, the thought that bears the stamp of our age and our geography—breaking up all the ordered surfaces and all the planes which we are accustomed to tame the wild profusion of existing things, and continuing long afterwards to disturb and threaten with collapse our age-old distinction between the Same and the Other" (Foucault 1994, xv). One of the items in the Chinese encyclopedia's list of animals that tickled Foucault's fancy is a startling and funny item—those "drawn with a very fine camelhair brush." This strange curiosity prompted Foucault to ask, "What is it impossible to think?"

Borges's surrealist and labyrinthine writings stretch the limits of what is possible to think, challenge our notions about the nature of reality, emphasize the ambiguity of language, strain the powers of the human imagination, and demonstrate the absurdity of looking for absolute knowledge. Borges enjoyed dabbling in philosophy (which he considered another type of literature), toying with philosophical paradoxes about the self, doubles, reading, writing, the intellectual problems of time and eternity, space, infinity, chance and destiny, fiction and reality. Borges assumes that objective reality, if it exists, exists independently of any description of it, because knowledge uses language and language is opaque—another thing within reality: "In a late poem, "The Other Tiger," Borges opposes to the tiger of the poem the real tiger, the one whose blood runs hot. Yet in naming it and trying to fix its world in words, it too becomes a fiction" (Bossart 2003, 55). Attributing existence or reality to the second tiger does not differentiate it from the tiger of the poem.

Similarly, in "A Yellow Rose" Borges demonstrates that a poet can mention or allude to a rose but never fully express it in words: "It was at that moment that the revelation took place: Marino saw the rose the way Adam must have seen it in Paradise. He sensed that it existed not in words but in its own timelessness. He understood that we can utter and allude to things but not give them expression, that the proud tall volumes that made a golden shadow in the corner of his room were not the world's mirror, as his vanity figured, but simply other objects that had been added to the world" (Bossart 2003, 5).

"The Three Versions of Judas" belongs to a collection of stories published in *Ficciones* (1944). In the prologue, Borges provides a list of the authors he rereads: Arthur Schopenhauer, Thomas De Quincey, Robert Louis Stevenson, Fritz Mauthner, Bernard Shaw, G. K. Chesterton, and Léon Bloy. Of the last author Borges says, "I believe I perceive the remote influence of the last mentioned in the Christological fantasy entitled 'Three Versions of Judas'" (Borges 1962, 106). Borges sympathized with the Catholic Léon Bloy, writing that they saw the world the same way. In a gesture to Bloy, Borges wrote "The Mirror of Enigmas" saying that Bloy saw the world as a language whose code we can hardly decipher. Bloy, a French writer zealously committed to the Catholic faith, who passionately searched for the Absolute, sadly lived life as a beggar. At times, Jacques Maritain, French Catholic philosopher, and his wife Raissa, a poet, recognized the genius of Bloy's radical Catholic spiritual vision and supported him financially. In his novels, essays, and poems, Bloy depicts history and the world as texts full of signs and symbols waiting to be deciphered (Monegal 1978, 314). Bloy died twelve years before Jean Baudrillard's birth.

"Three Versions of Judas," like Borges's short story "The Theologians," is a "scathing parody of theological reasoning" bringing together real and fictional people, blurring the distinction between reality and fiction. For instance, he quotes a disparaging comment on Nils Runeberg, the fictional protagonist of "Three Versions of Judas," and attributes that comment to none other than Maurice Abramowicz, lawyer and lifelong friend that Borges met in Geneva introducing Borges to Rimbaud's *Le bateau livre* (Borges 116).

Borges, fascinated by the problem of personal identity and the nature of the self, employs the rhetorical device of doubles often, inverting the role of hero and villain, a technique he uses in other stories in *Ficciones*. José Saramago, Portuguese winner of the Nobel Prize in literature (1998), similarly inverts the roles of God and Satan in his book *The Gospel According to Jesus Christ*. Likewise, Borges's story "The Shape of the Sword" is about a protagonist who tells a story of a betrayal as if he were the victim, not the betrayer. In this vein, Borges suggests that the hero is as much a villain as the villain is a hero pointing out that there "are two sides of the same character: man" (Monegal 1978, 385).

Borges's creative iconoclasm, to the great consternation of Christians, inverts the roles of Jesus and Judas in "Three Versions of Judas." The notion of Judas as the incarnation of God did not originate with Borges. In his sermons, journals, and essays, Ralph Waldo Emerson, whom Borges avidly read, and Theodore Parker, New England transcendentalist, separated Christ from the person of Jesus intimating that Christ, the oversoul, could be incarnate in anyone, including Judas.

Borges's protagonist, a fictitious theologian, Nils Runeberg, attempts to solve the theological mystery of Judas in three different works. The theological mystery associated with Judas concerns the question of why God became man. Theologians since the first century have offered various solutions to the question. Mark's Gospel says that Jesus died as a ransom for many. St. Anselm of Canterbury wrote the book *Cur Deus Homo?* (Why did God become man?), arguing that Jesus died to satisfy God's honor as supreme feudal lord who had been offended by human sin. Peter Abelard, a progressive medieval theologian, argued that Jesus died to give a moral example of how Christians ought to act. On close analysis, the question presupposes knowledge of God, at least knowledge of God's existence. Moreover, the question of the theological mystery expresses the human pretension to know the absolute. For Borges, theology exemplifies human overreaching, an absurd attempt to gain knowledge of the absolute. Runeberg is a caricature that serves as a foil for Borges to demonstrate the absurdity of theology, to establish the status of theology as fiction. Borges may not deny the historicity of Jesus, but he exposes theological doctrines about Jesus and interpretations of the significance of his death as fictional products of the human imagination.

First Version

Runeberg's 1904 work, *Kristus och Judas*, bears the epigraph "Not one thing, but everything tradition attributes to Judas Iscariot is false." In this first attempt at a solution of the "greatest" theological mystery, Runeberg offers a "metaphysical vindication" of Thomas De Quincey's (1780–1859) theory that Judas betrayed Jesus to set off a rebellion. By the way, De Quincey's popular book, *Confessions of an Opium Eater* (1821) was widely read in Latin America.

Judas's act of betrayal, reasons Runeberg, was superfluous, for Jesus was a public preacher known by the authorities. Runeberg concludes that the act could not have been accidental, given its important role in the drama of redemption, so he arrives at a conviction that church authorities would call blasphemous: that Judas's betrayal was an essential and indispensable part of the story of salvation. "Ergo, Judas's betrayal was not a random act, but predetermined, with its own mysterious place in the economy of redemption" (Borges 1998, 164). Moreover, if God were to submit to such an infinite sacrifice, a sacrifice of that metaphysical magnitude would require God's incarnation in a man who was truly representative of all sinners. Judas Iscariot fit the bill better than Jesus of Nazareth.

Platonism makes its stamp indelibly palpable in the "Three Versions of Judas," evident in the narrator's explanation. Plato's metaphysics postulates a hierarchy of being, a lower world of the senses and a higher world of the intellect. The lower world reflects the higher world but as shadows lacking substance. Accordingly, Judas "in some way" reflects the Word.

Theological critics quickly point out that Runeberg makes a mistake ignoring the doctrine of the hypostatic union of the Trinity. Personally, Borges deplored the doctrine of the Trinity, denouncing the paradoxical notion of one God in three persons as monstrous. For instance, Borges discusses three ideas of eternity in his nonfictional essay "The History of Eternity." Speaking about the second definition that relies on the concept of the Trinity, Borges writes, "Its conception of a father, a son and a specter, articulated in a single organism appears to be a case of intellectual teratology, a deformation to which only the horror of a nightmare could give birth. Hell is a mere physical violence, but the three inextricable Persons entail an intellectual horror, a suffocating infinity, as specious as that of contra posed mirrors" (Borges 1999, 130).

One critic specifically accuses Runeberg of committing the ancient heresy of Docetism, an early Christian movement that denied the integrity of Jesus's humanity. Again, Docetism rears its head in these discussions of Spanish and Latin American artists and writers. Does any conclusion follow from this observation? Because of this surprising iteration, it will be instructive to explain Docetism again briefly. "Docetism" derives from the Greek *dokein* meaning "to seem" or "to appear." The Docetics attributed evil to matter and goodness to spirit. God, who is spirit, cannot take on a human body because the body is evil. Therefore, Jesus appeared human but in reality existed only as a phantom because, as a spiritual being, he could not take on a real human body contaminated by evil. The author of the Gospel of John and I John purposely wrote to attack an early version of Docetism. St. Ignatius of Antioch attacked Docetism as heretical, for if God did not become fully human in Jesus, then Christ's Resurrection and ascension did not occur and, hence, there is no salvation.

Another critic chides Runeberg for overlooking Luke 22:3, a passage whose setting is on the eve of the Feast of Unleavened Bread, when the chief priests are looking for a way to kill Jesus. According to Luke, "Then entered Satan into Judas." This text purportedly undermines Runeberg's unorthodox interpretation. The critic reasons that if Satan entered into Judas, then Judas could not have been the incarnation of God. Stepping back from the story, the reader should note that in the Hebrew Bible, what one writer attributes to God, another ascribes to Satan. For example, the Chronicler, an anonymous Jewish historian, responsible for producing Ezra, Nehemiah, and I and II Chronicles (400 BCE) states unequivocally that Satan, not YHWH, moved David to take a census of Israel in order to determine the size of the army he could muster: "And Satan stood up against Israel, and provoked David to number Israel" (I Chronicles 21:1). The Deuteronomistic Historian, by contrast, at about the time of the Jewish exile in 586 BCE, writes in II Samuel concerning the same event that God provoked David to take a census: "And again the anger of the LORD was kindled against Israel, and he moved David against them to say, 'Go, number Israel and Judah'" (II Sam. 24:1). The Chronicler said that the devil did it; the Deuteronomistic Historian blamed God. Different Biblical writers attribute the same action to both Satan and God. Contrary to what some might think, including Borges, Runeberg does not stand on shaky ground when he attributes Judas's betrayal to God.

Because of the severe criticisms directed against him, Runeberg decides to write a new version, turning from theology to "oblique arguments of a moral order." Runeberg concludes that a charitable interpretation of the Gospels cannot attribute Judas's action to mere cupidity, what Augustine called inordinate desire or blameworthy cupidity. Recall that Jesus chose Judas to join his inner circle of apostles and sent him, along with the other apostles, to preach the good news of the Kingdom of God. Runeberg, reconsidering the real motive for Judas's action, finds it in an unmitigated commitment to total asceticism—asceticism, the narrator declares, that knows no bounds, not even temporal ones. Armed with the idea of a totalitarian sense of asceticism, Runeberg requires absolute self-denial on Judas's part. The ascetic merely mortifies the flesh; Judas mortifies the spirit as well. To be consistently ascetic, Judas repudiates the offer of redemption and the hope of salvation.

Runeberg revises this second version, entitling the third version *Dem Hemlige Fralsaren*, published in 1909 with a new prologue by the fictitious Bible scholar Eric Erfjord. The skeptical narrator, Borges, cannot accept the idea that all human evil and suffering throughout human history can be reconciled with the single temporal act of Christ's death on the cross: "To limit his suffering to the agony of one afternoon on the cross is blasphemous" (Borges 1998, 166). How can the few hours of Christ's suffering atone for all human suffering from the beginning of time—rapes, murders, tortures, mutilations, kidnappings, plagues, disease, wars, mayhem, destruction, pestilences, etc.? Thinking quantitatively, there is no measure for measure. In this regard, Borges seems to be making a valid point that requires an adequate theological response. A theologian could respond by saying that the difference is qualitative since the totality of all human suffering pales by comparison with the suffering of a divine being, whose suffering is infinite. This answer, however, assumes the paradoxical belief in the identity of the infinite and finite, and raises more problems, risking the slippery slope of an infinite regress.

Like Kierkegaard before him, Borges notes the contradiction inherent in the doctrine of the incarnation. On the side of theology, the contradiction is really a mystery or a paradox; on the side of philosophy, an absurdity. Theology asserts the sinfulness of humanity and the perfection of God; therefore, the narrator infers, "the attributes of *impeccabilitas* and of *humanitas* are not compatible" (Borges 1998, 166). How could a perfect God become human without losing perfection and acquiring sinfulness? Citing a fictional theologian, Kemnitz, the narrator admits that if the redeemer could feel hunger and thirst, then it is reasonable to admit that the redeemer could also sin and be damned. Incredulously, the narrator remonstrates that the story of redemption could not be limited to the "lonely day" of the Crucifixion. Borges, through the narrator, questions the integrity of Jesus's human nature. Is it not an inconsistency to hold that God became a man and that as a man God knew no sin? Where Kierkegaard accepts the paradoxical nature of the fundamental incompatibility of the infinite deity becoming a finite mortal, Borges considers the concept absurd. Kierkegaard assailed Georg Wilhelm Friedrich Hegel's claim that Jesus demonstrates the synthesis of the divine and the human. Karl Marx, too, rejected Hegel's claim that humanity is self-alienated God. For Marx, inverting Hegel, God is self-alienated humanity.

Borges demonstrates the absurdity of the incarnation in Runeberg's requirement that God adopt all the essential traits of human nature. Runeberg interprets Isaiah 53:2–3 as a prophecy of "the entire atrocious future . . . God was made totally man . . ." (Borges 1998, 166). The passage contains this quote from Isaiah: "For he shall grow up before him as a tender plant, and as a root out of a dry ground: he hath no form nor comeliness. . . . He is despised and rejected of men; a man of sorrows, and acquainted with grief." Borges, following Christian tradition, interprets the suffering servant of Isaiah 53 to be a prophecy about Jesus. An anonymous author (known as Deutero-Isaiah) writing this passage after 540 BCE, addresses post-exilic Jews living under Persian rule. For his original audience, the identity of the suffering servant is ambiguous. From a Jewish point of view, the suffering servant refers to Israel or the prophet. Interestingly, YHWH in Deutero-Isaiah calls Cyrus I the Persian Emperor "my servant."

By the consistency of Runeberg's logic, he concludes triumphantly that God chose a man who was the absolute opposite of Jesus: "In order to save us, he could have chosen any of the lives that weave the confused web of history; he chose an abject existence: He was Judas" (Borges 1998, 166). Borges the narrator intervenes to apply his circular nature of time; there is no novelty in history, anything experienced once is experienced repeatedly. He cites the fictional Erford's *Christelige Dogmatique* stating that the crucifying of God has not ceased, but happens again ceaselessly throughout all eternity: "Judas, now, continues to receive the pieces of silver; he continues to hurl the pieces of silver in the temple; he continues to knot the hangman's noose on the field of blood" (Borges 1962, 156).

The repetitive nature of time is a theme that Borges returns to repeatedly, no pun intended. In his nonfictional essay, "Circular Time," (1941) Borges examines the concepts of cyclical time and eternal recurrence. He sets out to define three modalities of the concept of circular time (incidentally, none are drawn from indigenous mythologies); the Platonic perfect year or celestial year; the Nietzschean idea of eternal recurrence; and Marcus Aurelius's concept of similar but not identical cycles.

"Plato's year" refers to the period described in the *Timaeus* as the time it takes all seven planets to return to their original point of departure. Such a period constitutes a perfect year. Astrologers after Plato inferred that if Plato's year is true of the solar system, it must be true of the universe. Taking this idea a step further, astrologers concluded that the "same individuals will be born again and will live out the same destinies" (Borges 1999, 225).

Nietzsche's related concept of eternal recurrence is based on the mathematical reasoning that x number of objects is only capable of a finite number of variations, and on the metaphysical claim that time is endless or infinite. Given finite configurations of objects and endless time, the same configuration of objects at some point in the past will recur repeatedly forever. Borges draws support for this idea from Hume's *Dialogues Concerning Natural Religion* (1779), where Hume states that "in an eternal duration, that every possible order or position must be tried an infinite number of times" (Borges 1999, 226).

The final modality—similar but not identical cycles—represents for Borges the most conceivable of eternal repetitions. It consists of the denial of the past and the future illustrated by Marcus Aurelius's observation that since all things move in orbits, it does not matter how many times a spectator views them, it is all the same. Aurelius wrote, "no one loses the past or the future, because no man can be

deprived of what he does not have." Dispensing with the past and the future dis-
poses the possibility of novelty. "There is nothing new under the sun."

Ultimately, the nature of the truth of the metaphysics of time does not really
perplex Borges. What matters for Borges is the quotidian sense of time that we
experience. He relishes the intuition that before we die, if we live long enough, we
will have experienced all emotions, perceptions, thoughts, sensations, and desires
possible for humanity.

At the close of "The Three Versions of Judas," the narrator strikes a depressing
note, revealing that Runeberg's 1909 version meets with indifference on the part
of the church authorities, libraries, publishers, book critics, and so on. Runeberg
humbly welcomes this silence, believing it to be providential so that God could
maintain his secret. Runeberg, fearing that he committed blasphemy for revealing the "terrible name" of God, suffers from insomnia. He wanders the streets of
Lund praying that he might share hell with his redeemer. Compare the chilling
passage from Camus: "When Heathcliff, in *Wuthering Heights*, says he puts his
love above God and would willingly go to hell in order to be reunited with the
woman he loves, he is prompted not only by youth and humiliation but by the
consuming experience of a whole lifetime. The same emotion causes Eckhart, in
a surprising fit of heresy, to say that he prefers hell with Jesus than heaven without Him" (Camus 1956, 19).

Borges pits himself against Unamuno declaring that unlike Unamuno he has
no desire for immortality: "What I said against Unamuno is that he is interested
in things that I am not interested in. He is very worried about his personal immortality. He says, 'I want to go on being Miguel de Unamuno.' Well, I don't want to
go on being Jorge Luis Borges . . . I want to forget all about him" (Bossart 2003,
163). Accepting Borges's sincerity, uncertainty remains about his meaning due to
the grammatical ambiguity of the antecedent of the third person pronoun "him."
Borges may be referring to the private person Borges or to the public person
Borges, the famous writer. To whom does he refer?

A few years after writing "Three Versions of Judas," Borges wrote another
scathing story about doubles attacking the pretentions of theology in the "The
Theologians" (1949). A copy of Augustine's *The City of God* was the only book that
survived the Huns' burning of books in Rome. The book contained a refutation of
the doctrine of eternal recurrence. Years later a theologian, Bishop Aurelian, heard
of a sect called the Monotoni who preached the doctrine of eternal recurrence. To
his chagrin, Bishop Aurelain discovered that another theologian, John of Pannonia had already written a polemic against the Monotoni. He determined to write a

treatise against the Monotoni refuting the cyclical teaching. His argument would surpass the rigor of Pannonia's polemic. Despite his efforts, the Church adopted Pannonia's work as its official position against the Monotoni.

Time goes by and another sect arises, the Histriones who reject the teaching of circular time. The Histriones also affirm that every person has a double in heaven and at death, the two become one. However, their linear concept of time becomes heretical. Writing a refutation of linear time, Aurelian writes a sentence of twenty words that he later discovers were written by Pannonia when the doctrine linear time was orthodox.

Forced to reveal the author of these lines, Aurelian names Pannonia. Consequently, Pannonia is arrested and convicted to be burned at the stake. As Pannonia burns, Aurelian catches a glimpse of his familiar face. Ironically, years later Aurelian is burned in a fire caused by lightening. In heaven, he learns that God is indifferent to theology and that he, Aurelian, and John of Pannonia are the same individual person (Borges 1998, 201–7). Inverting the roles of Judas and Christ, Borges brashly confronts the reader's comfort zone, short-circuiting his/her brain. Shifting the reader's standpoint results in what Slavoj Žižek calls a parallax view. A parallax view occurs when a spectator shifts standpoints, causing the object viewed to appear qualitatively different, even as something else. For example, Marx inverts Hegel and a shift from idealism to materialism takes place. Similarly, Carol Gilligan caused a parallax view. Examining Kohlberg's theory of the moral development of boys, she shifted the subjects of psychological investigation from boys to girls. The shift short-circuited Kohlberg's psychological theory of development and resulted in a different theory of moral development, undermining Kohlberg's universal pretensions. Borges's inversion causes a parallax view in which Judas, not Christ, is the incarnation of God. Notions of good and evil are upended in a Nietzschean mode. A similar inversion occurs in Borges's short story, "The Gospel According to Mark," where absolute notions or good and evil are questioned and where a modern double of Christ is tested in a crucible of a ranch house in the flooded plains of the Pampas.

THE GOSPEL ACCORDING TO MARK

"The Gospel According to Mark" is part of a collection of stories written by Borges in 1969 and published the following year in a book called *Brodie's Report*. In the prologue to *Brodie's Report*, Borges claims that "The Gospel According to Mark" is the best of the series (Woodall 1996, 226).

St. Paul, writing to the Galatians, says, "But when the fullness of the time was come, God sent forth his Son" (Gal. 4:4). At the beginning Jesus's ministry, Mark proclaims, "The time is fulfilled, and the kingdom of God is at hand: repent ye, and believe the gospel" (Mark 1:15). Divinity entered the temporal order, imparting theological meaning to history; history becomes salvation history. Understanding the historical significance of Christ's entry into time, sixth-century Christian monk Diogenes Exiguus divided history into two periods, BC and AD—in more modern nomenclature, BCE and CE. He sliced the historical timeline into two parts so that all human history looks either forward or backward to Christ. Borges's short story, "The Gospel According to Mark," looks backward to Christ to instantiate Christ forward in Borges's contemporaneous Argentina.

"The Gospel According to Mark" is a story about a medical student who becomes stranded in a ranch house during a flood while on vacation in the Pampas and reads Mark's Gospel to illiterate ranch hands to pass the time. The story ends shockingly. Borges's title intrigues us partly because of the use of the definite article in the title instead of the indefinite article. Use of the definite article suggests that this story is a repeat of the authentic, genuine, and original Gospel on its own right. Recall that for Borges the reading of a book is more original than the book itself, a theme familiar to Miguel de Unamuno. In Borges's "Pierre Menard," the protagonist attempts to write Cervantes's *Don Quixote*, not copy it, but rewrite it word for word. Menard's reworking of *Don Quixote* recalls Borges's well-known belief that a book is a manuscript undergoing infinite change because each reader gives it a different meaning and, in a sense, creates another book. For Borges, then, reading a book is the equivalent of rewriting it, which is precisely what Menard does. For this reason, Menard's "originality" lies not in the creation of a new text, but in demonstrating how an old text can convey new meaning (Bossart 2003, 125–26). Chesterton, Stevenson, and Kipling urged the conviction that literature is a rewriting of previous texts (Bossart 2003, 126). Borges read both the gnostic gospels and the canonical Gospels of the New Testament. Yet, he selected Mark.

In a highly provocative remaking of Mark's Gospel, the protagonist Baltasar Espinosa, an unwitting Christ figure, is a young man from Buenos Aires, intelligent, seemingly directionless, who leaves his requirements for completing medical school unfinished. Forebodingly, Espinosa is thirty-three years old and the story is set in the last days of March 1928. Espinosa's cousin Daniel, a rancher from the Pampas, the Argentine interior, invites Espinosa to spend the summer with him at his ranch, Los Álamos. Shortly after Espinosa arrives, as fate would have it, Daniel has to return to Buenos Aires on business, leaving Espinosa alone with the racially mixed, backward, and morally challenged farm hands, the Gutres. The father, son, and daughter are symbolic of the Trinity and, at the same time, the masses who reject Christ. Recall Orozco's hero/mass dialectic. A raging flood damages the Gutres' small house, forcing them to move into the ranch house with Espinosa. To pass time, Espinosa reads Mark's Gospel to them. Soon they identify Espinosa with Christ and follow him around the house as he reads the Gospel. After a fateful night encounter with the daughter, they lead him out, mocking him. Looking up, he perceives a cross in the beams of the broken roof.

In his philosophically reflective writings, Borges appears to accept George Berkeley's denial of an objective external world independent of the mind's perception of it. Consequently, there is no such thing as objective physical space and time (except in the mind of God). Curiously, Borges opens his narrative specifying the place and time of the story—"la estancia Los Álamos," "los últimos días del mes de marzo 1928"—calling to mind the Catholic significance of the Passion of Holy Week ending with the reenactment of the Crucifixion of Jesus Christ on Good Friday. Espinosa's fate is a token or instance of the archetype of the Crucifixion, echoing Nietzsche's doctrine of eternal recurrence.

Nietzsche's concept of eternal recurrence is based on several assumptions. First, a mathematical assumption that the world is a collection of a finite number of objects in which the possible number of arrangements is finite. Second, there is a metaphysical assumption that time is infinite. If there is a finite number of objects and a finite configuration of objects, on the one hand, and endless time, on the other, then the same configurations of objects will eventually recur innumerable times. David Hume, a British empirical philosopher and a source of Borges's philosophy, states in the *Dialogues Concerning Natural Religion* (1779) that "in an eternal duration, that every possible order or position must be tried an infinite number of times." Borges modifies Nietzsche and Hume, holding not to an exact replication of past events, but to the repetition of similar instances of archetypal patterns (Bossart 2003,110). Both of Nietzsche's assumptions are questionable.

At the beginning of the story, Borges adumbrates a moral opposition between town and country, recalling Marx's observation of the antagonism of town and country and reminiscent of Domingo F. Sarmiento's *Facundo: or, Civilization and Barbarism*. Buenos Aires represents civilization, higher education, a cosmopolitan port city open to the outside world, brimming with industry, commerce and welcoming novelty, foreignness, difference, and universality—but more than anything, a transplanted European city. It is the center of Argentinean life. The country, the Argentinean Pampas, by contrast, is the periphery and marginalized exteriority. Los Álamos Ranch signifies the absurdity of barbarism where, outside of the limits of civilization, life is bare, brutish, and savage. The second part of

Borges's short story, "The South" (1953), is set in the South, the exteriority, where dream and reality are confused, evoking Sarmiento's vision about the Argentinean conflict between civilization and barbarism.

Golgotha (the place of Christ's Crucifixion), too, stood outside of the city of Jerusalem, the center of ancient Israel. Jesus, remember, was a Galilean—"Can there any good thing come out of Nazareth?" (John 1:46). Jews from Jerusalem could detect the distinctive Galilean accent of Jesus and his apostles. A servant girl standing outside of Caiaphas's house on the night of Jesus's trial and pointed out Peter because of his Galilean accent, accusing Peter of belonging to Jesus's group of followers. Galilee, a rich agricultural region, a crossroads of international trading routes, contained a diverse population. Jews from Judea suspected that Galilean Jews were not pure Jews.

Espinosa, the name of the protagonist in "The Gospel According to Mark," means "thorny," suggesting the crown of thorns placed on Christ's head. Espinosa represents the ambivalent consciousness of Latin American youth of the early twentieth century formed by the push and pull of the countervailing forces of positivism and religious faith in the realm of ideology, and the antagonism of modernity and underdevelopment in the sphere of economics and society. His father taught Espinosa Herbert Spencer, a positivist sociologist; his mother, a devout Catholic, made Espinosa promise to say the Lord's Prayer every night. Espinosa embodies a conflict between science and faith—a perennial theme in Spanish and Latin American literature.

Borges portrays the Gutres unflatteringly. The father is nondescript, the son uncouth, and the daughter of an "uncertain paternity"—an allusion to the uncertain paternity of the Holy Spirit. Did the Holy Spirit proceed from the Father and the Son, as the Roman Catholic Church affirms, or from the Father only as the Greek Orthodox Church testifies? The narrator describes them as "barely articulate" or in Spanish, "casi no hablaban"—an ambiguous phrase yielding at least two possible interpretations. The Gutres are either quiet and soft-spoken or they are illiterate. In this case, "barely articulate" conveys the latter translation and fits the descriptions of the Gutres—son is "unusually uncouth," the daughter is of "uncertain paternity," and all are "tall, strong, and bony."

Espinosa, weary of Daniel's braggadocio, welcomes his cousin's departure to Buenos Aires to close a deal on cattle. Ominously, "Daniel," originally a Hebrew name, means, "God is my judge." Daniel's leaving evokes Christ's last words on the cross, "My God, My God, why hast thou forsaken me?" (Mark 15:34). One morning, pouring rain breaks the choking stranglehold of an oppressively hot summer, waking Espinosa to the cool moist atmosphere. Thanking God, he thinks that

everything will be all right. Espinosa, however, speaks too soon. The rain, unpre-
dictably, does not cease, rising waters become a flood, and the river Salado overflows
its banks. "The rain did not let up," emphasizes the narrator, conjuring the image of
Noah's epic flood (Borges 1999, 398). Floodwaters inundate the surfaces of all four
roads leading to the ranch, creating the image of a submerged cross.

"On the third day," a leak in the roof of the ranch hands' quarters makes living
there impossible. Espinosa, empathic about their plight but with some trepidation,
invites the Gutres into the main ranch house. Nature forces together the rational
and irrational, civilization and barbarity. Chaotic forces of nature erase the social
boundary between the sophisticated urbanite and the uncultured gauchos. When
separated by space, they live in different worlds; thrown together they experience
space as tension and time as anxiety. In proximity, they stand in a genuine face-to-
face ethical encounter capable of yielding peace, or more probably, confrontation.
In any case, ethics begins with proximity.

Living in close quarters, Espinosa eats his meals with the Gutres, intimating a
religious communion. Conversation is "difficult" owing no doubt to the fact that
the Gutres are barely articulate, but more importantly due to the obstacles generated by cultural distance and not bridged by physical proximity. The Gutres are
experienced ranch hands. Espinosa finds it surprising that they cannot explain
what they do.

Borges's short stories often depict language's inability to truly represent the
world. Speech is not always the revelation of thought or the most efficient vehicle
of communication. However, the question arises whether one really knows something if he or she cannot put it into words. St. Augustine was confused about the
nature of time, believing that he had an intuition of time but lacked the ability to
explain it.

The Gutres have no sense of time; they do not understand the temporal relationship between events, the nature of the past, or even the passage of time. Without a sense of time, there is little hope of memory, for without memory there is no
historical continuity. One night, Espinosa asks the Gutres whether people still
remember the Indian raids. They answer yes, but according to the narrator, they
would have said yes to any question about past events. Espinosa recalls his father
saying that in the Pampas any citation of a past event is a mix of bad memory and
a vague understanding of dates. Gauchos rarely know their birthday or the name
of their biological father.

Unable to leave the house because of the watery world outside, Espinosa, suffering from cabin fever, searches the house looking for reading material. Finding a
family English Bible, he discovers yellowing notes stuffed in its pages containing

genealogical information about ancestors, births, baptisms, and deaths, revealing the Gutres' Scottish lineage. Even though they are not religious, the Gutres still bear traces of Calvinist "harsh fanaticism" and the "superstitions of the pampas" (Borges 1999, 400). Leafing through the Bible, his fingers stop at the Gospel According to Mark. Espinosa begins the habit of reading Mark's Gospel to them after their evening meal.

Why did Borges choose Mark's Gospel rather than Matthew, Luke or John? He does not say why. There are, however, good reasons why one might select Mark. First, Mark's Gospel is the shortest Gospel and it has an air of urgency, due largely to the use of the adverb "immediately" more than one hundred times—a real page burner. Bible scholars tell us that Mark's Gospel is prior to and a major literary source for Matthew and Luke. Matthew and Luke begin with the miraculous virgin birth narratives absent from Mark and John. Borges, concerned with exploiting the symbolic value of the passion narrative, had no use for these; besides they would have provoked the superstitious nature of the Gutres. John's Gospel, drawing on gnostic and neo-Platonic language, would sound like babble to the Gutres and transcend Espinosa's elementary knowledge of theology.

A key turning point in the story occurs when Espinosa heals an injured pet lamb with some pills. This act stirs up gratitude and reverence toward Espinosa that startles him. The Gutres reverently follow him around the house. They eat crumbs from his side of the table, mimicking the saying of the Syrophoenician woman in Mark's Gospel:

> For a certain woman, whose young daughter had an unclean spirit, heard of him, and came and fell at his feet: The woman was a Greek, a Syrophoenician by nation; and she besought him that he would cast forth the devil out of her daughter. But Jesus said unto her, Let the children first be filled: for it is not meet to take the children's bread, and to cast it unto the dogs. And she answered and said unto him, Yes, Lord; yet the dogs under the table eat of the children's crumbs. And he said unto her, For this saying go thy way; the devil is gone out of thy daughter. And when she was come to her house, she found the devil gone out, and her daughter laid upon the bed. (Mark 7:25–30)

Jesus responds cruelly to the request of the Syrophoenician woman, comparing her to a dog. Palestinian Jews called non-Jews "dogs." In Mark's Gospel, Jesus is a Jew. This story, according to early Christian tradition, demonstrates the belief that the Gospel message addresses first the Jews and later the Gentiles. Using the

Jewish pejorative that Jesus labeled her with, the Syrophoenician woman turns it to her advantage saying, "Yes Lord: yet the dogs under the table eat of the children's crumbs," evoking Jesus' compassion. The Gutres astutely identified themselves with the Syrophoenician woman, or rather with the dogs that ate the children's crumbs. Conversely, the Gutres identified Espinosa with Christ.

Repetition stands out as a principal theme, allowing Borges to play with the concept of time. Having finished the Gospel, the Gutres want to hear it again: "Espinosa felt that they were like children, to whom repetition is more pleasing than variations or novelty" (2005, 478). Kierkegaard observes that repetition is an expression of the implicit belief that life is best lived in the present. Every Holy Week throughout Christendom the Passion story is reenacted—repetition. Reenactments of the Passion, like ritual practices everywhere, allow the participants to enter into a primordial time, the creation of the world, the setting of the sun in its orbit, the creation of the first man and woman, the heroic act or death of a hero or savior. Borges's story ends with what appears to portend a reenactment of the passion.

Later that night, while Espinosa lies in bed, the tall, thin, barely articulate daughter walks naked from across the house into his bedroom and climbs into bed with him. She leaves just as stealthily. Espinosa, feeling guilty and vowing secrecy admonishes himself not to tell anyone.

The next day, the father asks him whether Christ died to save man. Espinosa hesitantly replies that Christ died to save man from hell. Then the father asks whether the Roman soldiers who nailed Christ to the cross were also saved. Espinosa, whose theology is "dim," answers affirmatively.

By noting that Espinosa's theology is dim, the narrator implies that his own theology is not so dim. Borges read the Alexandrine theologians—Clement, Origen, and Athanasius—who formulated the doctrine of salvation not in terms of salvation from hell, but as salvation from death. Accordingly, Christ died to restore humanity to the divine image—immortality—lost because of Adam's sin.

The Gutres implore Espinosa to repeat the last chapters of Mark—the Passion narrative. Illiterate though they may be, the Gutres are sophisticated enough to realize that Mark's Gospel is really a Passion narrative. Afterward, Espinosa takes a nap. Awakened by the sounds of hammering, he gets up and goes into the gallery. The Gutres follow him as if participating in a religious procession. They bow to him and beg his blessing. Suddenly, they mock him, spit on him, and push him to back of the house. Espinosa senses what awaits him. When they push open a door, "he saw the sky. A bird sang out. A goldfinch he thought. The shed was without a roof; they had pulled down the beams to make the cross" (2005, 479). Here the story stops, but without an ending. The narrator leaves the reader with a presentiment, but not with a conclusion. Borges burdens the reader to fill in the conclusion, fulfilling Borges's conviction that reading is writing.

Critics castigated Kafka because he left many of his stories incomplete. Borges, however, admired this feature of Kafka's writing, incorporating incompleteness into his own stories. Given the uncertain endings of some of his stories, Bossart asks the relevant question, "how are we to read 'The Gospel According to Mark'? Does Baltasar undergo a religious conversion, or is he the victim of a misguided conversion on the part of the Gutres?" (Bossart 2003, 141). Balthasar Espinosa is a victim of irony. A skeptic, he reads the story of Christ to the ignorant, who, in turn, crucify him.

Borges' fictional portrayals of Christ are good examples of the extent to which Foucault's question can be applied: What is it not impossible to think? In both stories, "Three Versions of Judas" and "The Gospel According to Mark," Christ is absent and replaced by doubles Judas and Baltasar Espinoza. This supports the claim that Borges considers Jesus a fictional figure, a character whose plasticity yields an infinity of possibilities to a fertile imagination. The idea of Christ for Borges is a prompt for storytelling.

CHAPTER SIX

Richard Rojas

The Invisible Christ

L ittle known outside of Argentina, historian, statesman, and prolific writer Richard Rojas warrants our attention because of his modern spiritual classic, *El Cristo invisible*. Published in 1928, Rojas's *El Cristo invisible* (The invisible Christ) consists of three dialogues or conversations occurring over the course of three days between the author and an unnamed bishop from an anonymous interior province of Argentina. Learned, a world traveler, and a connoisseur of the arts, the anonymous bishop expresses a keen interest in debating with Rojas about the meaning of Christ. Of special interest for us is the first dialogue or debate concerning artistic representations of Christ, or "La efigie de Cristo" (the image of Christ).

On the eve of his visit to the provincial bishop's home, Rojas, a self-described scholar of Christian iconography, acquires a rare Spanish colonial painting of the Holy Trinity, *La Santísima Trinidad*, depicting the Trinity crowning the Virgin. Spanish colonial depictions of the Trinity as three identical bearded men appear widely throughout Latin America, even in the *santero* art of New Mexico (figure 6.1).

On Rojas's first visit to the bishop, he is painting. Rojas asks why the Catholic Church never established or sanctioned a standard or official image of Christ that could serve as a paradigm for religious art and devotion. Traditional European religious art represents the Holy Spirit with the figure of the dove (figure 6.2).

By contrast, Spanish colonial painting exhibits two features that appear to be radical departures from European art. First, a bearded man replaces the dove. Second, three identical bearded men represent the Trinity, sometimes as a single human with three bodies. Rojas succinctly captures the content of the painting saying, "The three persons in one simultaneous, rhythmic, and gestured action crown the Mother, the Virgin and fecund matter of the Cosmos" (Rojas 1929, 10). Not having encountered a similar image in Europe, Rojas hypothesizes that Spanish missionaries substituted the representation of a man for the image of a dove, fearing that otherwise the indigenous people would regress to zoolatry. Rojas's

FIGURE 6.1   Quill Pen Santero, *Trinity*, 1834. © Spanish Colonial Society, Santa Fe, New Mexico, 2017.

hypothesis may explain the motives of the Spanish missionaries who intended to destroy Amerindian polytheism.

Differences between European and Latin American depictions of the Trinity bring to the forefront the problem of the mutability of Christ's representation in Catholic art. The Catholic Church tolerates mutability in its iconography, in the bishop's view, as long as nontraditional images do not compromise sacred dogma. The Spanish colonial painting of the Trinity as three identical bearded men falls under the nontraditional category; however, both Rojas and the bishop agree that the painting is not heretical because it constitutes an exceptional case due to the

FIGURE 6.2   Hans Baldung Grien, *The Trinity and Mystic Pietà*, 1512. Oil on Oak,
112.3 × 89.1 cm. (NG 1427). © National Gallery, London/Art Resources, New York, 2017.

cultural peculiarities of Latin America. While the representation of the Trinity as
three identical men is a common image throughout Latin American and the American Southwest, it also exists in European art. Examples of the Trinity depicted as
three identical men in European art include the *Allegory of the Holy Trinity*, a medieval fresco in Perugia showing one head with three faces; the *Trinity*, a fifteenth-century fresco in Vercelli, Italy, at the Church of St. Peter and St. Paul; the sixth-century
Hospitality of Abraham, a mosaic with three identical men representing the Trinity at
the Basilica of San Vitale, Ravenna, and so on.

Reluctantly conceding the existence of a uniquely "American" Trinity, the bishop adamantly denies the existence of a European analogue: "But in Europe there is nothing like it, and this Trinity that we will call 'American' only shows the precaution the church had to take in presenting doctrine to the rudimentary consciousness of the Indians" (Rojas 1929, 21). Cultural adaptation and contextualization of the church's message, explains the bishop, accounts for the uniqueness of the Latin American image.

On further consideration, Rojas astutely observes that adaptation and contextualization of religious symbols presuppose some standard or archetypal model. Does the church, he asks perspicaciously, sanction an archetypal image of Christ? Operating within the framework of Platonic realism, Rojas enquires after some archetypal form instantiated in particular representations of Christ. Along these lines, there must exist some kind of demarcation between the concrete, temporary, visible images of Christ and the universal form of the invisible Christ they represent.

Reasoning hypothetically that if the depictions of Christ in Catholic art represent Jesus, then the church must have some idea of an immutable, official, dogmatic image of Jesus/Christ. Rojas appears to make some kind of distinction between Christ and Jesus. The terms of the distinction are not clear. One possible distinction is that between depictions of Christ in art used by the church and the Jesus of the Gospels. Another is the distinction between the dogmatic Christ of the church's official teaching and that of artistic rendering. A third distinction could be that between the historical Jesus of flesh and blood and the mystical Christ abiding in heaven. Many such distinctions could be drawn ad infinitum. Initially, the bishop takes Rojas to be assuming the traditional identification between Christ and Jesus, the continuity between the Jesus of flesh and bone and the glorified Christ of dogma. Identity and continuity go together because identity presupposes continuity—no continuity, no identity. Whatever continuity exists between Jesus and Christ, one conceivable difference immediately stands out— the historical Jesus was visible during his lifetime and, arguably, the Christ of faith is invisible (Rojas 1929, 23). In which case, Rojas reasons, the image of Jesus should be immutable in Catholic art, but it is not. Defending the church's Christological dogma, the bishop declares that God is manifest in Christ and Christ is manifest in Jesus. Christ is the eternally preexisting second person of the Trinity incarnate in the human form of Jesus.

Christian mystical literature, abounding with an unlimited diversity of metaphors, symbols, and images of Christ, testifies to mutability and plasticity necessary to the representability of Christology. For instance, Fray Luis de León (1527–1591) in his book *Los nombres de Christo* (The names of Christ) explores some of the most notable and enigmatic names of Christ in the Bible. Fray Luis's "Faces of God" is a metaphor for the names and virtues of Christ. Attributing numerous names to God is common in theistic religions. Islam, for example, gives God ninety-nine names, one short of one hundred, a number that symbolizes perfection. The hundredth stands for God's unknown name, for the limited human mind cannot know all the attributes of an infinite deity. Among the Eastern religions, Hinduism employs many names and images of divine reality leading some to give Hinduism the moniker "the religion of thirty-three million gods." Rojas points out that in the *Bhagavad Gita*, for example, God is called Supreme Soul, Lord of the Holy Union, the Ancient Principle, Indivisible, Time, Hari, Krishna and so on (Rojas 1929, 25–26).

Rattled by the comparison between Christianity and Hinduism, the bishop denounces the Hindu gods and goddesses as "monstrous." Borges, recall, used the same language in reference to the Catholic Trinity. Hideous portrayals of the image of Kali, mouth agape revealing bloody pointed teeth, and wearing a necklace of severed hands and a belt of severed heads, make her appear monstrous on purpose to signify her role in frightening away the demons that threaten Dharma. Ganesha, Shiva's son, a popular deity depicted with the body of a man and the head of an elephant, strange to Western eyes, symbolizes good fortune. Hindu deities sporting blue skin and waving multiple pairs of arms do not suit the bishop's aesthetics, but somehow, the irony of a pregnant virgin and dead God fail to offend the sensibilities of the dogmatic bishop.

Historical debates about the use of religious icons during the Byzantine period, Rojas argues, threatened to rip the church apart just like the heated debates regarding the canon of the New Testament. The iconoclastic controversy ignited when Emperor Leo III prohibited the use of icons. Fearing a backlash from the Muslims who deemed religious images idolatrous, Emperor Leo III suppressed the veneration of religious icons—richly decorated two-dimensional images of religious figures. John of Damascus rose to the defense of icons, arguing that they constituted a continuation of the incarnation of Christ and that they were necessary for evangelizing the illiterate masses. The Seventh General Council (787 CE) resolved the conflict, ruling that icons served a sacred function in the church, as long as they were not objects of worship but only of veneration, a kind of deep respect. Note that the creation of a division between worship and veneration functioned to accommodate different, even opposing, perspectives.

When Constantia, sister of Emperor Constantine, wrote to Eusebius of Caesarea requesting an image of Christ, he replied, "Which one? The true unchangeable one or the one in the form of a slave?" For Eusebius, the historical Jesus is the only true and unchangeable image of God. For Emperor Constantine V, an icon of Christ could not be the true image unless it was identical with the Christ of faith. Consequently, for Constantine only the Eucharist represented the true image of Christ (Pelikan 1999, 85–87).

Even before the iconoclastic controversy, after Chalcedon (450 CE), some theologians claimed that since Christ is the true image of God and God is nondescript, so Christ is beyond description. Chalcedon affirmed the two natures of Christ and the unity of his person. Thus if an artist were to create an image of Christ's divinity they would violate his essential nature by attempting to describe the indescribable (Pelikan 1999, 85–87).

Iconoclasm, by trying to preserve the integrity of Christ's divinity, results in degrading the integrity of Christ's humanity. Defenders of icons, by contrast, held that since the incarnation of Christ made Jesus an icon of the true image of God, God in this manner justified the use of icons. After all, an icon is an image of the true image of God. John of Damascus defended this view in his apt description of God as the "first and the original image-maker of the universe" (Pelikan 1999, 89).

Considering these matters, Rojas raises a thought-provoking question: In what sense is Jesus the image of God? There is no description of the physical appearance of the historical Jesus in the four Gospels of the New Testament. Admittedly, the Book of Revelation opens with a description of the heavenly Christ. According to St. John's mystical vision, "His head and his hairs were white like wool, as white as snow; and his eyes were as a flame of fire; And his feet like unto fine brass, as if they burned in a furnace; and his voice as the sound of many waters (Rev. 1:14–15). Unfortunately, John's mystical vision of the postpaschal Christ cannot assist in a description of the physical appearance of the historical Jesus. Rojas seems to be asking about the physical appearance of Jesus and its representation of God.

One single canonical image of Jesus would serve as a counterexample to Rojas's argument that the church does not possess an official image of Jesus. Self-assured of the existence of such a counterexample, the bishop smugly brings up the example of Veronica's veil as the image consecrated by the church's tradition—"painted with the sweat and blood" of Jesus (Rojas 1929, 29). Skeptical about the authenticity of the image and the story behind it, Rojas presses him to answer whether Veronica was a real woman. Exasperated by Rojas's skepticism, the bishop unequivocally declares, "Yes!" Without waiting for the bishop to elaborate, Rojas immediately pounces, recounting the legend and providing a source that refutes the folktale:

> Tradition has it that a woman of privilege left her palace, following a pious
> custom in Jerusalem for those condemned to the cross, to wipe the face of

Jesus when the Lord was on his way to Calvary. However, the canonical Gospels do not give the name of Veronica nor do they refer to the anecdote, nor do they affirm the miracle of the figure transferred to the cloth. All of this comes from other less authoritative sources that attribute to the woman the name of Bernice or Veronique; moreover, [Giovanni] Meile affirms that the name of Veronica comes from an anonymous book. It is from this source that is derived the mistaken Vero-ikon, true icon, authentic picture—a little barbaric given the etymology. As you can see, we are walking in an uncertain zone of myths. One word can create a legend. (Rojas 1929, 31)

The existence of the icon is not in question, only its authenticity. In his counterargument, Rojas reasons that if the Veronica veil were authentic, the church would have consecrated the image as the official archetype or paradigm of Christian iconography. The church failed to do that. Therefore, the conclusion must be that the church does not recognize the authenticity of the icon. Considering that the church finally adopted a canon (an authoritative list of books) for Christian scripture after centuries of volatile debate and dissension, one would expect the church to have canonized a representation of Christ. Instead, the church left the representation of Christ free to the artistic imagination (Rojas 1929, 33).

The twenty-seven books that now appear in the New Testament did not appear as a complete list until the Easter Letter (367 CE) of St. Athanasius, the bishop of Alexandria. As early as the second century CE, Christians certainly recognized the Gospels and some of St. Paul's letters as scripture. Marcion, a wealthy Christian (140 CE), rejected the divine authority of the Hebrew Bible and only accepted Luke and the letters of Paul as canonical and revelatory. Marcion's Canon provoked debate about canonization. Papias, an early Christian bishop, in his "Expositions of the Oracles of the Lord" (130 BCE), lays out a list of books recognized by the early church as the Word of God. Irenaeus, Bishop of Gaul at the end of second century, wrote the *Adversus Haereses*, a polemical work directed against the Gnostics, in which he acknowledges the canonicity of some New Testament books. The Muratorian Canon from the end of the second century, is the universally acknowledged first but incomplete canonical list of New Testament books. Early Christians looked suspiciously at Hebrews, 2 Peter, and 2 and 3 John because they did not appear apostolic (written by an apostle); they rejected James because of the emphasis on salvation by works in contradiction to Paul's doctrine of salvation by faith alone. Early Christians largely rejected the Book of Revelation because of its highly charged symbolism and obscure apocalyptic language. Documented lists of New Testament books prior to the Council of Nicea (325 CE) undermine Dan Brown's claim in his best-selling novel *The Da Vinci Code* that the Emperor Constantine intervened, settling the problem of the New Testament canon (Brown 2003, 234). For centuries, the early Christians argued about the New Testament canon.

The lack of a standard or canonical image, argues the bishop, is because the Veronica veil ruled as the unofficial but true image of Jesus. Rojas reasons that if the icon ruled as the unofficial image, it would have served as the reference point for later religious artists. That never happened largely because of the unintelligibility and vague form of the Veronica veil. Blurred and smudged, the icon does not depict a coherent identifiable face. From the image one cannot tell whether Jesus is dark skinned or white, longhaired or short haired, bearded or beardless, old or young. Rojas concludes that the icon's lack of clarity may be the reason why the church allowed such latitude to artistic imagination, which it does not tolerate in translations of the Gospels.

Later paintings purportedly based on the Veronica veil share little resemblance. For example, an anonymous fifteenth-century Franciscan painting of the suffering Christ lacks the crown of thorns; yet a painting by Guillermo de Colonia in a Munich gallery depicts Christ wearing a highly stylized crown. Gabriel May's *Ecce homo* vaguely suggests a crown and depicts a figure "smoky as in a dream." De Pavia covers the head of Jesus with a Moroccan turban. Even if these artists purportedly follow the Veronica veil, they used different models since the church never canonized the image of the Veronica veil or any other representation of the physical figure of Jesus. Rojas concludes his demonstrating asserting, "All these images pretend to reproduce the Cloth of Veronica but they are not copies of the presumed original and represent diverse human types varying in color, etc." (Rojas 1929, 34–35).

Shifting the theme from the nonexistence of an archetypal image, the discussion turns to a problem in aesthetics. What is the function of art? One response in the history of art theory that appears to satisfy Rojas is the representation theory of art. Art objects represent some physical object or idea. With respect to religious art, the content purportedly represents Christ or some aspect of Christ. Rojas is motivated by the question, what do representations of Christ in art express about the idea of Christ? (Rojas 1929, 43). With this question, Rojas implicitly denies that a representation is a copy of the original sensible object. On the contrary, Rojas appeals to Plato's theory of forms, which posits an invisible world of abstract objects. Attempting a solution at the pedestrian level, the bishop voices the commonsense opinion that the images of Christ represent the Biblical Jesus and not some invisible ideal, essence, idea, or notion. In so doing, he unwittingly reintroduces the copy theory of representational art, the very theory that Rojas is backing away from. Underneath the debate between the copy theory and the ideational theory is the metaphysical problem about the relationship between the Christ of faith and the historical Jesus.

What is the nature of the relationship between the historical Jesus and the Christ of faith? Is Christ identical with Jesus? If so, in what way? Is Christ a divine entity inhabiting the material body of Jesus? Is Jesus merely one instance of possible incarnations of the divine Christ? Is there a continuity between the historical Jesus and the Christ of faith? If so, what kind of continuity is this? Historical? Metaphysical? It is easy to say that the Christ of faith represents the historical Jesus or that, conversely, the historical Jesus represents or symbolizes the Christ of faith. It appears that the debate begins by assuming that representations of Christ express some feature of Jesus but shifts to consider in what sense Jesus represents some feature of the preexisting Christ.

Following the dialogue carefully, the reader notices that Rojas appears to be referring to Christ as a spiritual idea. Jesus, then, in some way, symbolizes this idea. At one level, there is a dyadic relationship between Christ and Jesus, a simple relation between sign and signifier. At a superficial level, there is a triadic relationship between Jesus, the heavenly Christ, and Christ represented in theology, art, literature, and history. However, the heavenly Christ collapses into the representational Christ. The dyadic relation returns, but it creates further problems. First, the referent of the name Jesus is ambiguous, picking out either the Jesus of the Gospels or the historical Jesus. The Gospels present more than one representation of Jesus, for the Jesus of the synoptic Gospels is different than the Jesus of the Gospel of John. Additionally, Gospels are evangelical tracts whose purpose is not to record history but to persuade hearers and readers to convert to the Christian faith. In any case, the character of Jesus in the Gospels is the work of Christians projecting their own representations of Jesus forged by different traditions of Christianity. In short, the Jesus of the Gospels is already an expression of the Christ of faith and not just the source of later representations of Christ. Rojas seems unaware of these hermeneutical nuances. Nonetheless, his apparent concern is with the artistic depictions of Christ and the idea they purportedly represent. At this stage of the discussion, Rojas does not show his cards; rather he appears content simply to declare that Christian art represents the ideal or idea of Christ, which, for the moment, remains a mystery, a mystery awaiting unveiling before the end of the dialogue.

Rojas runs into a grave logical difficulty. He cannot claim that artistic images of the Christ of faith represent the historical Jesus without falling into circularity.

He has already made clear that depictions of Christ represent some feature of Jesus, and Jesus symbolizes Christ or the spiritual idea of Christ, but at the same time Jesus is the source for the depictions of Christ. The circularity of Rojas's reasoning makes interpretation difficult and indicates that Rojas was confused.

Recall that for Rojas, pictorial representations signify ideas. Commonly, people believe that a picture represents by resembling some object. A depiction of Jesus/ Christ in painting, then, is authentic when it resembles Jesus/Christ. How does one determine whether a resemblance is established? One way is to look for a correspondence between the features of a picture and those of a Gospel story. Then, it is just a matter of whether the picture captures the look and feel of what a story brings to the imagination. Superficially, this is what pictorial representation means.

This explanation reflects the bishop's viewpoint on this matter. Rojas's inquiry takes him to a deeper level. Besides the look, the resemblance, or the correspondence between picture and story, Rojas seeks the idea of Christ. Assume some grand idea lies behind the representations of Christ. Let this be the idea of Jesus's personality, for both Rojas and the bishop claim that the human personality of Jesus is the key for getting at the idea of Christ, both the "spiritual idea" of Christ—the ontological second person of the Godhead according to Catholic Christianity—and the Christ represented by art.

Suggesting that the personality of Jesus is the key to the idea of Christ, Rojas appears to hold some type of personalism. Personalism is a philosophical view, popular from the second half of the nineteenth century through the first half of the twentieth century, which asserts that the highest being and/or value in the universe is personality. Personalism influenced many Latin American thinkers before World War II, thus it is not surprising that Rojas makes personality central to his interpretation of the Christ idea. Jesus's personality, for Rojas, evokes something transcendent, expresses the existence of the incommunicable behind the veil of the communicable, and represents the universal good instantiated in a great kaleidoscope of historically diverse particular images—human personality.

In the history of Christian art, images of Christ typically depict a young human male—bearded or clean-shaven. Early Christians also resorted to non-human images—fish, anchor, lamb, cross—to represent Christ or the Christian faith. The most enduring, emotional, and memorable images of Christ are those of the body of Jesus. Consider, then the human body as a symbol of the spiritual, the bearer of personality "a veil that covers that which is beyond all forms." For this reason, Rojas engages Christian icons to ferret out "la verdad del Espíritu invisible que en ellas se esconde" (the truth of the invisible spirit that is hiding in them) (Rojas 1929, 47).

To reiterate, religious depictions of Christ, whatever the content, convey some essential idea about Christ. What is this essential idea? This essential idea, whatever it may be, is the object of Rojas investigation. Artistic images of Christ are signs signifying ideas whose meaning requires deciphering: "All that I hope to accomplish is to decipher the significance of these images if it is the case that they possess any significance" (Rojas 1929, 47). An unstated assumption motivates Rojas's investigation, namely that all images of Christ convey a common hidden meaning. The body or the humanity of Jesus is the principal clue. Assuming that personality is the expressive essence of a human being, then, it follows that the meaning behind the religious symbol has something to do with embodied personality.

Wrongly thinking that he and Rojas agree, the bishop affirms that the Biblical Jesus is the original source and model for subsequent religious images about Christ. Historically, artists drew inspiration from the Gospel stories to fuel their religious artistic creations. However, the bishop misses the point, because Rojas's Jesus is ambiguous, denoting either the historical man of flesh and bone or the character of Jesus in the Gospels. There is always the possibility that Rojas is confusing the two. If the latter is the case, Rojas, and probably the bishop, too, is mistaken. The historical Jesus and the Gospel Jesus are not identical. The Gospel writers are expressing faith for evangelistic purposes. Along the way, they may capture some aspect of the historical Jesus or the historical environment in which Jesus lived, but that is not their overriding purpose. Jorge Luis Borges makes a similar point in his short essay "Borges y yo" (Borges and I), in which he draws a distinction between Borges the famous writer and Borges the man—the public person and the private person. He ends the essay enigmatically: "I don't know which of the two is writing this essay" (Borges 1961, 186).

Rojas observes that the church places on its altars not only a great variety of images of Christ, but also conflicting ones. He observes, rightly or not, that the images seem to get more pagan the closer they are to the first century: "We only get the phantasms of Veronica or the suspicious picture of Esmeralda among various apocrypha, reliquary, or symbolic polymorphism of the Catacombs in whose dark crypts penetrates the declining light of pagan mythology disconcerting us in every way" (Rojas 1929, 50). In other words, early Christian depictions of Christ drew on Greek art and mythology. This was the case for Renaissance artists as well.

Shocked to hear that Greek art and mythology served as sources and models for Christian artists during the Renaissance, the bishop incredulously asks, "Do you believe that their false gods . . . have influenced the iconography of the true God?" (Rojas 1929, 50). Unbridled by the bishop's consternation, Rojas gleefully declares, "In the Christian heavens roam the shadows of the ancient Olympians" (Rojas 1929, 50). As an example, Rojas points out a bronze statue of St. Peter in Rome, claiming that it was originally a statue of Jupiter, a pagan statue "whose feet are kissed by Catholics." The bishop is unwilling to give Rojas the benefit of the doubt. Undaunted, the bishop stubbornly remains skeptical about pagan sources in the face of a plurality of evidence to the contrary. Hoping to break down the bishop's recalcitrance and incredulity, Rojas points out the striking resemblances between Renaissance images of Christ and those of Apollo, Orpheus, and Hermes: "During the early centuries of the Christian era, in the Catacombs, Christ was represented by a species of Orpheus with his lyre symbolizing thereby the power of his word over the passions and instinct, the beasts tamed by music in the Orphic mysteries. He is also represented like Hermes Kriophoros, Hermes bearing a lamb in Greek mythology, strictly translated by the figure of the Good Shepherd, a beardless youthful male with his sheep over his shoulders is profusely repeated" (Rojas 1929, 50–51).

The bishop interjects, making a good point, in principle at least, that pagan sources are not necessary since there are Biblical symbols of the good shepherd and the fish. For example, Luke tells the parable of the good shepherd, who goes off in search of his missing sheep. Psalm 23:1, a beloved Psalm, likens God to a shepherd: "The Lord is my shepherd, I shall not want." The hieroglyph of the fish finds sources in Jesus's feeding of the five thousand and in calling his disciples to be fishers of people. While the bishop's argument appears defensible in principle, it overlooks the fact that Renaissance artists did indeed turn to Greek models, especially those of the youthful Apollo, to represent the adolescent Christ, as Rojas argues:

> If I had before me some of the adolescent Christs, you would see that they are
> not the nonsense of my imagination. Take for example, [the adolescent Christ]
> of Bernardino Luini in the Ambrosiana de Milan and Beltraffio's youthful
> Christ in the Academy of Pergamum. How can one deny the difference
> between those Christs of Apollonian lineage and the other suffering, bearded,
> and barbaric Christs—Dionysian in their bloody virility . . . *The Redeemer*
> from the Communal Academy of Brescia painted by Raphael at the height of
> the Renaissance under Pontifical patronage is a beardless and naked youthful
> Christ. His front side is luminous, his right hand raised upward; no one
> looking at this image can free themselves from thinking that this is an image
> of Apollo. (Rojas 1929, 54–55)

Allowing the possibility that Greek art seduced Raphael, the bishop cannot conceive that Greek art could have a similar effect on Michelangelo, the church's artist. Unfortunately for the bishop, Rojas demonstrates that Michelangelo, just as Raphael, turned to Greek sources:

> Michelangelo's Christ in *Jesus Cursing the Reprobates*, in the Sixteenth Capilla, is not about the youthful Jesus or any Jesus in the Gospels but the glorious Christ Excelso of the Last Judgment. Nevertheless, the artist has painted his body smooth and bare exuding youthful vitality in the torso, the face enveloped in celestial light as if he were himself a god of light. This Christ of Michelangelo, spiritual archetype of the Messiah, is a perfect Apollo and it is found as you can see for yourself in the Vatican itself where the Pope rules over Christianity. (Rojas 1929, 55)

Unsettled by Rojas's identification with Michelangelo's Christ and the Greek God Apollo, the riled bishop loses his temper and accuses Rojas of heresy. Shrugging off the accusation the way one brushes off lint, Rojas softens his tone, replying that he is only seeking a universal Christ. Rojas does make a justifiable comparison that is worthy of further explanation. However, Raphael and Michelangelo also made drawings of Apollo. It is possible that Rojas, at times, is mistaking an image of Apollo for that of Jesus/Christ.

For the first time in the dialogue, Rojas supplements a representational view on art with an expressionist slant stressing that religious art gives expression to human feelings and beliefs beyond what written texts can convey. Representational art and expressionist art are not mutually exclusive, as evidenced by the work of Orozco. Art that represents also evokes a perlocutionary effect. Artistic depictions of ageless Christs, sexless Christs, and so on, target human emotions as well as stimulate the optic nerve and light up the shorter and taller cones.

Earlier Rojas stated that the personality or humanity of Jesus is a clue to the mystery of Christ. Later in the dialogue, he specifies that the symbolism of Jesus is ambiguous in that the humanity of Jesus both reveals and conceals the mystery of Christ. What is the mystery of Christ? At this point in the discussion, Rojas limits the mystery of Christ to the passion and death of Jesus. Why did Jesus suffer and die? According to an old adage, the manner of one's death reveals the essence of a person's life. The way Jesus died unveils something of the mystery. There are, says Rojas, masculine and feminine ways of dying. To die a masculine death is to die for an abstract idea, such as one's nation or the ideal of freedom. To die a feminine death is to die for people or for personal happiness. Jesus died a feminine death since he died for people. Socrates died a masculine death because he refused to betray his ideals (Rojas 1929, 71–72). Saying that Jesus died a feminine death does not resolve the mystery but leads us closer to the unveiling of the mystery. Jesus's death, as well as Jesus's personality, reveals a clue about the mystery of the significance of Christ. Moreover, like Jesus's personality, the death of Jesus is an essential feature of being human.

One thing is clear: something about Jesus's humanity conveys a notion of divinity or some ultimate value. For this reason, Rojas highlights features of Jesus's humanity when mentioning the mystery of Christ:

> I say that the mystery appears when one considers other characteristics of
> Jesus, like his maternal love for children, his indulgence toward feminine sins,
> the sweetness of his voice and his habitual manners. This is what some
> renaissance artists saw while other modern artists prefer to represent him
> under the aspect of an abrupt and unclean revolutionary. . . . He possesses in
> himself all races, since he transcends them; all ages in that he feels like a child
> and speaks like an elder; and he has perhaps all the mystery of the carnal man,
> the Adam/Eve whose fall he redeemed was a fall of love. (Rojas 1929, 72–73)

Clearly, the mystery of Christ resides in the very humanity of Jesus. In short, human nature is divine in every aspect of bodily life, including sex. For this reason, Rojas draws attention to human sexuality. It makes sense that if humans are sexual creatures, and Jesus is human, Jesus was a sexual being. This idea was not lost on Nikos Kazantzakis in his creative retelling of the life of Jesus in *The Last Temptation of Christ*. Martin Scorsese's movie based on the book approaches Jesus's sexuality boldly yet ambiguously.

Discussing Jesus's sexuality makes many people, especially American Christians, uncomfortable, and this fact about Christians reveals the persistence of Docetism in common American Christian beliefs and attitudes toward Jesus. Rojas raises a crucial question with anthropological implications: Could Jesus have been human without awareness of his sexuality, without experience of sexual desire or sexual self-awareness? People may live their whole lives without having had sex with another human being, but is it possible that they live their whole lives without sexual self-awareness?

Accompanying sexual self-awareness is suffering—as many know first hand. Rojas is probably right when he suggests that Jesus could not have taken on human suffering in its depth and breadth if he did not experience the suffering produced by love and sexual desire:

The greatest afflictions of man, the most human, are those that proceed from sex. Love is the road of salvation and the path to perdition, for man and for woman. For many years of Jesus' life, we know nothing about him, and it is not presumptuous to imagine that he bore in that period of his early youthfulness the characteristics of his age and sex. If that had not been the case, then he could not have known earthly suffering, the great human mystery. Love could enter into his divine life, as it entered the sacrifice of his death without the flesh overcoming the spirit. (Rojas 1929, 73–74)

To further his argument about the centrality of sexuality in human life, he mentions the role of eroticism in classical art and literature, and gives the examples of the "The Sleeping Hermaphrodite" also known as the "Borghese Hermaphroditus" (1620), erotic and bucolic poetry, and Suetonius's history of Roman emperors.

Downplaying the role of sexuality in classical literature, the bishop boasts that the triumph of Christianity over the Greeks and Romans demonstrates the depravity of the classical cultures and moral superiority of Christianity. St. Francis of Assisi and Dante Alighieri prove the victory of the spirit of Christ over the lust of the flesh and the lust of the eyes. The bishop's rhetorical victory is brief, for Rojas unrelentingly provides more examples and suggests that if Jesus bore all human sufferings, he must have experienced love and sexuality:

The phallic engravings on the chairs in the stupendous Cathedral of Ciudad Rodrigo indicate that the flesh has not been entirely overcome. In the Renaissance, an artistic genius like Leonardo de Vinci, an ambiguous person himself, lived under this disquietude, and painted on his canvases beautiful youthful males that looked like women. . . . Do not forget that Christ was the hero of universal love, of spiritual love transcending all limits. He kept in his consciousness the mystery of both sexes the way that Shakespeare knows all too well the secret of Hamlet and that of Ophelia. Jesus looked into the interior of souls and lived the life of all human beings given that he himself bore their sufferings. (1929, 75–76)

Leo Steinberg's eye-opening, controversial book, *The Sexuality of Christ During the Renaissance*, offers myriad examples of artists' renderings of Christ's sexuality as an infant, at his Crucifixion, and his resurrection. Innumerable examples like these undermine the naïve Docetism of a sexually repressed Christianity.

Predictably, the bishop remains staunchly unmoved, holding tenaciously to the traditional belief that Jesus is a model of purity. Sexuality in Christian art, he explains, is due to artists taking extremes, creating ambiguous figures of Christ. Jesus's purity is the result of a wishful projection coming from a guilt-ridden humanity. Rojas earns admiration when he boldly calls Christ's purity a fiction of Christian idealism. Jesus lived life in the flesh. Flesh and spirit are antithetical concepts in St. Paul's writings.

Jesus's humanity and ontogenetic human development fortuitously enlarge the scope of the possibility of variability in the imagination of the artists. On this point, there is a rare agreement between Rojas and the bishop. Variability in the images of Jesus is easily explained by Jesus's own biography, argues the bishop. Accordingly, he reasons that different images would be required to represent Jesus at different stages of his life: the infant Jesus, the twelve-year-old Jesus in the temple, Jesus cleansing the temple, Jesus in the Garden of Gethsemane, the crucified Christ, the resurrected Christ, and so on. Changes in cultural aesthetics, artistic styles, and techniques also help explain the variability of the images of Jesus. Therefore, the Christ of the Byzantine era, naturally, appears differently than the Christ of the Renaissance. Having marshalled an impressive argument, the bishop exudes a smug confidence that he has settled the issue of the diversity and variability of the images of Christ. Expressing an unabashed sense of victory, the bishop brashly concludes, "Desearía que este modo de considerar la cuestión bastara para satisfacer vuestras objeciones" (I would wish that this way of considering the question sufficiently answers your objections) (Rojas 1929, 81).

The variability and plasticity of the images of Christ is necessary given the developmental stages that Jesus underwent, and considering the cultural differences and national origins of artists. Rojas, however, believes that the bishop misunderstands the problem of plasticity by stressing the superficial accidents of change and variability with regard to form. Rojas's core concern lies with the idea or concept behind the form. By shifting the focus from the human form to the idea expressed in the form, Rojas applies a Platonic realism that exalts the invisible universal over the visible particular.

Perceiving an inconsistency in Rojas's realistic metaphysics, the bishop jumps to the conclusion that Rojas is denying the existence of Jesus Christ. Dodging the misdirected charge, Rojas says that the existence of Jesus is not the issue, but the variability the church allows in the representations of Jesus. In the churches of southern Italy and Andalusia, Christ is generally dark-haired; in northern Italy and in Germany, Christ is usually blond, he observes. Unfazed, the bishop reminds Rojas about the need for contextualizing the Gospel: "Jesus and the characters of the Gospels always take on the dress and appearances of the culture and era of the artists who conceive their images" (Rojas 1929, 83). Suddenly self-conscious and embarrassed by his unconscious commitment to historical relativism, the bishop beats a quick retreat back to his avowed conservative position defending the church's dogmas about the divinity and canonicity of the Gospels. Allaying the bishop's fears somewhat, Rojas confides that he is seeking in the images of the Jesus the "Cristo invisible" (Rojas 1929, 85).

Since the church has not adopted a canonical prototype for the image of Christ, Rojas boldly declares that he is entitled to construct his own. Toward this goal, Rojas enigmatically refers to a sixteenth-century crucifix of wood made by a converso that depicts Christ as a mulatto (1929, 86). Not only that, says Rojas, but also, in North America, blacks believe that the devil is white since blacks have suffered so much evil at the hands of whites. Therefore, they reason that Christ must be black. At the time, Rojas could not have foreseen that the 1960s black leaders Elijah Mohammed and Malcolm X would label whites "white devils." Black theologian James Cone in his 1968 work, *A Black Theology of Liberation*, uses whiteness as a symbol for evil. Aghast at the notion of a black Christ, the bishop argues that if we are to assign a racial label to Christ, the proper label is that of a Galilean Jew in keeping with the Gospel stories. Unwittingly, by identifying Jesus as a Galilean, the bishop makes Jesus's racial identity even more ambiguous, for as Rojas notes, "I have read that the name 'Galilee' comes from the term '*Gelil hag-goyim*,' which means, 'circle of the gentiles.' This is the place name of Jesus's homeland, a place inhabited by Phoenicians, Syrians, Arabs, Greeks in great numbers even though many of them were Jewish converts; moreover, Roman magistrates and soldiers governed the country. With these facts the racial question loses importance if you presume to infer from his native people the physical type of the Nazarene" (Rojas 1929, 89).

Rojas's account about the etymology of Galilee is correct. However, his comment about the makeup of the population is anachronistic. After Assyria's defeat of the Northern Kingdom of Israel (722 BCE), Assyria resettled foreigners from many nationalities into the region. By the first century CE, however, the population in Galilee was largely Jewish (Coogan 2010, 1752).

Dismissing the ethnic question altogether, the taciturn bishop seeks the safe refuge of Catholic theology: "In any case, the ethnic question loses importance when you consider that Jesus was engendered by the Holy Spirit." Quoting from Galatians, feeling sure that he is on solid ground, he says that in Christ there are no longer Jews or Gentiles. When the messy problems of being human muddy people's perceptions of Jesus, they often turn to the divinity of Jesus. The bishop does just that emphasizing the spirituality and divinity of Jesus. In doing so, he inadvertently finds shelter in a type of Docetism unintentionally impugning

Christ's human integrity. Rojas, by contrast, constructs a Jesus who is an ambiguous ontological figure marked by a dialectical tension between divinity and humanity (Rojas 1929, 90).

Decisively splitting asunder the identity of Jesus and Christ, Rojas asserts that Jesus died, but Christ rose from the dead in a form "astral like the spiritualists' ectoplasm." Sensing a contradiction in describing Christ as both invisible and astral, he quickly dismisses the significance of the visible or astral form of Christ saying that what matters are the spiritual, mystical values and ideals of Jesus. Most importantly of all, Jesus death functions as a human symbol of universal love expressing the reality of an "invisible God" in every human being (Rojas 129, 92). Rojas's Christology uneasily affirms an identification between the visible Jesus and the invisible muted by the underlying theme of the visibility of humanity and the invisibility of divinity.

Rojas appears to emphasize the visibility of Jesus especially at the Crucifixion but shifts emphasis to the invisibility of Christ as the center of religious gravity. The invisible Christ subordinates the visible Jesus. For instance, doubting Thomas would not believe until he saw with his own eyes the stigmata of Jesus. Jesus, however, reproached him saying, "Because thou hast seen me, thou hast believed: blessed are they that have not seen, and yet have believed" (John 20:29).

To protect himself against confusion, the bishop draws a cynical bead on Rojas, accusing him of claiming that Christians invented Christ. Intuitively, the bishop is onto something, but he is mistaken about Rojas's intention. Rojas intends to unveil the mystery of Christ that is veiled by the human corporeality of Jesus.

Rojas assigns to Jesus the function of representing Christ as if Jesus is analogous to artistic representations of Christ. For him, the history of Christian art yields an ambiguous aesthetics in the representations of Jesus/Christ. One type of representation is that of the youthful beardless Apollo-like Jesus/Christ and the other is that of the virile, bearded, masculine Jesus/Christ:

> I have said that, but I want to point out that for now I am only referring to the corporeal figure as the object of this dialogue through the knowledge of which I hope to find the significance of the spiritual figure. It is evident that the image of Christ unknown in its origins hides in the esoteric symbols of the lamb and the fish or in the pagan allegories of Hermes Christopher or portalira Orpheus. From the child that the Magi adored and the youthful Apollos that persisted until the epoch of Michelangelo, there alternates the bearded man that will become in following centuries the dominant figure in a profuse imaginary. This virile type, roughly sketched in the first centuries, is

definitive in the renaissance when art in the fullness of expressive means and humanism in the fullness of its creative sympathies shapes the consensus of the Human archetype. That is, in my opinion, a new symbol . . . the aesthetic creation and the mystical creation work in two different spiritual directions inspired by the tradition of messianic Hebraism. (Rojas 1929, 105)

The image of the bearded, older, masculine Jesus/Christ is a token of the ugly Christ or Cristo feo that finds its biblical anchor, for Christians, in Isaiah 53, a chapter on the suffering servant: "he hath no form nor comeliness; and when we shall see him, there is no beauty that we should desire him" (Isaiah 53:2b). Clement of Alexandria and Justin Martyr, according to Rojas, adhered to this vision but did not fully develop the notion of the ugly Christ.

In contrast to the ugly Christ, the beautiful Christ finds biblical support in Psalm 45:2, where the Psalmist speaks of the anointed one: "Thou art fairer than the children of men." An alternative reading says, "You are beautiful, the most beautiful of the sons of man." St. Ambrose and St. John Chrysostom, so Rojas claims, anchored their Christologies in the affirmation of Christ's beauty. Rojas may be stretching things a bit when he claims that these two visions are at the source and origin of all subsequent images of Christ in religious art.

Finding no real contradiction between the ugly Christ and the beautiful Christ, the bishop blithely remarks that these two visions merely reflect the multifaceted dimensions of Christ's nature and work. Nonetheless, he admits that he personally prefers the beautiful Christ expressed in the work of Raphael and finds it to be more in concert with the Christian ideal. Maybe so, answers Rojas, but the ugly Christ finds expression in the Renaissance work of Andrea Mantegna and Albrecht Dürer, and in modern art like that of Gustave van de Woestyne's *Jesus Christ Showing His Wounds*.

Rojas disapproves of the bishop's implication that the beautiful Christ is more authentic than the ugly Christ. The beautiful Christ, Rojas contends, is a later artificial creation. To support this contention, he quotes from a twelfth-century letter known as the *Publius Lentulus*, as the source of the idea of the beautiful Christ. The purported letter may be spurious since Rojas writes that it is apocryphal.

A singularly virtuous man has appeared and lives among us. His followers call him the Son of God. He cures the sick and raises the dead. He is tall and attracts looks. His face simultaneously inspires both love and fear. His hair is long, blond, straight to his ears, and then curls loop to the shoulders, a streak

in the middle separates them falling on both sides according to the custom of
the Nazarenes. He has rosy cheeks, a short nose, and a well-formed mouth.
His thick beard is parted in the middles with the color of hazelnuts just like
his hair. His look reveals wisdom and candor. His blue eyes are covered with
subtle shadows. This man, generally likeable in conversation, becomes fearful
when he reproaches. But, even in such cases, there emanates from him a
serene self-consciousness. No one has seen him laugh, although frequently, he
has been known to cry. The tone of his voice is grave, reserved, and modest.
He is as beautiful as a man can be. His name is Jesus, son of Mary. (Rojas
1928, 109–10 [author's translation])

The bishop admits that the *Publius Lentulus* may have served as a model for
some later artists. Discussing the virtues of the *Publius Lentulus* reminds the
bishop of his own preference for the Spanish Christs. In particular, he likes a
painting in the Prado by Juan de Juanes, the *Sacred Heart in the Palm of the Hand*,
Diego Velásquez's famous *White Christ*, and El Greco's work entitled *Salvator
Mundi* (Savior of the World). Rojas arrogantly replies that he does not know what
it means to prefer a particular Christ. Appearing disagreeable, he confesses that he
dislikes Spanish religious art with its sanguinary forms and sensuality of torment
that he attributes to the Spanish spirit: "La Inquisición y la Tauromaquia juntas,
color de sangre y belleza de pasión" (Both the Inquisition and the art of Bullfight-
ing express the color of blood and the beauty of passion) (Rojas 1929, 116).

Approaching the end of the first dialogue, Rojas begins to unveil the mystery of
Christ hinted at earlier: the images of Christ reveal that humanity is the secret to
the significance of Jesus's spirituality. Fully developing his thesis, he boldly ven-
tures the claim, "The image of Christ, subject to change, as we have seen resolves
itself, therefore, into the image of Humanity and therefore its spiritual image; the
image of Christ—multiple, undulating and dynamic—resolves itself into a divinity, a living and human divinity" (Rojas 1929, 116).

In a confessional mood, Rojas explains that exposure to artistic depictions of
Jesus in his youth secured for him the belief in the existence of Jesus Christ. Aesthetics, not theology, brought him to faith. Along the way, he studied the history
of Christian iconography. Eventually, he became disconcerted by the lack of an
original prototype. In time, he reluctantly accepted the fact that there is no original image of Jesus. He traveled to Rome hoping to assuage his doubts, only to have
them confirmed:

The Church does not possess any authentic graphic documentation of the
physical person of Jesus comparable to the authoritative portrayal of his

spiritual personality found in the Gospels. The obscure figure of Christ appears confused with enigmatic signs and pagan myths; the church left it to each artist to represent its founder according to their own imagination, changing local projections, or the ideal envisioned by the interpreter. The figure of Jesus has shown great variation over the course of twenty centuries, reflecting race, epoch, culture, schools of thought, and individual tempera-ments. (Rojas 1928, 121–22)

In the modern age, Rojas observed a new shift of emphasis in Protestantism, rationalism, romanticism, liberalism, and philosophical neo-mysticism, giving rise to a new type of individualism. The examples he gives of the romantic individual ideal include the tormented expressions in Woestyne's *Christ Showing His Wounds* and Eduard von Gebhardt's *Christ the World Wanderer*, depicting Christ as a beg-gar, a vagabond aged by misery until he no longer resembles the traditional Christ neither in age nor in type. But he especially rejoices over some modern works such as the following: Antoine Wiertz, *Los partidos jugados por el Cristo*; Jean-Hippolyte Flandrin, *Jesus Cries over the City* (the modern city); Bertel Thorvaldsen, *Come Unto Me* (figure 6.3); and Leonardo Bistolfi, *Christ*.

These works of art exemplify for him the humanization of God. In them, he recognizes the idea of the mystery of Christ, that Christ in humanity lives in the modern world, promoting a democratic and individualistic spirit:

> Every true artist is a true believer. Jesus of Nazareth, as incarnation of an invisible Master, is a son of God, and as realization of an incarnated Christ, the Son of Man. The multiform iconography of Jesus is explicable because Jesus Christ is not a man, but 'the man' or, better yet, all human beings. Iconography presents him as child and adult, short and tall, ugly and beauti-ful, dark and blond, gentleman, and rebel, Jew and Gentile. Each one of us can be his image. Christ is the human being in all its forms. That is the way the Church has given him to us, and from this fact, there emerges a new interpretation of Christianity. (Rojas 1928, 128)

Concluding the first dialogue, Rojas sharpens the focus of the meaning of the mystery of Christ by specifying it as love for the sake of humanity. Christ's cross represents humanity's love for humanity: "The Cross of Christ, unlike the Swas-tika and the Tao, is the figure of a shadow projected over the face of the earth, beneath the light of Heaven, the body of Humanity with open arms for the sacri-fice of love" (Rojas 1929, 130).

Artistic representations of Jesus raise the problem of the meaning of Jesus as

FIGURE 6.3   Bertel Thorvaldsen, *Come Unto Me*, 1839. Marble statue of Christ in the
Church of Our Lady, Copenhagen. © Art Resources, New York, 2017.

signifier. At one level, Jesus signifies the Christ; however, in this case, we merely trade one signifier for another and then the question becomes what does Christ signify? Rojas reasons that since the material signifier of Christ is the human body of Jesus, then the idea represented by the humanity of Jesus is just that: humanity. In other words, the mystery of Christ unveiled reveals that the meaning of the Jesus event is that humanity is divine. Christ in Jesus is the divinity in humanity or simply the revelation that human life is sacred. Rojas's message is ultimately a humanist message that human life is the ultimate value in the universe. His invisible Christ denotes humanity. Does Rojas overcome Docetism with his affirmation of humanity as the meaning of Christ's symbolism? The surprising answer is no. Since humanity is an abstraction, the assertion that humanity is the denotation of the invisible Christ still roams within the ambit of Docetism. The only way to overcome Docetism is to identity Christ with the historical Jesus. Alas, this identification is another version or representation of Christ. On the other hand, Rojas's emphasis on the abstract concept of humanity as the denotation of the Christ foreshadows the concept of the liberator Christ in Latin American liberation theology.

CHAPTER SEVEN

Liberation Theology

Christ the Liberator

P ope Francis, in his *Evangelii gaudium* (2013), apparently endorses liberation theology's teachings on social justice, in stark contrast with his immediate predecessor Pope Benedict XVI who, as Cardinal Joseph Ratzinger, issued an order on May 9, 1985, imposing an indefinite period of silence on Brazilian liberation theologian Leonardo Boff. The immediate stimulus for Ratzinger's action came from Boff's work *Church, Charisma, and Power*, which criticized the hierarchical structure of the Catholic Church and promoted the development of extraecclesial grassroots church movements led by laity. Prior to the silencing of Boff, Ratzinger had criticized Catholic theologians Edward Schillebeeckx, Hans Küng, and the pioneer of Latin American liberation theology, Peruvian priest Gustavo Gutiérrez.

In the 1960s, Gutiérrez began reflecting on the social and political implications of the Christian faith from the perspective of the poor and the oppressed. Rereading the Gospels from the underside of history, Latin American theologians asked social questions that traditional theology ignored: What does it mean to love my neighbor if my neighbor is an oppressed class? What are the political implications of faith in Christ? They recognized the presence of God in the pitiful bodies and faces of the poor and suffering, identifying God with the poor, *el Dios pobre*, the poor God. In their constructive theology, they transformed the traditional representation of Christ from a personal spiritual savior into Christ the sociopolitical liberator. Calling for a radical reformation of church and society, they demanded that the church make a preferential option for the poor and take sides with the poor in a class struggle.

Liberation is not a new theme in Latin America. The spirit of liberation burned brightly at the beginning of the Spanish conquest, when figures like Father Bartolomé de las Casas stood against Spanish abuses and defended the rights of the Indians. In Valladolid, Spain, Las Casas vigorously championed indigenous rights against conservative scholastic theologian Juan de Sepúlveda, who doubted the rationality (and humanity) of the Amerindians and justified their oppression and slavery. More recently, beginning in the 1930s, robust liberation movements— Catholic youth organizations, Catholic worker, and worker priest movements— linked faith with social and political commitments. Historical events in the world and in the region cultivated the soil, preparing conditions favorable to the development of liberation theology. The 1959 Cuban Revolution, for instance, proved that United States hegemony could be overthrown, raising hopes for liberation throughout Latin America. The Second Vatican Council II (1962–1965) modernized the church, indirectly sowing the seeds for the emergence of liberation theology.

Pope John XXIII convened the council tasked with opening up the church to the modern world, an opening that he called *aggiornamiento*. Key documents produced at Vatican II redefined the church as the people of God, including lay people in the new definition. Prior to Vatican II, the official definition of the church only included the clergy. Vatican II promoted interfaith dialogue and called for a new spirited engagement with the sciences, especially the social sciences, in order to make theology more relevant to the needs and interests of modern society. Pope Paul IV, who adjourned Vatican II, extended its reforms in his famous encyclical *Popularum progressio*, setting forth a theology of development that reflected the developmentalist programs of the 1960s, asserting the right of oppressed peoples to overthrow tyrannical regimes, and echoing Thomistic theories of just war. Capitalist ideologues promoted developmentalist socioeconomic theories assiduously and unashamedly advancing a realpolitik idea that in reality cloaked a utopian ideal that capital investment, economic expansion, technological advances, and structural adjustment policies would spur socioeconomic growth, eventually eliminating social inequalities, poverty, and injustice caused by underdevelopment.

Political and revolutionary theologies reacted against the merely reformist attitudes of the theology of development. First articulated in 1966 at the Church and Society meeting of the World Council of Christian Churches in Geneva, Switzerland, a theology of revolution challenged the socioeconomic theories of development underlying the World Bank, the International Monetary Fund, and Kennedy's Alliance for Progress. The theology of revolution sought to substitute a theory of dependence for a theory of development as a more adequate theoretical model explanatory of the actual global conditions of poverty, inequality, oppression, exploitation, and marginalization. According to dependency theory, poverty in third world countries directly results from global capitalism. Theologians turned to social theories in order to equip theology with the analytic and hermeneutic tools necessary for adequately interpreting social conditions in light of the Gospels and the Gospels in light of social conditions and social theory.

Latin American theologians joined in a fruitful conversation with social scientists who espoused dependency theory and Marxism, not that they necessarily go hand-in-hand. In 1964, theologians met in Petropolis, Brazil, to discuss the meaning of faith in contemporary Latin America. Among these theologians, Gustavo Gutiérrez came to play a catalyzing role in the development of liberation theology. Three years later in Montreal, Canada, Gutiérrez, an unpretentious but brilliant Peruvian priest, presented a groundbreaking paper on church and poverty. Later, he expanded these notes into an epoch-defining book, *A Theology of Liberation* (1971), setting forth the fundamental outlines of a theology of liberation.

At the Second Latin American Episcopal Conference meeting in Medellín, Colombia, in 1968, bishops adopted Vatican II reformations in order to adapt them to Latin America. Present as a theological consultant, Gutiérrez probably wrote the rough drafts for the Medellín documents "Peace," "Justice," and "Poverty." These innovative documents introduced a radically new theological vocabulary informed by progressive social science—"institutionalized violence," "structural sin," and "integral liberation."

In *A Theology of Liberation*, Gutiérrez expresses the worry that a genuine and authentic Latin American Christology, relevant and responsive to the needs of the poor, was sorely missing. Surprisingly, he failed to provide the missing Christology in his classic text *A Theology of Liberation*, but he did sketch the basic outlines of the idea of Christ the Liberator (Gutiérrez 1975). Raising similar concerns, Brazilian theologian Hugo Assmann warned theologians that unless they paid attention to Christology and hermeneutics (the art and science of the interpretation of ancient texts), liberation theology would lack relevance (Assmann 1973, 100). Throughout the seventies liberation theologians wrestled with the problem of creating a relevant and responsive Latin American Christology adapted to the challenges facing Latin America. Ignacio Ellucaría, Spanish philosopher teaching in El Salvador, and Raúl Vidales, Peruvian theologian, echoed the concerns of Gutiérrez and Assmann, boldly emphasizing the urgency of constructing a truly authentic Latin American Christology (Ellucaría 1976, 26).

One key feature of the emerging Christology gaining everyone's attention was the pressing concern of the political implications of the Gospel and the political consequences entailed by a genuine Christian commitment and the contextualization of the Gospel in Latin American circumstances (Segovia 1985, 98). Contextualizing Christ in postcolonial Latin America raised many difficulties, leading some theologians to express skepticism about the possibility of constructing an authentic Latin American Christology. By the1980s, it seemed obvious that the only consensus on a Latin American Christology was that there was no consensus except that Christ represented liberation. What kind was disputed.

Historical preoccupation over Latin American identity and frustration caused by a growing awareness of Latin American dependency upon the United States and Europe prompted the search for an authentic Latin American Christology as part of a general anxiety about the possibility of a genuine and authentic Latin American culture. Agosto Salazar Bondy, Peruvian philosopher, addressed the question of the possibility of an authentic Latin American philosophy in a now famous paper, "The Meaning and Problem of Hispanic American Thought." He begins by tracing the historical outline of philosophy and currents of thought in Latin America from the sixteenth century to the 1960s. Scholastic philosophy, exemplified by the works of Francisco Suárez and Francisco Vitoria dominated official thinking in Latin America for three hundred years. By the early nineteenth century, trends in modern European philosophy finally entered Latin America and eventually liberalized political thinking. Many currents of thought streamed into Latin America from Europe—French Enlightenment ideals, romanticism, materialism, German idealism, utilitarianism, and liberalism. The last half of the nineteenth century saw the rise of positivism to a preeminent hegemonic position throughout much of the region, becoming especially influential in Mexico and Brazil. In the early part of the twentieth century, antipositivistic sentiments found expression in the writings of José Martí, José Enrique Rodó, Antonio Caso Andrade, and José Vasconcelos. Phenomenology and pespectivalism became widely influential after 1925 due to the introduction into the region of José Ortega y Gasset's journal, *Revista de Occidente*, followed by existentialism—Husserl, Heidegger, and Sartre—and Marxism. By the 1960s Anglo-American analytic philosophy established itself as the official voice of philosophy in regional universities.

From this summary, Salazar Bondy derives a negative conclusion regarding the quality of Latin American philosophy, namely that nothing in the philosophy reflects the history, culture, and circumstances of Hispanic America. What he discovers, echoing the views of Mexican philosopher Samuel Ramos, is a history of imitative thought. In his words, "On the contrary, what we find in all our countries is a succession of imported doctrines, a procession of systems which follows European, or, in general foreign unrest. It is almost a succession of intellectual fashions without roots in our spiritual life" (Salazar Bondy 1968, 387). Because Hispanic thought is largely the translation and transmission of European thought in Latin America, it follows, for him, that Hispanic thought is inauthentic.

Cultural, political, social, and economic dependency of Latin America on Europe and the United States is the cause of inauthenticity. Consequently, a genuine and authentic Hispanic philosophy, one arising out of genuine reflection upon Latin American reality is only possible if Latin America can break free from dependency on "cultures of domination." Liberation is a possibility, an option that philosophy should create (Salazar Bondy 1968, 398). Gutiérrez and the other liberation theologians hoped for an authentic Latin American Christology for the same reasons that motivated Salazar Bondy to suggest the possibility of a philosophy of liberation—the need for serious reflection on the Latin American reality itself.

Claiming that the lack of an authentic Christology constituted the worst gap in Latin American theology, Assmann bemoaned the absence of consciousness or awareness of the crisis concerning the problem of inattention to the historicity of Jesus. Aggravating matters, liberation theology offered no improvements on the "current slogans." Inquiring into the nature of this gap, he uncovered a disturbing tendency toward ecclesiastical abstractionism in the doctrines of the person and work of Christ, concluding that political movements manipulated popular and Biblical images of Christ to suit ideological agendas (Assmann 1983, 136–37). To minimize the risk of ideological distortion, Latin American Christology would have to confront the distinction between the Jesus of history and the Christ of faith.

Since the late eighteenth century, Bible scholars operated under the assumption that layers and layers of tradition and interpretation of the Christ of faith stand between the reader and the Jesus of history. Where nineteenth-century Protestant Bible scholars gave up the search for the historical Jesus, Latin American liberation theologians arrived at the opposite position, concluding that the Jesus of history and not the Christ of faith had to serve as the point of departure for constructing a genuine Latin American Christology. Since the Christ of faith results from tradition, imagination, official creeds, and the teaching of the church, liberation theologians inferred that the Jesus of history, his life and teachings, prior to the church's interpretation, constituted the only possible basis for the construction of a genuine Latin American Christology.

By all accounts, Latin American liberation theologians agreed on an investigation of the historical Jesus as the only possible starting point. Brazilian theologian Leonardo Boff began his book on Christology, *Jesus Christ Liberator*, with a study of the historical Jesus, arguing that theology in general must begin with Christology as its starting point (Boff 1975, 47). Jon Sobrino, a theologian working in Central America, unambiguously takes his theological starting point in the historical Jesus in his work *Christology at the Crossroads*. Pastoral theologian Segundo

Galilea, elaborates a Christian spirituality with the historical Jesus as the point of departure for Christian mystical reflection. Gutiérrez, in a preface to Hugo Echegaray's *La práctica de Jesús* points out that the book's real value lies in its faithful depiction of "the historical humanity of Jesus" (Echegaray 1984, 3). However, the growing consensus among liberation theologians appeared merely formal. On the material level of content, they diverged from each other, following different and conflicting interpretations. Latin American Christology did not yield an agreed-upon archetype or paradigm other than the ambiguous term "liberator Christ."

Motivated to correct ahistorical Christologies, liberation theologians turned to the historical Jesus as the point of departure for the possibility of a relevant and authentic Latin American Christology. Consequently, liberation theologians found themselves trying to tease out the political implications of Christ's mission: "The political character of his mission is also obscured by the ahistorical cast of various traditional Christologies which do not take Jesus' historical life very seriously in trying to construct themselves" (Ellucaría 1976, 24).

Opposition to the ahistorical Christ of traditional faith and worship stemmed from the widely shared conviction that such abstractions are too weak to confront real social injustices. Latin American liberation theologians held the conviction that only teaching and preaching based on the Jesus of history could effectively drive home the point that social injustices are not to be tolerated: "No authority can allow just anything whatever, justice and exploitation are not so indiscernible that way, and Christ died to show that not just anything is permissible. But, not just any Christ. The historical Jesus is definitively irreconcilable with compromise and opportunism" (Miranda 1973, 9). Political implications of Jesus's actions and teachings are more salient than the vague spiritual and mystical attributes of the abstract Christ of dogma. Since dogmatic Christology abstracts from the historical Jesus, it tends to obscure the grounds for authentic Christian ethics.

Before considering Boff's paradigmatic liberation Christology, Assmann's account of the conflict of Christologies in Latin America is worth a closer look. His account begins with the polemical claim that abstract treatments of Christ end up "sabotaging Christology" (Assmann 1983, 23). Lacking a foundation in the actions and teachings of the historical Jesus, ecclesiastical abstractions and ideological formulations generate conflicting Christologies. Working under the assumption of the materialist concept of history, Assmann argues that understanding Christologies requires analysis within a conceptual framework, taking into account the sociopolitical conflicts that characterize the circumstances and real historical social contradictions that produce images of Christ. No real resolution to conflicting and opposed Christologies is possible without first finding a solution to social conflicts. Fearing that there will always remain revolutionary Christs and reactionary Christs, Christs on the left and Christs on the Right, conservative Christs, bourgeoisie Christs, liberal Christs, and liberator Christs, in the end Assmann offers realistic lines of thought for progressive Christians. He counsels a realistic acceptance of the fact that the liberator Christ will probably maintain a subordinate position in society, subordinate to the civil Christ authorized by social convention and sanctioned by church doctrine.

Since class struggle epitomizes the structure of social antagonism of contemporary capitalist societies in Latin America, the Liberator Christ representing the interests of the dominated classes will inevitably clash with the bourgeois Christ. Following the downfall of Allende in Chile, two representations of Christ stand out for Assmann: The *tercerista* Christ (the moderate Christ of the third way) and the Christ of the coup d'état. Advocates of the Liberator Christ project toward the future and toward life. Progressive ideas of Christ project Christological metaphors to revolutionary heroes like Che Guevara in the slogans "*el Che vive*" (Che lives) and "Che died for all the children of the world" invoking a utopian forward-looking Christ (Assmann 1983, 137).

Especially abhorrent for Assmann are the Christs of folk religion who function as "specialists in specific domains according to their special attributes regionally differentiated, just like the saints and virgins that populate the symbolic universes of cultures." For the popular religious consciousness, Christ is just another saint, with no more power than the image of the Virgin. Assmann compares popular religious treatment of Christ to the villagers' treatment of a corpse in Gabriel García Márquez's short story "The Handsomest Drowned Man in the World." The fictional story is about the sudden appearance of a man's body on the beach of a fishing village. Shrouded in mystery, endowed with good looks, the man's large body becomes an object of devotion for the villagers and a catalyst for their transformation.

Working within the framework of historical materialism, Assmann insists that neutrality is not an option because stepping outside of the domain of class conflict is impossible. Like Pascal's wager, the Christian faces a forced option. The believer must choose either the bourgeois Christ or the revolutionary Christ. The progressive Christian does not have the luxury of avoiding the conflict between the ideologies of Christ. Not to choose is to choose the status quo that favors the powerful. Christians must ask questions such as the following: What is the political relevance of Christ in the world today? Where is Christ acting in the world today? Assmann presumes that if Christ is acting in the world today, then Christ is working through people, movements, institutions, political parties, governments, governmental agencies, and nongovernmental organizations. Given the antagonistic nature of social conflict, Christ cannot be neutral but must take sides. Christ is a partisan of the oppressed, and the Christian, to be true to Christ, must be a partisan in the struggle between classes, striving for the liberation of the oppressed (the Exodus paradigm). Consequently, if Christ's action in today's world is more than spiritual, the liberation of the oppressed will take concrete forms in social movements. However, a commitment to the partisan Christ, Assmann warns, does not entail uncritical commitments to particular political parties or specific social movements. Christians must always make an eschatological reservation vis-à-vis particular social movements and political groups, refusing to absolutize any political party, ideology, institution, movement, or group.

Emerging from a context characterized by class conflict, widespread poverty, political repression, conflict, and domination, Christ the Liberator motif presupposes a prior commitment to radical social change raising the question: Whom is the liberator Christ supposed to address? The obvious answer for liberation theologians is the poor, the victims of social injustice, women, people of color, the unemployed, the homeless, the peasants, and the working class—socially oppressed and politically dominated. Commitment to Christ the Liberator means that Christians as individuals and the church as a whole must show preferential treatment to the poor.

Concrete historical and social circumstances shape, frame, and mold every Christology. If this premise is true, then changes in historical and social circumstances, the emergence of new needs and interests, calls for changing Christologies. "Christology must take cognizance of what sort of situation it finds itself in and on what level it is situated" (Assmann 1975, 347). Real social differences allow for the identification of class, ethnic, and racial Christologies—a Latin American Christology, an Asian, African, European, and a North American Christology. Of course, analysis calls for more specificity as the focus becomes more and more localized. Assmann's assessment of the difficulty of constructing an authentic and liberating Latin American Christ leaves one pessimistic of the possibility of its actualization.

Convinced that the historical Jesus must become the point of departure for a Latin American Christology in order to overcome the pitfalls of ahistorical conceptions of Christ, Leonardo Boff opens his 1972 book, *Jesus Christ Liberator*, with a historical overview of theological attempts to recover the historical Jesus. In the nineteenth and twentieth centuries, New Testament scholars and theologians pried open many layers of tradition and faith constituting the Gospels in order to obtain an untarnished image of the historical Jesus of Nazareth. As Boff puts it,

Protestant scholars tried to get at the historical Jesus before the early Christian traditions converted him into the Christ of faith. Boff concludes that no consensus of a single biography of Jesus is possible: "There is not, nor can there be a single biography of Jesus" (Boff 1972, 4). Assuming that the Gospel portrayal of Jesus is largely interpretative and expressive, not descriptive, inevitably leads to this conclusion. In fact, the impossibility of forming a consensus of a single biography led some New Testament scholars to the denial of the historicity of Jesus. Rudolf Bultmann, a German New Testament scholar who studied under the German existentialist philosopher Martin Heidegger, accepted and promulgated the interpretative and mythical nature of the Gospels; yet for all that, Bultmann did not deny the historical existence of Jesus, only his relevance.

One of the problems facing any attempt to get at the historical Jesus is the host of hermeneutical problems. Take Gutiérrez's claim, for example, that the historical Jesus is the basis of theological reasoning. Note that this claim already presupposes theological reasoning to establish that the historical Jesus is the basis of theology. On close inspection, circular reasoning is taking place: a particular notion of the historical Jesus is necessary for theological thinking, but theological thinking already posits Jesus as the point of departure for theology. Theologians refer to this problem as the hermeneutic circle.

As Boff points out, the hermeneutic circle stands in the way of a reliable portrait of the personality of the historical Jesus. One common way to think about the problem is the following. In order to understand part of a text, an understanding of the text as a whole is presupposed. Paradoxically, in order to gain an understanding of the whole text requires an understanding of the part, hence the circularity. The chief problem facing interpreters of texts, ancient texts in particular, is the problem of entering into the circle. How and where does one enter it?

Complicating the matter further is the incontestable fact that entering the text is never unbiased or neutral. Personal experience and social perspective colors any reading of a text. The preunderstanding shared by other members of reader's world is also a function of a constantly receding curved horizon. Thus, preunderstanding is not fixed but dynamic. In addition to the reader's horizon of understanding, there is also the world horizon of the history and tradition that embedded and enframed the writers of ancient texts. The original historical context, or contexts given the shifting horizons in the transmission of texts, situates the text within its own horizon of meaning. Can these two horizons, that of the contemporary reader and that of the ancient text, be bridged?

Hermeneutics is the method by which to bridge these two horizons and make understanding of a text possible. Hermeneutics, a theory of interpreting scripture and classic texts, began with Friedrich Schleiermacher in the nineteenth century and Wilhelm Dilthey in the twentieth. For Schleiermacher and Dilthey, the objective of interpretation is to understand the meaning of a text from the past—the meaning and intention it had for the author and those whom the author addressed. However, interpretation has another purpose as well, and that is to find out the significance or truth the text has to us today given our questions, needs, and interests. For Bultmann, the latter is the main reason we do Biblical exegesis.

Bultmann argued that hermeneutics is necessary because the reader or interpreter brings presuppositions, both conscious and unconscious, to the reading of a text: "Reflection on hermeneutics (the method of interpretation) makes it clear that interpretation, that is exegesis, is always based on principles and conceptions which guide exegesis as presuppositions, although interpreters are often not aware of this fact." Because of this psychological fact, Bultmann advises readers to become aware of the presuppositions and preconceptions that they bring to the text and to ask which of these presuppositions are helpful and which are not, if it is possible to make this distinction (Bultmann 1958, 46).

Questions for which the reader seeks answers motivate the reader, so that to understand a text properly also requires awareness and knowledge of the questions that motivate the reader. One's questions, Bultmann notes, frame conceptions of the object of inquiry. For example, says Bultmann, if you ask questions about the psychology of a Biblical character, then you already entertain certain conceptions about psychology. Derived from our own psychology, these conceptions show that interpretation presupposes a relationship between the interpreter and the content of inquiry: "You obtain the conceptions from your own psychical life" (Bultmann 1958, 50).

The resulting or corresponding presupposition of exegesis is that the reader stands in a particular relation to the subject matter—in this case the relation of interrogation between the psychical life of a reader and a particular text: "Our relationship to our own psychological conditions implies that we already bear in ourselves certain conceptions about the psychology of human life." Interpretation presupposes that a reader already has a "certain understanding of the matter in question, and from this understanding grow the conceptions of exegesis" (Bultmann 1958, 50). Because of the reader's preunderstanding, any reading enriches, making possible new and deeper readings in the future. Without awareness of preunderstanding, "it is impossible to understand any text." Preunderstanding is the basic presupposition for every form of exegesis "that your own relation to the subject matter prompts the question you bring to the text and elicits the answers you obtain from the text" (Bultmann 1958, 50–51).

Juan Luis Segundo emphasizes the significance of the meaning of a text for ourselves, but Segundo goes beyond Bultmann, identifying the addressee as the faith community of which the interpreter is representative. Both methods are concerned with showing how the word of God given in the past relates to the present. Segundo defines the hermeneutic circle as a continuous, dynamic change in our interpretation of the Bible as our current reality changes. Circularity necessarily occurs because each new change of social reality calls for a new reading of God's revelation, and with this new reading a corresponding challenge to change reality that leads to a new rereading of revelation, and so on successively (Segundo 1975, 12).

Segundo lays down two hermeneutical conditions for the possibility of a genuine liberation theology. First, the interpreter must interpret current events in such a way that they provoke questions sufficiently general, basic, and rich to challenge us to question our conventional beliefs about life, death, knowledge, society, politics, and the world. Second, theology needs to ask new and decisive questions. However, if theology responds to the new challenges without revising its conventional reading of the Bible, it shuts down the dynamic movement of the hermeneutic circle. On the other hand, if interpretation of the scripture does not keep up with the changes in historical circumstances, then the latter will remain without response or will receive old and outdated responses. A complete hermeneutic circle, on the other hand, satisfies the condition of raising suspicions about current circumstances that lead to a new interpretation of the Bible (Segundo 1975, 4).

Boff grabs the problem of circularity by both horns, describing the hermeneutic problem in relation to the historical Jesus as a circle from which the interpreter cannot escape. Can we reconstruct a history of Jesus without at the same time having already interpreted it? Historians approach their objects with the eyes of their time, with the interests dictated by, for example, the concept of the scientific scholarship that they and their time possess. Boff believes that no matter how much they attempt to withdraw themselves as subjects, historians can never escape the socially constructed self and arrive at the unsullied meaning of the object. For this reason, concludes Boff, every biographical interpretation of the life of Jesus will necessarily reflect the life of its author. There will always be elements of our biography in our interpretation: "It is a circle from which no one can escape" (Boff 1972, 5).

Since history, context, and tradition condition both the reader and the text, the unwary reader probably misses the point aimed at the original audience. Consider one of Jesus's parables, for example, the parable of the Pharisee and the tax collector who went to the temple to pray:

The Pharisee stood and prayed thus with himself, God, I thank thee, that I am not as other men are, extortioners, unjust, adulterers, or even as this publican [tax collector]. I fast twice in the week, I give tithes of all that I possess. And the publican, standing afar off, would not lift up so much as his eyes unto heaven, but smote upon his breast, saying, God be merciful to me a sinner. I tell you, this man [the tax collector] went down to his house justified rather than the other: for every one that exalteth himself shall be abased; and he that humbleth himself shall be exalted. (Luke 18:11–14)

More than likely, the modern reader misses the point of the parable. Two thousand years of tradition stand between Gospels and the reader. Today's reader customarily regards the Pharisee as a nefariously despicable figure—a self-righteous hypocrite. English language reflects this bias. For example, the English word *pharisaical*, meaning "hypocrite," derives from the noun "Pharisee." Modern day readers anticipate that Jesus will exonerate the tax collector.

In its original context, however, the conclusion of Jesus's parable shocked the Jewish Palestinian audience. Unlike the common people, the Pharisee strictly observed the dictates of the Torah, prayed publically, fasted religiously, tithed scrupulously, and, thus, exemplified righteousness. On the other hand, Jews despised the tax collector, who worked for the Romans and defrauded the people, lining his own pockets. Jesus's original audience fully expected Jesus to approve the Pharisee and to condemn the tax collector. Jesus inverted their values, shaking their worldview. Our modern worldview, however, remains unflinched. Our psychic equilibrium remains unfazed.

Given the problem of the hermeneutic circle, Boff concludes, theologians necessarily emphasize the primacy of the Christ of faith over the historical Jesus. Bultmann, for example, discouraged attempts at reconstructing the historical Jesus and advised exclusive concentration on the Christ of faith (Boff 1972, 7). As Boff explains it, *Historie* (historical work) relies upon texts, factual data, in order to reconstruct what really happened. Without accessible and verifiably reliable historical facts at the scholar's disposal, a biography of Jesus is likely impossible. *Geschichte*, another German term for "history," does not denote historical facts but connotes the meaning or significance of historical events. As Boff points out, "Only in this latter sense is Jesus of interest" to Bultmann and his followers. While Bultmann may minimize the importance of the historical Jesus, Boff believes that the search for the historical Jesus is inevitable, for, as he accurately observes, eventually, the question about the origins of the faith in Christ must face facts about Jesus.

Turning to the historical Jesus is justified on practical grounds as well. Boff worries that placing the primacy on the Christ of faith makes it difficult to distinguish honest preaching about the historical Jesus from the ideological manipulation of Christ as religious symbol. Without recognition of such distinctions, Boff warns, there is a risk of identifying Jesus with church dogma. At stake is the risk of losing "every critical element and the possibility of legitimate protest." The loss of a critical attitude immunizes the church. It is impossible to adopt a critical attitude toward the church's doctrine of Christ if the only possible standpoint of interpretation is the understanding of Christ constructed and disseminated by the church itself (Boff 1972, 10–11).

In contrast to Bultmann's Christ of faith, Boff's Christ is "above all a historical being—conditioned, datable." Boff insists on the unity and continuity between the historical Jesus and the Christ of faith. The mere fact of the existence of Christologies indicates the "greatness and sovereignty perceived in the historical Jesus." Boff argues that the unity and continuity of the historical Jesus and the Christ of faith is secured by the preaching of the early church: "The continuity between the historical Jesus and the Christ of faith consists therefore in the fact that the primitive community made explicit what had been implicit in the words, demands, attitudes, and comportment of Jesus. Christology should clarify how Jesus revealed God in his own words and deeds; for, in the Gospels we encounter the historical Jesus proclaimed the Christ" (Boff 1972, 11–13).

Distancing himself from Bultmann's primacy of the Christ of faith, Boff, nonetheless, adopts Bultmann's eschatological interpretation of the significance of Christ: "Faith says that Jesus is the future of human beings and the world, that he is the maximum realization of our religious desire to be in communion with the divine, that he is God himself incarnate" (Boff 1972, 17). Jesus represents the possibility of a new human reality, a new mode of being human that might instill hope about the future. Thus, in this sense the historical Jesus remains glued to the Christ of faith.

Since Boff aims at constructing a contemporary and sociohistorically relevant Christology beginning with the historical Jesus, he must also account for his own sociohistorical context as a Latin American. Consequently, his Christology is self-consciously a Latin American Christology. That is, a Christology fashioned out of the real-life sociopolitical concerns and needs of the Latin American people and, at the same time, a Christology relevant to and reflective of contemporary Latin America: "a Christology thought out and vitally tested in Latin America must have characteristics of its own" (Boff 1972, 43).

Boff acknowledges that contextualizing Christology within the peculiar realities of Latin America, especially given the impossibility of arriving at a single biography of the historical Jesus, risks creating another contextualized Christology alongside many other contextualized Christologies—African, Asian, etc. Another risk is making Christ too subjective and relative to particular cultures. Contextualized Christologies address needs and concerns of particular groups of people at the cost of failing to address universal human needs and concerns. Ironically, the view articulated here pushes the historical Jesus to the vanishing point on the distant horizon and embraces Bultmann's emphasis on a personal existential encounter with Christ. Boff confirms these suspicions, holding that in speaking of Jesus Christ the goal is to define the human being confronted with the mystery of Christ.

Inexplicably, the resolute return to the historical Jesus to establish an intellectually appropriate point of departure for theology does not prevent fanciful reconstructions of the Christ of faith. In the case of many liberation theologians, the turn to the historical Jesus results not in a clearly delineated and fact-supported profile of Jesus but in the derivation of purported universally valid norms and transcendent values. Boff is deeply committed to the proposition that transcendent values appear in the story of Jesus that can guide our way through challenging historical and concrete situations.

Worry about Jesus's relevance to political commitments in current present history does not constrain Boff from waxing metaphysical about cosmological union between divine reality and human nature at some future omega point. Starting not with the historical Jesus but with a faith claim, Boff asserts that the Resurrection shows a cosmic unity between God and humanity. The Resurrection appears as a proleptic eschatological event in which the true destiny of human nature is revealed as the product of the evolutionary process. In effect, Christ shows us the future of our own being. Christ is the *telos* of God's plan for human history and for the cosmos. Christ represents the ultimate unity of the cosmos, humanity, and divinity. For Boff, Jesus's Resurrection represents a springboard for interpreting our own future (Boff 1972, 208).

Oddly, taking the historical Jesus as his point of departure, Boff ends up constructing an imaginary cosmic Christ purportedly present in all dimensions of reality and in every particle of the universe. The cosmic Christ is also present in history, for the incarnation is a "historical fact known through faith." Divinity through the person of Jesus makes its way into humanity, in the "vital part of matter." Jesus's physical body is part of the evolution of the cosmos; his incarnation and resurrection represent the convergence of cosmic forces of materiality and spirituality: "As body-spirit, Jesus of Nazareth was also a nexus of relationships with the totality of human

and cosmic reality that surrounded him. By means of his resurrection, Jesus trans-
figures not only his body but also the human body and materiality, completely
revealing the fullness of human nature—*homo revelatus*. New Testament Christology, therefore, is an elaboration of a cosmic and transcendental Christology showing
that all of reality is converging in Christ" (Boff 1972, 209).

Taking Christology to the rarefied heights of an unrestrained speculative imaginary, Boff leads the reader to consider the possible significance of Christ to the
universe, partly in order to overcome objections to a Ptolemaic conception of the
cosmos implied in traditional accounts of Christology. He asks the age-old question that plagues the wondering mind: "Might there not be other spiritual beings
inhabiting other planets in other systems?" Anticipating the objection that he is
raising "idle" questions, Boff defends the right to ask any questions whatsoever,
especially when reflecting on religion. He points out that other great theologians
speculated on such possibilities, noting that Teilhard de Chardin argued for the
indefinite evolution of human consciousness headed on a trajectory to an omega
point of convergence with cosmic reality. Quoting Pascal, he boldly claims that
consciousness is nobler than physical reality because it can think and it can love:
"A single act of love, noted Pascal, is worth more than the whole physical universe"
(Boff 1972, 214).

Reflecting upon the evolutionary mysticism of Teilhard de Chardin, Boff
argues that the affirmation of the unity and totality of the universe presupposes a
satisfactory account of the nature and cause of a harmonious universe: "What is it
that makes the world a unity and a totality? What is the principle that unifies
beings in being and an invisible totalizing structure?" Believing that science cannot provide an answer, Boff turns to metaphysics. He proposes that the resurrected or cosmic Christ is the answer to Leibniz's concept of a substantial bond
that holds everything in harmony. Christ is precisely that bond: "It is the resurrected Christ who overcame these limitations, and is now present, not physically,
but pneumatically" (Boff 1972, 215).

To the question whether there are other rational beings in the universe, Boff
argues that there is no good reason to consider it an idle question. If the universe
is unimaginably immense, then it is reasonable to assume the existence of extrater-
restrial rational beings. Assuming, then, that there are other rational beings in the
universe, it follows that Christ, who is pneumatically present throughout the universe, must relate to them according to their own special evolutionary conditions.
In other words, the earthly Jesus was only one avatar of Christ. There are many
others: "Just as the eternal Logos, which fills all reality appeared in our flesh and
assumed the evolutionary coordinates of our galaxy, nothing prohibits this same

eternal Logos from having appeared and assumed the spiritual and evolutionary conditions of other beings in other systems" (Boff 1972, 216). On close inspection, the historical Jesus, in Boff's account, mediates universal and transcendent values. In that case, contrary to Boff's privileging the historical Jesus over the Christ of faith, the Christ of faith trumps the historical Jesus. If universal and transcendent values are what really matter in the end, what is the point of a Christology based on the reconstruction of the historical Jesus?

Breaking with the status quo Christ of official Catholicism, liberation theologians turned to the historical Jesus as the point of departure for a new Christology, purportedly resulting in the doctrine of Christ the Liberator. Ironically, the liberator Christ becomes, at times, something far removed from anything that could resemble a first-century Palestinian Jew. Boff, for all of his insistence on beginning with the historical Jesus, eventually develops a speculative cosmic Christology, a panchristism locating Christ's presence in all things and setting up Christ in Teilhardian fashion as the omega Christ toward which all the forces in the universe are converging: "The goal toward which human being and the cosmos itself marched was manifested in Christ: total cosmic-human-divine revelation and fullness" (Boff 1972, 210). Teilhard de Chardin's evolutionary Christology is unmistakable in Boff's early work, *Evangelho do Cristo cósmico* (1970), where Boff emphasizes not the historical Jesus but the resurrected Christ of faith: "It is the resurrected Christ who overcame these limitations and is now present not physically but pneumatically" (Boff 1972, 215). Implied in Boff's panchristism is the idea that there exists a Christic structure to creation and that the world religions are sundry forms of latent elements of an implicit universal Christianity.

Mexican economist and Bible scholar José Miranda, insisting that only a theology based on the historical Jesus can work as a counteracting force against injustice, eventually converts Jesus into a moral imperative. Based on an exegesis of the Johannine writings, Miranda concludes that the Logos is a moral imperative of justice and love to the neighbor. According to Miranda, God is only accessible through the historical Jesus, yet at the same time, God is only accessible through the moral imperative of acts of love and justice.

Likewise, Sobrino and Gutiérrez arrive at universal concepts of Christ, making thin the idea of beginning with the historical Jesus. Gutiérrez, for example, universalizes the incarnation of Christ to such a degree of rarefaction that the doctrine of Christ loses concrete relevance and particularity. He says, for instance, that the internalization of God's presence in Christ, because of Christ's incarnation, will make true the claim that "humanity, every man, history, is the living temple of God." At times, both Sobrino and Boff identify Christ as an instantiation of the Kingdom of God. For Sobrino, an understanding of the Kingdom of God is a necessary condition for understanding Christ. However, in order to understand the concept of the Kingdom of God, one must first understand the meaning of Christ. Boff, for instance, echoing early church father Origen, portrays Christ as the self-manifestation of the Kingdom of God. Latino theology in the United States seems to have settled on the notion of Christ as the mestizo Christ.

CHAPTER EIGHT

The Mestizo Christ

L atina/o theology is a species of liberation theology and its origins arguably trace back to the Mexican American priest/theologian Virgilio Elizondo, who conceived the idea of the mestizo Christ. To understand Elizondo's Mexican American Christology, a discussion of José Vasconcelos's book *La raza cósmica* (The cosmic race) will provide necessary background information.

Vasconcelos (1882–1959), a Mexican philosopher and statesman inspired both by Cuban writer and activist José Martí and Uruguayan writer José Enrique Rodó, promoted a robust vision of mestizaje (hybridization), a racial mixing that purportedly results in a new human type. In Vasconcelos's reconstruction, mestizaje is a cultural biological process, a historical-racial mechanism, and a spiritual force analogous to natural selection. Mestizaje drives the course of races, the development of nations, and the formation of peoples toward a common utopian future and cosmic humanity ruled by love and beauty. Chicanas and Chicanos in the heyday of the civil rights revolution in the late sixties and early seventies recuperated Vasconcelos as their prophet and identified Vasconcelos's *raza cósmica* (cosmic race) with Chicanas and Chicanos labeling themselves *La Raza* the People or the Race with special reference to the mestizo people. Historically, the moniker "La Raza" refers ambiguously either to the common people or to the nation. At the heart of Vasconcelos's book *La raza cósmica* is the essay entitled "Mestizaje." Regarded a classic of Chicana and Chicano literature, it may have been adopted by Chicanas and Chicanos because they saw in it, unconsciously perhaps, a way to overcome or at least compensate for a socially internalized inferiority complex. Affirmation of mestizaje emboldened Chicanas and Chicanos to believe that collectively they constitute a special race endowed with vital powers enabling them to overcome racism through a renewed liberated self-consciousness in which they recognize their own marginalized group as a new synthetic race that recapitulates and supersedes all other races.

For critics, it remains unclear whether to interpret the concept of the raza cósmica metaphorically or biologically. Vasconcelos was partly responsible for the biological/racial interpretation. Yet in his 1948 edition of the book, he expressed doubts about his earlier optimistic view of racial mixing conveyed in the 1925 edition of *La raza cósmica*. He confessed that he found his faith in mixed races ironic. Vasconcelos vacillated about the potential transformative value of racial mixing, writing, "Nevertheless, it remains to be seen whether the unlimited and inevitable mixture is a favorable factor to the increment of culture or if, to the contrary, it will produce decadence" (Vasconcelos 1979, 3–4). After declaring the book a "notorious mistake" in 1944, Vasconcelos nonetheless agreed to the publication of a new edition in 1948 (Jaén 1979, xvii). In the prologue to this edition, Vasconcelos reveals that he reluctantly entertained a biological/racial interpretation of the raza cósmica and bemoaned the possibility that the results anticipated from mixed race stock may take many centuries (Jaén 1979, xvii).

In the prologue to the 1948 edition of *La raza cósmica*, Vasconcelos writes, "various races of the earth tend to intermix at a gradually increasing pace, and eventually will give rise to a new human type" (Vasconcelos 1979, 3). On this occasion, however, he emphasizes spirituality and not biology as the constituting principle of the raza cósmica. Additionally, tempering his optimism, he utters suspicions that racial fusion could result in degenerative features. Contrary to his earlier optimistic attitude about mestizaje, he approved the mixture of more racially similar groups like that between the Spanish and Italian exemplified by the Argentine population. He dropped his earlier sanguine attitude about the interracial mixing of dissimilar racial groups such as the Spanish and Amerindian that constitutes the racial makeup of the majority of the Mexican and Central American populations.

Earlier, in the 1925 essay, he blamed underdevelopment in Hispanic nations on the strong presence of Amerindians. However, equipped with a Darwinian understanding of time and evolution, he held out hope that over the long run, evolution would combine the positive features of racially dissimilar groups. To the chagrin of postcolonial readers, Vasconcelos applauds the Christianization of the Amerindians as a positive force that transformed cannibals into civilized people: "Christianity made the American Indians advance, in a few centuries, from cannibalism to a relative degree of civilization" (Vasconcelos 1979, 5).

Despite Vasconcelos's palpable racist attitudes toward Amerindians, blacks, and Asians, *La raza cósmica* directed, ironically, a polemic against the Aryan thesis of white supremacy; however, this work barely targets the Aryan thesis. Ostensibly, he aimed at refuting the claim that "pure" races are superior to mixed ones, a fundamental assumption underlying Aryanism. Rather, he argues for the superiority of Latinism or Hispanicism over Anglo-Saxonism, a theme common among Latin American writers after the 1898 defeat of Spain by the United States.

In the aftermath of the Spanish–American War, Hispanic intellectuals throughout Latin America felt inferior compared to Anglos. In the 1800s the turn to liberal political ideas and the widespread acceptance of a positivist concept of science and history led many intellectuals, such as Domingo Faustino Sarmiento and Juan Bautista Alberdi to blame Latin America's underdevelopment on the inheritance of anachronistic, patristic, and medieval Spanish ideals and values. Hence, the demands for the de-Latinization and de-Hispanization of Latin America, and, at the same time, the promotion of Anglo values of individualism, materialism, and technology. Andrés Bello, the Venezuelan intellectual who was once personal assistant to British utilitarian philosopher Jeremy Bentham, argued that independence from Spanish rule did not suffice for total emancipation. Complete liberation requires independence from the Spanish spirit. Similarly, the Argentinean Esteban Echevarría proclaimed, "We cannot accomplish the social emancipation of Latin America unless we repudiate our Spanish heritage" (Nuccetelli 2009, 200).

Against this spirit of *nordomanía* (Nordic craze), Uruguayan José Enrique Rodó reminded his youthful readers that the spirituality, sentimentality, sympathy, and idealism of Latin Americans rose morally above the rank individualism, crude materialism, and greedy spirit of the Yankees. Drawing from Shakespeare's *The Tempest* and Renan's interpretation of it, Rodó identifies the gringo with Caliban, the Island savage. By contrast, Ariel, the winged spirit, symbolizes the incarnation of Latin values of beauty and idealism.

Inspired by Rodó's romantic and idealistic defense of Latinism, Vasconcelos makes the bold statement that "Our age became and continues to be a conflict of Latinisms against Anglo-Saxonism. . . . A conflict set in the New World" (Vasconcelos 1979, 10). Vasconcelos blames the failure to unify Latin America on the demoralization of the populations brought on by the hegemony of the United States. Latin Americans sought refuge in nationalisms, and thereby lost sight of the larger unity of the Spanish race as a whole. Echoing Unamuno, Vasconcelos insists that Hispanos in Latin America should feel as Spanish as the Spaniards of Spain. Geographical barriers, understandably, are obstacles to unity, but consciousness has to transcend such barriers. Rodó and Vasconcelos represent Hispanic intellectuals who felt sympathy for the Spanish *patria* (homeland).

Vasconcelos rejects the Indigenist objection that Mexican culture is not entirely Spanish because it contains many Indian elements. The Indian, according to the Indigenist argument, did not entirely yield to the Spanish. Against the Indigenist objection Vasconcelos argues, "Even the pure Indians are Hispanized; they are Latinized, just as the environment is Latinized" (Vasconcelos 1979, 16). Vasconcelos's narrow historical vision biased toward the Spanish heritage marginalizes the

Amerindians even to the point of relegating them to a forgotten historical past. As Vasconcelos asserts, "No race returns" (Vasconcelos 1979, 16).

Affirming a biological determinist theory of culture—cultural patterns are pre-existing ideas genetically innate in the races—he denounces the post-Darwinian doctrine of the survival of the fittest for two reasons: the doctrine condemns the weak, and it gave rise to Nazism. In Vasconcelos's words, "the Darwinist doctrine . . . origin to the theory of pure Aryanism, defended by the English, led to an aberrant imposition by the Nazis" (Vasconcelos 1979, 3). Defenders of the Aryan thesis that the pure races are superior to mixed races or "mongrel" races readily accepted the doctrine of the survival of the fittest. Jointly, these beliefs fortified the foundations of Nazism. Spurred on partly by the sense of inferiority that Latin Americans developed in the face of Anglo-American dominance in the region, Vasconcelos combated not Nazism in 1925 but the claim of Anglo superiority over Latin culture. Disturbed by the "mixed breed" epithet that Anglos used to label Mexicans, Vasconcelos took it upon himself to prove the converse, namely that the mixed race peoples are superior to the so-called pure races. His defense of hybridization is auxiliary to his argument for the superiority of Latins or Hispanics over Anglos. His main thesis states that Hispanics, a synthesis of former world civilizations, are a sign of the promise of a new humanity, the bridge to a utopian raza cósmica, and an expression of biological perfection that "eventually will give rise to a new human type, composed of selections from each of the races already in existence" (Vasconcelos 1979, 3).

History, in this deterministic teleological account, is inexorably pulled forward by the irresistible force of a preordained destiny—the realization of a new humanity. Attributing agency to history, Vasconcelos makes history the efficient cause of collective human outcomes. Along the way, each race plays out its determined role. Whites, for instance, by mechanizing the world, are laying down the global technological and economic conditions for the final stage of the ultimate biological and cultural fusion of the races mediated by Latin civilization.

Vasconcelos does not contend with the white race. He takes his fight to the Anglo-Saxon, one of the two major conquering ethnic groups of whites that played defining historical roles in the Americas. The other ethnic type is the Latin. Of these two, the Latin, however, plays the decisive role of carving out the ultimate path to the raza cósmica. Given the hegemonic dominance of Anglos over Latinos since the defeat of Spain in 1898, how does Vasconcelos justify his exuberant claim? His answer is that history chose the Latin over the Anglo-Saxon because the former has a hearty and inherent predisposition to mix with other races. The Latin to some extent romanced the dark other. Anglo-Saxons, by contrast, in attempting to preserve the purity of their race, dispossessed, displaced, or destroyed the dark other. For these reasons, Vasconcelos concludes that the Latin is better suited to the historically novel mission of incorporating other races. Spanish openness to marriage with other races is proof that Hispanics possess a moral quality of sympathy lacking in Anglos.

The moral quality of sympathy is a spiritual trait that gives a spiritual and moral advantage to Hispanics over Anglos. Therefore, reasons Vasconcelos, Hispanics deserve to be the people chosen to assimilate and to transform humanity into a new type. As he sees it, endowed with an abundance of love, the Spanish created a new race with blacks and Indians, generously sharing "white ancestry" with them.

With typical hyperbole, Vasconcelos one-sidedly blames the English for annihilating the indigenous, as if genocide of the Indians were a divine mandate. Because Anglos absolutized their particular racist attitudes, attributing a divine origin to them, America belongs to the Spanish, whose "predestination obeys the design of constituting the cradle of the fifth race into which all nations will fuse with each other to replace the four races that have been forging history apart from each other" (Vasconcelos 1997, 19).

Sympathy is a moral trait that Vasconcelos believes uniquely endows Hispanics with an innate capacity for blending and mixing with other races. Sympathy is a gift, a divine mission, and a mysticism embraced by Latinos, unlike Anglo-Saxons, who limit themselves to racial purity. As a result, history condemns Anglo-Saxons to biological and cultural decadence. Anglos transplanted Europe to the New World; hence, their mission is almost complete. By contrast, the historical role and spiritual/biological mission of Hispanics is unfulfilled. Ultimately, Hispanics will realize the new humanity, because in their genes all racial groups are summed up as evinced by the "depth in the pupil of the red man . . . sensuality and dance in a drop of Black blood," and "the clear mind of the White." Pulled inexorably toward the future, the Hispanic American necessarily fulfills her divine mission through reproduction, forming the raza cósmica (Vasconcelos 1979, 21–22).

Though he speaks acrimoniously of Anglo whites and sardonically decries their global imperialism, Vasconcelos does not exclude them from the raza cósmica: "Naturally, the fifth race has no intention of excluding Whites just as it does not propose to exclude any race; the norm of its formation is the appropriation of all capacities for the greater integration of power" (Vasconcelos 1979, 25). By aesthetic selection, due to the trait of sympathy, the fifth race will accept whatever superior traits whites possess, but reject their "arrogance." Earlier, Vasconcelos asserted that history had forgotten the native peoples, but now he writes that because they con-stitute one of the parent cultures of Latin American mestizaje, they necessarily functioned as a natural bridge for it. However, the mission of creating the cosmic race falls squarely on the shoulders of the mestizo (Hispanic). Vasconcelos envi-sions the teleological thrust of history and the process of evolution as converging in Latin America to consummate the entire process of hominization to bring about the new human type and global solidarity. Historical, spiritual, and biolog-ical tendencies of evolution selected Latin America, not Anglo America, for the former has proven itself suitable for bringing about this cosmic transformation by means of its natural facility to integrate races and its sympathetic acceptance of the stranger.

Envisioning a future society characterized by beauty and love, not law and order, Vasconcelos makes room for whites but worries that their defining traits may inevitably predominate. Surprisingly, the possible eventuality of the predom-inance of white traits does not worry Vasconcelos as long as these traits arise not out of arrogance but out of refined personal taste in mate selection. Personal taste formed by a mysterious aesthetic will or force guides the choice for mates, provi-dentially selecting the right person out of a multitude of potential mates. The mysterious process develops in stages but will eventually submit "all life to the superior norms of feeling and fantasy" (Vasconcelos 1979, 28). Vasconcelos identi-fies the spiritual factor of the aesthetic force as Christian. Hence, in the future utopian society, human behavior will be guided by a Christian aestheticism simi-lar in form to Henri Bergson's *elan vital* (creative feeling): "A refined aesthetic sensibility and a love of profound beauty . . . all that is necessary for the third period impregnated with a Christian aestheticism" (Vasconcelos 1979, 38).

Since the Latin people have been faithful to the "divine" mission of miscegena-tion in America, they are the ones naturally called on to bring about the utopian future. As Vasconcelos puts it, in spite of defects, Latin Americans possess the traits and dynamism to assimilate and to convert all races through the mestizo. All races and peoples are genetically represented within the blood of the mestizo race of Latin America. The genius and blood of all races will produce the raza cósmica, a synthesis of human culture engendered by mestizos in Latin America, a people endowed with true brotherhood and gifted with a real universal vision. Progressive spiritualization and aesthetization of human history inevitably will lead to the convergence and emergence of the raza cósmica and the inauguration of a utopian aesthetic era. Ethnic barriers will lose their force and the mixture of races will increase to the point that a new, fully mixed race will charge through equipped with the superior qualities of all the previous races, surviving by the instinct of natural selection, whose mechanism is love. Retrospectively, it will be clear that the mixing of races was a necessary condition, the sine qua non for the emergence of a new utopian age.

Pierre Teilhard de Chardin (1881–1955), in *Phenomenon of Man* (1935, 1955), proposes a similar version of evolution, one that culminates in the emergent fusion of human kind with divinity. Vasconcelos, Teilhard de Chardin, and Henri Bergson reacted against the mechanistic interpretation of evolution found in Darwin and Henry Spencer. Bergson's work, *Creative Evolution* (1907), painted a picture of evolution guided by a free, creative, vital impulse. Teilhard de Chardin advanced a hypothesis reminiscent of Vasconcelos's theory of the fusion of the races. Didier T. Jaén, author of the introduction to the 1997 edition of *La raza cósmica*, quotes Chardin to great effect in this respect: "The most vigorous human branches are by no means those in which some isolation has preserved the purest genes; but those, on the contrary, in which the richest interfecundation has taken place . . . The most human collectivities always appear in the last resort, to be the product not of segregation but of synthesis" (Jaén 1997, xii). All these writers foresaw both a biological determinism that guides the formation of a genetic unity of the human race and a universal, moral teleological force leading to the formation of a global ethics: "To admit, in fact, that a combination of races and peoples is the event biologically awaited for the new and higher extension of consciousness to take place on earth, is at the same time to define in its principal lines and internal dynamism, the thing that our action stands most in need of: an international ethic" (Jaén 1997, xiii).

Like many Mexican Americans in the Southwest, Mexican American priest Virgilio Elizondo, inspired by Vasconcelos's classic essay, identified himself as a member of *La Raza* (the Race). (It should be noted that Fray Angélico Chávez did not identify himself in this manner but as an Hispano.) Born on the west side of San Antonio, Texas, an urban area densely populated by Mexican Americans and Mexican immigrants, Elizondo writes that he grew up painfully experiencing being pulled in two directions—American and Mexican. As a child, the young Elizondo imagined San Antonio to be a city cut down the middle by an invisible border dividing the United States and Mexico. Living in the borderlands that define San Antonio, Elizondo experienced the alienating feeling that he was both an insider and an outsider with respect to both "parent" cultures. At some point, he concluded that he did not have to choose between one or the other identity or even a bicultural identity (signified by "hyphenated" national or ethnic names). Rather, as if seeing a divine revelation, he envisioned the borderlands as a living organism brimming with new possibilities for human life; the borderlands came to signify for him "the cradle of a new humanity," a living laboratory fusing the north and the south. Hispanic Mesoamerican scholar Davíd Carrasco exuberantly celebrates Elizondo's mestizo future as a "Brown Millennium" when "the United States is entering the fuller recognition that it is a world of racial, cultural, and political shades. The many-hued, multicolored America—with Asian, Latin American, African peoples mixing, enriching and challenging our democracy—will be neither a black world nor a white world" (Elizondo 2000, xxiii).

Elizondo first employed the terms "mestizo" and "mestizaje" in his 1975 work, *Christianity and Culture: An Introduction to Pastoral Theology and Ministry for the Bicultural Community*, but the terms take on greater significance for interpreting Mexican American reality in his books *Galilean Journey: The Mexican American Promise* (1983) and *The Future is Mestizo* (1988). Both books wistfully express a projectivist belief in an analogical resemblance between Jesus's Galilean experience and the Mexican American experience.

Elizondo boldly supplements Vasconcelos's mestizaje with a second mestizaje, similar in magnitude to the birth of mestizaje in sixteenth-century Mexico. The second mestizaje has been taking place in the southwest United States since the Treaty of Guadalupe Hidalgo (1848). The Spanish–Indian encounter gave rise to the first mestizaje in Mexico, but in the United States, the second mestizaje, primarily cultural, is gradually evolving in the multifaceted interactions between white American and Mexican cultures, resulting in the cultural hybridity that is the Mexican American. Mexican descendants in the United States are certainly part of the demographic reality in the Southwest. However, Elizondo seems to ignore the robust racial mixing in the region that reveres the integration, assimilation, and acculturation of numerous ethnic and racial groups brought together by complex historical forces. The anthropological result is a rich demographic that transcends the simplified Mexican/Anglo binary. Many people loosely labelled Hispanic or Mexican American, embody many different bloodlines—Spanish, Mexican, Comanche, Apache, Pueblo, Navajo, Anglo, French, African, German, Swedish, Scottish, Jewish, Chinese, Vietnamese, and so on. These are the rich ingredients of the savory stew of the demographics of the Southwest.

Reviving the anachronistic Latina/onglo discourse of the turn of the twentieth century, Elizondo follows Vasconcelos in sharply demarcating the difference between Spanish America and Anglo-America by noting that the Spanish conquest gave birth to a new people, whereas Anglos merely transplanted the British tradition. Anglos, in Elizondo's pessimistic estimation, are ethnocentric, racist, Nordic Europeans arrogantly posturing as the superior race. Fueled by a racist attitude, they uprooted indigenous people and enslaved Africans. Painting a dark picture with broad brushstrokes, Elizondo acrimoniously protests that whites did not "hesitate to offer Indians and blacks to the gods of profit and greed" (Elizondo 1983, 8). Elizondo cautiously uses more tempered language conceding that although the Spanish were racists, they were not racial purists and voluntarily cohabitated with the Indians. "Racial mixing," notes Elizondo, "was not discouraged by the Catholic kings of Spain or by the Vatican" (Elizondo 1983, 10).

The "Nordic conquest" of Mexico (1845–1848) initiated the second mestizaje—the birth of Mexican American people. From the beginning, Anglos perceived Mexicans as inferior, lazy, unreliable, and superstitious, and incapable of assimilation into American culture. Believing in manifest destiny, land-hungry whites provoked the Mexican–American war in 1845. It resulted in Mexico's defeat and the ratification of the Treaty of Guadalupe Hidalgo in 1848, which forcefully absorbed Mexico's northern territories into the United States. As a result, the formerly Mexican citizens of the Southwest became a marginalized population in the United States. Theoretically, they were citizens, but in practical terms, they lacked the privileges and rights of citizenship that whites took for granted.

Anglos did not accept Mexican Americans as equal citizens, perceiving them as Mexicans, foreigners, and immigrants. In their colonized homeland, Mexican Americans faced institutional discrimination and social hostility. Feeling rejected, undergoing discrimination and alienation, Mexican Americans resigned themselves to different degrees of assimilation into Anglo culture, an option increasingly imposed on them. On the one hand, social demands forced them to become more like Anglos; on the other, Mexican Americans faced the raw perception that they are incapable of assimilation. On the other side of the border, Mexicans rejected Mexican Americans as *pochos* (rotten fruit).

Trapped between two worlds, like orphans abandoned by both parents, Mexican Americans suffered from the unenviable stigma of mestizaje—to be both inside and outside at the same time: "To be an insider and an outsider, as is the mestizo, is to have closeness and distance from both parent cultures" (Elizondo 1983, 18). Elizondo perceives positive features in mestizaje—an openness to novelty and hybridity that inevitably endow Mexican Americans with the power to integrate and to synthesize the best qualities of both cultures, generating something new and original. However, like Vasconcelos before him, Elizondo fears that hybridity also poses the danger that new hybrid features may be degenerative. In any event, mestizaje promises the emergence of a new culture that incorporates the best and the worst of both parent cultures. Mexican Americans, therefore present a new cultural anthropological type, representing a novel unity of the greatness of both Latin American and Anglo-Saxon cultures. Keep in mind that Elizondo's conception of novel unity emphasizes cultural integration, not biological hybridity.

Thinking morally about the ethical implications of mestizaje, Elizondo argues along the lines of Vasconcelos that mestizaje comes with an inbuilt ethical imperative. Since Mexican Americans represent the best of both cultures, an ethics of responsibility commits them to live out the radical meaning of mestizaje by pioneering ways of forging a new humanity and a radically different kind of society. Seeking to avoid a biological determinist understanding of morality of mestizaje, Elizondo mystifies and spiritualizes mestizo morality. However, there is a concrete moral obligation that falls on the shoulders of Mexican Americans. They are to serve as moral role models who live exemplary lives of the new human type. On close inspection, however, the obligation to pursue a new human type assumes that current human types and social forms fail or fall short in some way or other and presupposes the need of a politics of ideology critique to question the false assumptions that undergird legitimacy claims of ruling political and dominant social institutions. Elizondo does engage in a systematic ideology critique but he eagerly denounces structures of social sin and unquestioned ideals like those of free enterprise, democracy, political pluralism, progress, the American dream, and so on.

Elizondo warns against the risks of American assimilation on the one hand and Mexican conservatism on the other. In his book *Race Matters*, Cornel West warns against similar risks facing African Americans. Given these risks, a live option challenges Mexican Americans "to bring their better elements into the birth of a new people, a new creature." Influenced by liberation theology, Elizondo urges Mexican Americans to forge bonds of solidarity with the poor in the struggle for a new global humanity. From a theological perspective, Elizondo interprets mestizaje as an eschatological sign announcing the inauguration of God's reign. Like the reign of God, mestizaje represents a "new universalism that bypasses human segregative barriers." As an analogue of Christ, the mestizo incarnates the Gospel in today's world, proclaiming "in flesh and blood that the longed for kingdom has in fact begun. La Raza is the promise of the future" (Elizondo 1983, 124).

According to his autobiography, early in life, Elizondo knew only theoretically the Christ of faith—the abstract second person of the Trinity; only later did he discover the significance of the historical Jesus for Mexican Americans—the mestizo Christ. As a first step in constructing the identity of the mestizo Christ, Elizondo brings out the particular features of the historical Jesus's Galilean Jewishness that may make for an analogy between Jesus and Mexican Americans.

Elizondo shifts emphasis from the high Christology that affirms belief in Christ as the Son of God to the low Christology that focuses on the historical

Jesus from the small rural town of Nazareth set in agriculturally rich Galilee. Jesus's situation in this region in the first half of the first century CE conditioned the person, actions, and beliefs of Jesus. Unless people understand the historical, social, political, economic, and cultural situation of first-century Palestine, Jesus cannot be understood. Consider Nathaniel's words to Philip: "Can there any good thing come out of Nazareth?" (John 1:46).

Nazareth was located in Galilee. In the first century CE, Galilee was a social, economic, and cultural crossroads because of major trading routes that criss-crossed it; consequently, its social environment was more diverse than that of Judea. For this reason, Elizondo assumes that diversity in Galileae weakened ideas of Jewish exclusiveness both ethnically and religiously. For Elizondo, on consideration of first-century Galilee, there are similarities with the American Southwest. In particular, both functioned as sites of mestizaje: "A natural, ongoing biological and cultural mestizaje was taking place" (Elizondo 1983, 51). As a result of the process of mestizaje, their respective populations suffered similar consequences. Both populations—Galilean Jews and Mexican Americans—suffered alienation from each of their parent cultures.

He likens the attitude of Jerusalem Jews toward Galilean Jews to the attitude of Mexicans to Mexican Americans. Jerusalem Jews doubted the Jewish integrity of the Galilean Jews just as Mexicans question lo mexicano of Mexican Americans. By the same token, the way Greco-Romans perceived Jews as beyond assimilation is comparable to the way Anglo-Americans perceive Mexican Americans as not capable of assimilation (Elizondo 1983, 52). Elizondo contends that Jesus as a Galilean Jew, like the Mexican American, suffered the alienating consequences of not being fully accepted by either parent culture. Noting the early rumors that Jesus was the child of a Jewish girl and a Roman father, Elizondo describes Jesus's opponents as Jews that regarded him not only as a cultural hybrid but possibly even as a biological one. Elizondo seizes on the possibility of Jesus's hybridity to strengthen the connection with the hybridity of Mexican Americans.

Jesus's purported hybridity motivates Elizondo's positive affirmation of Mexican American mestizaje. Elizondo muses that being a Galilean Jew in Judea was similar to being a Mexican American in Texas. His quest for Mexican American identity finds in the concept of Jesus's hybridity a reason for a joyous affirmation of ethnic identity as well as the possibility of social and cultural resistance against the Anglo-Saxon forces of assimilation, racism, and colonization.

Elizondo's concept of the mestizo Christ stands or falls on the facticity of Jesus' hybridity. Current scholarship on southern Galilea and Nazareth lessens the rhetorical force of Elizondo's analogy. Southern Galilea, it has been found, was highly urbanized and densely populated. The social system consisted of regional cities served by satellite towns and villages. Archeological discoveries attest to the existence of Nazareth at least by the beginning of the second century BCE. Tombs have been unearthed containing inscriptions displaying evidence that Nazareth was a small town whose population was loyal to the Romans but proudly Jewish (Crossan 1992, 15–19).

Elizondo's portrayal of Jesus as a mestizo Jew does not fare well in the light of modern scholarship. To attribute mestizaje to Jesus results not from a correct historical reconstruction of the Jesus of history, but from the projection of a personal basic human need to identify some feature of Jesus with a comparable feature of oneself or one's group. Latina/o theologians following Elizondo's example adopted Vasconcelos's concept of mestizaje or its related twin *mulatez* (the state of being mulatto) as a hermeneutic key for interpreting the US Hispanic condition or that of Afro-Latina/os. Arturo J. Bañuelos compiled and edited a book entitled *Mestizo Christianity: Theology from the Latino Perspective*, which introduces the reader to the "core canon" of Latino theology. Its bibliography represents the work of forty-seven authors, of whom twelve are women, thirty-five men, nine Protestants, and thirty-eight Catholics. The majority of these writers either belong to the Academy of Catholic Hispanic Theologians in the United States (ACHTUS) or La Comunidad of Hispanic American Scholars of Theology and Religion (Bañuelos 1995, 3). According to Bañuelos, mestizaje is a core paradigm for theology's attempts to articulate the Latino experience; it is a *locus theologicus*, a field or object domain for theological investigation. Néstor Medina makes mestizaje the central theme of his book, *Mestizaje: (Re)Mapping Race, Culture, and Faith in Latina/o Catholicism* (2009). Medina, like Bañuelos, adopts mestizaje as a theological category or locus theologicus, but emphasizes mestizaje as a religious experience, an ethical moral choice, and a symbol of inclusion and cultural resistance. At the same time, he notes the ambiguity of the term. He's right to highlight its ambiguity, but the term is also vague, for there are degrees of mestizaje.

Latina/o theologians, among Latina/o writers and scholars, are not unique in adopting the concept of mestizaje. Chicana feminist writers employ the term as profusely as the theologians do. Interestingly, Chicana feminist Gloria Anzaldúa used the term mestizaje to describe the consciousness of the Mexican American woman for whom the Christian Christ is a repugnant religious symbol and replaces Christ with the symbol of the Aztec goddess.

Gloria Anzaldúa, celebrated Chicana feminist writer, glorified mestizaje without taking recourse to the mestizo Christ. Appropriating the concept of mestizaje as a conceptual tool for interpreting her own experience, she rejected the Spanish

Catholic Christ and embraced Coatlicue, the Aztec goddess of earth and sexuality. Anzaldúa replaced the patriarchal Catholic Christ with the Amerindian feminine-empowered antichrist of Coatlicue. Contemporary American evangelical Christianity represents the antichrist as an apocalyptic ruler of evil controlled by the devil who wreaks havoc in the last days, persecuting Christians to death. The term *antichrist* only occurs four times in the New Testament, all in the first and second letters of John, and always with reference to proto-gnostic Christians who deny that Jesus came in the flesh. In the context of this chapter, *antichrist* refers to any religious symbol that substitutes for Christ. The English preposition *anti* derives from a Greek preposition that can be translated either as "against" or "instead of." The recuperated Aztec goddess in Anzaldúa's writing does not symbolize the servant of the devil, the evil antichrist of apocalyptic Christianity, but the "instead-of-Christ" in sacred Chicana pagan feminist morphology.

Gloria Anzaldúa's work exemplifies Chicana feminist recuperation of mestizaje for cultural and sexual self-identification. In her modern Chicana classic, *Borderlands/La Frontera: The New Mestiza* (1987), she mindfully teases out the complex dimensions and the multifaceted implications of the ambiguous nature of her mestizaje/borderlands identity forged by the confluence of many cultures that informed her own psychic structure and inscribed effects on her bodily experience: "Because I, a mestiza, continually walk out of one culture and into another, because I am in all cultures at the same time, alma entre dos mundos, tres, cuatro, me zumba la cabeza con lo contradictorio. Estoy norteada por todas las voces que me hablan simultaneamente" (a soul between two, three, four worlds, my head is buzzing with the contradictory. I am steered by the voices that speak to me simultaneously" (Anzaldúa 1999, 99). Ripped by forces pulling her in all directions, she relentlessly pursues a dodgy question: to what collectivity does the dark woman belong? The key identifier is not Hispanic or Latino but "dark woman," indicating that her Amerindian race and feminine gender stand at the center of her psychic preoccupations and anxieties about group belonging. Although she identifies herself as mestiza, she chooses to celebrate the Indian element of her heritage above all ethnic identifiers. Anzaldúa's phenomenological description of her inner life emphasizes the perplexities, anxieties, fragmented identity, and multifarious voices the mestiza consciousness experiences. Drawing from her own mental states, Anzaldúa describes the mestiza as confused because of the conflicting information she receives about life and world. She uses the term "cultural collision" to describe the fragmented subjectivity experienced by the mestiza in the postmodern condition. Ilan Stavans similarly describes the Hispanic condition as schizophrenic.

In grappling with the complexity of her own identity, Anzaldúa draws security by tapping into the transformative potential of mestizaje, in her case, a passionate, mystical, and lesbian feminist experience of ambiguity. Her ruminations on mestizaje echo to some extent the work of Vasconcelos's *La raza cósmica*. Unlike Vasconcelos, who locates the future utopia in the Amazon, the space that forms and constitutes Anzaldúa's mestiza consciousness is located further north, *en el norte*, in the borderlands of the United States and Mexico, which she poignantly describes as an open wound where the third world meets the first world and bleeds: "The U.S.-Mexican border *es una herida abierta* where the Third World grates against the first and bleeds. And, before a scab forms it hemorrhages again, the lifeblood of two worlds merging to form a third country—a border culture. Borders are setup to define the places that are safe and unsafe, to distinguish us from them. A border is a dividing line, a narrow strip along a steep edge" (Anzaldúa 1999, 25).

Anzaldúa's sanguinary description of borderlands mestizaje rises out of her own painful experiences and observations. Her vivid and sometimes painful descriptions use terms such as internal strife, ambivalence, and multiculturality, which express instability, insecurity, and uncertainty about personal identity. Nevertheless, for all that, she regards mestizaje as a vital spiritual resource bearing liberating potentialities for self-making. Facing the ambiguity of identity head on, she comes away not with a reason for resignation and despair but with a motive for celebrating diversity in unity.

To a certain extent, the term mestizaje seems to denote a type of schizophrenic psychosis. Yet from this dark abyss, Anzaldúa reaches down and finds a psychological coping mechanism in the attitude of tolerance. Surviving ambiguity requires an ethic of tolerance for contradictions. Anzaldúa writes about tolerance as more than a mere coping mechanism. For her, it is a necessary condition for creating a new synthetic unity, a new identity, a new consciousness: the new mestiza consciousness. In Anzaldúa's clever hands, the mestizaje consciousness is transformed into the new mestiza consciousness. Like Shiva, the new mestiza consciousness is destructive and creative, breaking down dualistic essentialist barriers in order to create the conditions for the emergence of holistic thinking, a liberating consciousness necessary for the struggle to inaugurate a mestiza utopia: "A massive uprooting of dualistic thinking in the individual and collective consciousness is the beginning of a long struggle, but one that could, in our best hopes, bring us to the end of rape, of violence, of war" (Anzaldúa 1999, 102).

Moving effortlessly from one site of cultural struggle to another, she strategically positions herself as a feminist rejecting machismo in the Anglo and

Indo-Hispanic worlds. Rejecting the Christian traditions of her dual religious lega-
cies—Protestant and Catholic—she revives a Mesoamerican neopaganism uncovering the secret that the mestiza's redemption lies with the Aztec female deities, not
Christ. The Spanish Catholic vision of the divine female represents a patriarchal
psychological fantasy preempting the matriarchal all-powerful mother: "The first
step is to unlearn the *puta*/virgin dichotomy and to see *Coatlapopeauh-Coatlicue* in
the Mother, Guadalupe" (Anzaldúa 1999, 106). From another side, she celebrates
jotería (gay affectation) as a sign of a harmless new type of masculinity that will
certify a man as an acceptable candidate for admission into the new violence-free
world of the mestiza. The struggle against binaries includes the struggle against
racism. Her overriding message is that the possibility of a redemptive cultural
identity depends on overcoming essentialist the dualities male/female, straight/
gay, and white/colored, while at the same time celebrating contradiction and toler-
ating ambiguity.

Anzaldúa both assumes and challenges the existence of a socioracist hierarchical structure in which white culture denigrates Chicana culture, and Chicana culture, in turn, demeans indigenous culture. There's a joke among Chicanas and
Chicanos that if you're poor, then you're Mexican; if you're working class, then
you're Mexican American; if you're middle class, then you're Hispanic; but if
you're rich, you're Italian. This joke illustrates the awareness of a socioracist hierarchical structure in the Hispanic/Latino community itself.

Anzaldúa's phenomenology describes the mestiza standing at the intersection
of three cultures, facing a confusing array of possible ways to forge her identity—
transgressing, embracing, combining, forgetting, synthesizing, creating, accepting, and rejecting. A confusing place of paralyzing perplexity, the crossroads
nevertheless signifies possibilities, hopes, and dreams. The one clear possibility
highlighted by Anzaldúa is the exciting but ominous one of simply walking away
from the crossroads and carving her own path. That may be the only option for
the mestiza, since boundaries are elastic and identities are fluid. A question must
be raised that, unfortunately, Anzaldúa is no longer around to answer: How is
walking away a real option when the crossroads designates a mental space where
different subjectivities are continually crisscrossing?

More marvelous yet for Anzaldúa is the realization that the mestiza does not
have to opt for any particular identity. She does not have to choose between Anglo
or Hispanic cultures. Unable or unwilling to choose a fixed path, Anzaldúa writes,
the paradigmatic mestiza embraces and celebrates ambiguity, contradiction, and
uncertainty, hoping therein to find liberation in tolerance, plurality, diversity, and
the fuzziness of identity. Despite her celebratory acceptance of ambiguity, she

nonetheless privileges her purported Aztec heritage, choosing the path of the irrational forces of the unconscious symbolized by the Aztec goddess of gods, the Lady of the Serpent Skirt, Coatlicue; the mother of Huitzilopochtli, the god of war; and his sister, the mutilated Coyolchauxui. Anzaldúa's turn to the chthonic female deities of the Mesoamericans epitomizes mestiza rejection of Western civilization, the Christian church, and enlightenment rationality. Like Kierkegaard, she takes a leap of faith into the darkness, but her darkness is subterranean, surrounding the chthonic forces of Dionysius—passion and vitality.

Chicana writer Helena Viramontes, too, seems to reject the Christ of Christianity in her first novel, *Under the Feet of Jesus* (1996), which portrays the Christian faith as a superstitious relic of a cultural past. Viramontes tells about the sad lot of thirteen-year-old Estrella and her migrant family struggling for meaningful existence on the margins of social life as Mexican American farm workers in California. Arriving at their dilapidated home, Estrella's father hastily builds a crude domestic altar in the kitchen by setting up wooden crates in a corner. On top of the crates, Estrella's mother, Petra, places plaster cast statues of Jesus, the Virgin Mary, and Joseph—the Holy Family, the true Trinity of Hispanic folk Catholicism. These are not only symbols of the Christian faith, tokens of the belief in the sacredness of the family; above all, they are magical amulets or fetishes. Petra places the family's papers underneath the statue of Jesus, symbolically entrusting the fate of the family to him. One day, through Petra's fumbling, the statue falls and breaks. Faith is misplaced in the illusionary power of religious symbols.

If there is any original contribution to Christology by Hispanics, it is that of the mestizo Christ or the hybrid Jesus who represents the hybridity of US Hispanics, a mixed-race people. Despite the originality of the mestizo Christ, Hispanic theology needs to formulate more adequately sufficient the conditions for the possibility of constructing an imaginary mestizo Christ. Forty-five years after Gutiérrez bemoaned the lack of a Latin American Christology, the same lament echoes in Hispanic theology. In her article "Jesus," published in *Handbook of Latina/o Theologies*, Michelle González declares that while the centrality of the crucified Christ in Latina/o communities is clear, the centrality of Christology in Latina/o theologies is not (Gonzalez 2006, 22–23). She also notes that Ada María Isasi-Díaz, a leader in the Hispanic theology movement and founder and proponent of *mujerista* (womanist) theology, recanted her earlier position that Jesus was not central to Latina/o beliefs (Gonzalez 2006, 23).

What accounts for this glaring lacuna in Hispanic theology and the absence of Jesus in Hispanic literature? Could the absence of Christ in Hispanic writing testify to the relative insignificance of Christ in Hispanic folk religion? Certainly, there exists a prodigious proliferation of images of Christ in popular culture—crucifixes inked on skin, painted on the hoods of low riders, drawn on *paños* (cloths), dangling on necklaces, and the ubiquitous crucifix made of wood, plastic, or plaster hanging on bedroom walls, adorning the walls of church naves, and so on. How could Christ be considered insignificant in Hispanic/Latina/o culture?

Hispanic culture portrays Christ primarily as the crucified Christ—a corpse, a dead body, a signifier of death. Psychologically, the function of this particular signifier serves as a mechanism for coping with human morality. In the Latina/o perspective, Christ accomplished his work in the past, at his Crucifixion. Therefore, he is a remote deity. By contrast, the Virgin Mother is a living, accessible, and caring deity.

In popular Hispanic Catholicism, the Virgin Mary uses up most the religious oxygen in the symbolic atmosphere. She is the go-to person for people clinging to a last ditch effort for a concrete hope. She is the true intercessor between the believer and God the father, the remote Creator, the Ancient of Days, inaccessible and far away. When Jesus/Christ signifies every son, then he is a living symbol. The religious symbolism of Jesus and Mary is a projection of familial sentiment between sons and mothers, so the mestizo Jesus is a heavenly projection of the sacredness or exalted pride of Hispanic ethnicity. The mestizo Jesus symbolizes the worth and dignity of Hispanic. Maybe Anzaldúa got it right, that is she saw through to the religious core of Hispanic culture. She cut through veil of Our Lady of Guadalupe to the essence of the Aztec goddess, who rightly takes over the sacred space that Protestants reserve for Jesus.

EXCURSUS: THE NAME GAME—HISPANIC OR LATINA/O?

A cursory reading of Hispanic/Latina/o literature reveals that Hispanic/Latina/o self-perception in the United States generates and constructs polymorphous forms of identity and a kaleidoscope of multivalent ethnic, racial, cultural, religious, and national images. It is no mere coincidence that ambiguity stands out as one of the most predominant and pressing themes in Hispanic/Latina/o literature. Ambiguity is a problem of identity that requires ontological and epistemological criteria of clarification and, at the same time, conceptually employed strategies in diverse forms of counterhegemonic resistance, with varying degrees of effectiveness and communicability, in a society constituted by classist-racist hierarchy.

US Hispanics continually and anxiously face a perplexing situation in which non-Hispanic society unproblematically construes and manipulates Hispanic identity according to a set of unexamined stereotypes, and at the same time,

Hispanics themselves cannot pin down a fixed and nonelusive ethnic identity that satisfies the many and diverse groups denominated Hispanic/Latino. The media, the government, and the public face little difficulty and generally escape critical scrutiny in their use of labels *Hispanic* or *Latino* in one broad sweep as though identification of the apparently targeted population is both easily fixed by some determinate and definable racial essence. Even use of the term "targeted population" implies the existence of a unitary and identifiable group.

Ilan Stavans, author of *The Hispanic Condition* and a self-described Jewish Mexican immigrant from Mexico City, tells the heart-wrenching story of the painter Martín Ramírez to illustrate the liminality of the immigrant experience, and thereby, to show the labyrinthine quality of Hispanic identity. Ramírez was a field worker in Mexico when the turbulence of the Mexican Revolution and the incipient industrialization of Mexico drove him from job to job as a laundry worker and then as a railroad worker. The push of the upheavals brought about by the revolution, and the pull of the American demand for cheap labor, took him north across the border. He somehow lost the power of speech and wandered about the streets of Los Angeles. Only Mexico City boasts of a larger Mexican population. Authorities diagnosed him as a schizophrenic and hospitalized him in a sanatorium. By the end of World War I, a college professor discovered Ramírez and encouraged his art. Eventually hailed by art critics, his work is displayed around the world—New York, Chicago, London, Washington, DC. Psychologists concluded that difficulties and challenges of adapting to a new, or better yet, an alien culture caused his psychic disturbance.

Stavans too hastily makes Ramírez a representative of the "entire plight of Hispanic cultural experience in the United States," characterizing Hispanics in general as culturally schizophrenic. Regarding this characterization, one should note that Ramírez was an ethnic immigrant and not a national minority. Ethnic immigrants originate outside of the territory of the United States and come to the country voluntarily. National minorities forcefully incorporated into the United States are assimilated to a greater degree than ethnic immigrants. Two questions remain unanswered. Did the immigrant experience play a determinative role in the development of Ramírez's schizophrenia? Or was Ramírez schizophrenic before he left Mexico? In any case, it is a bold leap of several octaves to move from a description of Ramírez's particular condition to a generalized characterization of Hispanics. Perhaps the outspoken character of Caliban from Shakespeare's *The Tempest* better exemplifies the underlying rebellious spirit of the Hispanic condition than the mute artist Martín Ramírez. Caliban the savage learned to curse Prospero the colonizing master with the same language he learned from Prospero.

At the very least, any adequate concept of Hispanic/Latino identity must convey the notion of historical fusion of many cultures, nationalities, ethnicities, and races. Synthesis, acculturation, assimilation, and integration drive the adoption and adaptation of mutually foreign biological and cultural traits in the formation of new human groupings and social realities. Any account of Hispanic/Latino identity eventually succumbs to a problematic slipperiness of conceptual formulation and ideational clarity generated by the internal complexities lying within the notion itself. As a result, explorations of Hispanic/Latino cultural expressions require, as a precondition for genuine understanding, an honest recognition of the conceptual difficulties in clarifying Hispanic/Latina/o identity. Historically, ethnic identity occupies the discursive center of gravity in the narrative constructions of individual and collective autobiographies in the Hispanic/Latina/o pursuit of historical self-understanding, recognition, demand for respect and sociopolitical entitlements.

The problem of identity raises a host of semantic, ontological, and epistemological concerns when applied to the identification of ethnic groups, ethnicity, and the choice of ethnic names. A subordinate set of issues raises questions about the necessity, adequacy, justification, and denotative function of ethnic names. Recently, Hispanic/Latina/o philosophers in the United States have taken up these questions about the terms *Hispanic* and *Latino*. What is the source or origin of the unity of Hispanics? Do we need either ethnic label? Do the terms *Hispanic* and *Latino* fit the groups expressed by these terms? Is one term to be preferred over the other? Is there any epistemic justification for the use of *Hispanic* or *Latino*? What is the correct use, if any, of these terms?

Recent debates among Hispanic/Latina/o philosophers contest issues about ethnic identity. In particular, there is considerable disagreement over whether *Hispanic* or *Latino* better expresses the identity of the people of Latin America and their descendants in the United States. I will explore the recent years-long debate between eminent American philosophers Jorge Gracia and Linda Martín Alcoff. Since they have written extensively on race and identity, the following discussion cannot do full justice to the depths and complexity of their theories and arguments.

In his philosophical approach to ethnic identity *Hispanic/Latino Identity: Philosophical Perspectives*, Jorge Gracia argues that ethnic names are necessary against the objections of name nihilists. For the name nihilist, an ethnic name such as *Hispanic* or *Latino* is useless and confusing because it does not have a clear connotation, a set of properties, by which it can determine the extension, denotation, or reference of the things it names. The nihilist argument holds that without a clear connotation, an ethnic name cannot denote anything in particular. Therefore, ethnic names are arbitrary or conventional. Gracia observes that the nihilistic account stands or falls on the essentialist assumptions it makes about ethnic names. Gracia worries that if the name nihilist's argument is correct, then there could be negative practical consequences in using ethnic names seriously. For example, if ethnic names are arbitrary or conventional, they may give false information about the groups they identify. False information may be harmful or dangerous.

Against the nihilistic account that ethnic names appear vacuous, Gracia's counterargument raises powerful objections. One such objection is that ethnic names are necessary for effective communication about certain groups of people in particular contexts. Ethnic names, he claims, are similar to common names and proper names in that the members of a class denoted by such names share common relevant features. Common names are required to move about the world. Likewise, claims Gracia, ethnic names are necessary to make meaningful utterances about different kinds of groups of people in the world. Proper names, like common names, are necessary because they anchor terms to particulars in the real world. Gracia concludes that ethnic names, like common names and proper names, are necessary for effective and meaningful communication.

Is Gracia correct that ethnic names function like proper nouns and common names, picking out particulars in the real world? The noun *unicorn* functions like a common noun, but it doesn't pick out any particular object in the actual world the way that *lion* or *tiger* denote classes with members. *Santa Claus* is a proper noun, yet it does not anchor onto any person in the actual world. If *Latino* is a proper name, what singular class does it pick out in the real world?

Probably influenced by the theory of definite descriptions, Jorge Luis Borges playfully demonstrates in his short story, "Tlön, Uqbar, Orbis Tertius," that strings of adjectives, verbs, and adverbial nouns could substitute for nouns in effective and meaningful communication. If this is the case, then communication may be possible without the use of ethnic names. Gracia seems correct in saying that it is necessary to speak about groups of people with shared ethnic and racial features. A circularity, however, is present in Gracia's argument. To claim that it is necessary to speak about ethnic groups is to presuppose the existence of ethnic groups. If ethnic groups exist and they are referred to, then they must already be named, labeled, classified, or categorized as such. Assuming, as Gracia does, that there is a relation between ethnic names and the groups denoted, is there any reason for thinking that the relation is anything but accidental? That an ethnic name must denote a ethnic group makes linguistic sense. There may be good reasons for claiming that ethnic groups exist and that ethnic names are necessary. Does it follow from this premise that *Latino* or *Hispanic* must denote a particular group? It would be a mistake to take this idea for granted.

Second, Gracia rightly points out that ethnic name nihilists are essentialists because the nihilist claims that it should be possible to pick out those and only those properties that jointly specify the necessary and sufficient conditions for the concept of ethnic identity to apply. On Gracia's construal, essentialism about identity is the view that a property or set of properties always and only characterizes the things called by the same name. A name should effectively point to something in the real world, names attach to things, and words link to the things they denote. In the nihilist view, since no property or set of properties always and only characterizes the group and subgroups called Hispanic, the term *Hispanic* fails to denote anything. It follows, therefore, that name nihilism assumes that a correct account of ethnic names must be an essentialist account. The same conclusion applies to the term *Latino*. Gracia convincingly demonstrates that defining the essence of an ethnic group—picking out those and only those properties that jointly specify the necessary and sufficient conditions for ethnic identity—proves insurmountable. Therefore, to overcome the ethnic name nihilist argument, Gracia must provide an argument for a nonessentialist account of ethnic names.

Gracia's alternative to essentialism has to give an adequate account of what unifies the group because whatever it is that unifies the group constitutes the key to its identity. In a way, this sounds like essentialism, but it is not. Gracia is not seeking a set of properties that always characterize members of a group. He agrees with name nihilists that in the case of ethnic identity, identity is not based on a conception of a shared property or set of properties, but Gracia does not conclude that ethnic names are vacuous. Instead, he construes an alternative account of ethnic identity, a construal based on a theory of familial and historical relations. The problem facing Gracia is to show that it is meaningful to talk about the identity or unity of a group of individuals without specifying a common set of properties.

Ludwig Wittgenstein's theory of family resemblances fits the bill for Gracia. Ludwig Wittgenstein pondered a similar problem with regard to games. Games, said Wittgenstein, are diverse and there is no common feature characteristic of all and only games; however, people are successful in using the term *game* in reference to the kind of activity people consensually call a game. There may be some resemblance between some kinds of games, but there may be little or no resemblances between one kind of game and another. Some kinds of games are played in fields of grass or turf; others are played on or in water. What resemblance does football bear to peek-a-boo?

Gracia notes that resemblances are distributed unequally among differentiated members of a group of particulars, in this case games. Games do not all share the same features, but game A may possess some of the traits as game B, and game B may share some of the same traits as game C, but A and C may not have any features in common. Yet games A and C are linked together by family resemblances they share with B. Likewise, in a family, the parents and offspring do not share all the same features, but there are enough resemblances among them to show that they constitute a group. This is the family resemblances theory that Gracia employs to establish the unity in diversity of Hispanics.

Even name nihilists can agree with Gracia's observation that there are many nationalities and ethnicities in Iberia, Latin America, and the United States that do not share a set of common features but are ordinarily referred to as Hispanics or Latinos. According to Gracia, this is because of family resemblances that tie them all together, albeit not in the same way. Gracia's appropriation of Wittgenstein's family resemblance theory, at this stage of the argument, sounds plausible but remains incomplete. One problem is to account for the difference between relevant and irrelevant resemblances. What constitutes a relevant resemblance? Secondly, what is the cause of resemblance? If relevant resemblances are spontaneous and random, then relevant resemblance has no power of explanation. What explains the diversity of shared resemblances among members of an ethnic group? If the idea of family resemblance can be transferred to an ethnic group, then some causal mechanism must account for the distribution of resemblance among the members. Genetics accounts for family resemblance. Genetics cannot be the causal explanation of ethnic identity without presupposing essentialism. That is something Gracia seeks to avoid. Auxiliary questions arise: Do some traits matter more than others? What if some resemblances link members of the group *Hispanic* to non-Hispanics? Would that make those non-Hispanics eligible for membership in the group? If resemblances are properties, some account must be given about the relation between resemblance properties and the particulars to which they are attached. Gracia's account treats resemblances as relations, not properties, and that resemblances are historical relations. Relations are either internal or external. It is unclear whether Gracia's historical relations are internal or external.

Gracia claims that historical relations unite Hispanics uniquely and separates them from others not so connected to the history that ties the people of Iberia and the Americas together. He employs the metaphor of a web to picture the set of external relations that unite Hispanics. "What ties them together, and separates them from others are history and the particular events of that history rather than the consciousness of that history; a unique web of changing historical relations supplies their unity" (Gracia 2000, 49). A web of shared historical relations is the mechanism that accounts for Hispanic ethnic identity. Hispanics do not all share the same features, but a history of interconnected events constitutes the mechanism for their unity.

The account of a web of historical relations begins with the 1492 encounter between the Spanish and Amerindians, a reasonable date to begin such an account. One wonders, though, whether US Hispanics could not have come about without the 1492 encounter. It is conceivable that the historical events surrounding the 1492 encounter would not have resulted in the emergence of US Hispanic/ Latina/os, or of Latin Americans for that matter. Factually, 1492 is the date that began the web of historical relations leading to the emergence of Latin Americans and their descendants in the United States. However, this is not a necessary fact but a contingent one.

On charitable grounds, assume that the familial resemblances/web of historical relations account adequately explains the unity/identity of Hispanics. What ethnic name best expresses the unity/identity of this group in this case? What is the most adequate and historically relevant name—*Hispanic* or *Latino*? On the grounds that it allows a better understanding of the historical reality underlying that unity, the term *Hispanic*, argues Gracia, possesses greater representational power than the term *Latino*, and operates like a window on reality. Therefore, he urges the adoption of *Hispanic* over *Latino*: "In short, my proposal is to adopt 'Hispanic' to refer to us: the people of Iberia, Latin America, and some segments of the population in the United States, after 1492, and to the descendants of these peoples anywhere in the world as long as they preserve close ties to them. Moreover, I have argued that the use of this term does not imply that there are any properties common to all of us throughout history. Its use is justified rather by a web of concrete historical relations that ties us together, and simultaneously separates us from other peoples" (Gracia 2000, 52). Underlying this proposal is an essentialist presupposition that something Spanish—language or origin, perhaps—is the common element that holds Hispanics together. For this is the only way it can be understood that the name *Hispanic* operates like a window on reality.

In her 2005 essay, "Latino vs. Hispanic: The Politics of Ethnic Names," Alcoff takes issue with Gracia's historical account for the justification of the use of the term *Hispanic* and offers a rival historical narrative that favors the term *Latino*. Alcoff raises the following question: Do ethnic names signal political views? Affirmative in her response, she answers that ethnic names signal political views about assimilation, cultural nationalism, and race. For this reason, Alcoff challenges

Gracia's argument that *Hispanic* has better descriptive and explanatory advantage in delimiting the unity of the Iberians, Latin Americans, and their descendants in the United States.

Her challenge consists of two arguments. The first makes the case that the choice of ethnic names implies political considerations, and the second claims that *Latino* fits historical reality better than *Hispanic*. Alcoff asserts that the choice of ethnic names is "inherently political" or at least that the choice of ethnic names "signals" political views. To support her argument, she claims that contestation over ethnic names has been an integral part of political movements among Latinos in the United States since the 1960s. Moreover, she observes that Latina/o immigrants often experience a change of ethnic labels upon entering the United States, endowing Latinos with an epistemic privilege to know the dynamism and instability of names. Because of this firsthand experiential knowledge, Latinos also understand the inherent relationship between names and social status. Therefore, she concludes, Latinos are relatively sophisticated about the socially constructed character of ethnic names (Alcoff 2005, 4).

That ethnic names are socially constructed lends plausibility to the claim that ethnic names signal political views. However, showing that ethnic names are social constructs does not ipso facto imply that ethnic names signal political views. She must explain more clearly how social construction implies political commitments. To this end, she argues that the choice of names relates to struggles over power and that social ontologies hook up with political self-images. The choice of names legitimizes narrative, and for this reason, social construction of names implies political views and commitments.

Her most solid argument holds that the complexity of social and historical reality means that empirical evidence is underdetermining. Contestations over names follow. Moreover, contestations of names are really contestations over historical interpretation, political analysis, and alternative configurations of intracommunity relationships. Therefore, the choice of ethnic names signals political views. If the choice of ethnic names implies contesting interpretation, political analysis, and so on, social contestations of the choice of names signal political views only broadly and loosely. Contestations in civil society may or may not entail legislative intervention.

Alcoff risks undermining her own argument because of the underdetermination of historical and empirical evidence. It follows, then, that choice for ethnic names is underdetermined. Undermining her argument further, Alcoff argues that naming is always an open question. If, for instance, *Latino* is the term of choice, it remains an open question whether the term possesses sufficient denotative clarity.

Nonetheless, she argues convincingly that because of the historical and empirical underdetermination of ethnic names political considerations are necessary in choosing ethnic names makes a strong case. As she puts it, "This underdetermination both calls for a political solution and makes a political solution possible in the sense that it makes a space to interject political considerations in the discussion, as one consideration whose importance will vary depending on the strength of other factors" (Alcoff 2005, 9).

In the second part of her essay, she rejects Gracia's choice of the term *Hispanic*, maintaining that the term *Latino* has a distinct advantage over *Hispanic* in that the former term better expresses the colonialism constitutive of the people named Latina/o. In making her case, she places a strong emphasis on the historic date 1898, when the United States defeated Spain in the Spanish–American War. For Alcoff, the historical moment of 1898, not 1492, better signals the constitution of Latinos and the legitimacy of the use of the term *Latino*. Eighteen ninety-eight signals the end of Spanish colonialism in Latin America and the beginning of US colonialism in Latin America. In effect, 1898 symbolizes a transfer of colonial power from Spain to the United States, signifying a crucial turn in the "imaginary of modern/colonial world system." Therefore, 1898 is of much greater political and cultural relevance for understanding Latinos/Hispanics than Gracia's preferred date of 1492.

The defeat of Spain by the United States actually works against Alcoff's argument because the events of 1898 generated in Spain and in Latin America the movement known as *Hispanidad*. Latin American intellectuals, feeling nostalgic for the motherland, sought ways of reviving Spanish traditions and customs in Latin America. The depth of feeling for Spain led Latin Americans to identify with Spain in their preference for the self-identifying monikers "Hispano" or "Hispano-Americano." In his master's thesis, Ignacio Martínez ably defends his claim that 1898 generated the Hispanidad movement in Latin America and Spain: "It was at this time (1898) that *Hispanismo* gained its most loyal advocates in Latin America, and is what this thesis considers to be the beginning of this moment." (Martínez 2006, 41). The disaster created "a pro-Spanish/anti-American movement that functioned on different levels." Because of its poverty, Spain could not meaningfully reconnect with Latin America except in the realm of ideas. Martínez defines post-1898 Hispanicism as "a trans-Atlantic ideology that aimed to promote the solidarity of all Hispanic peoples based on their common language, race, tradition, and geographic proximity, in an effort to find an authentic Hispanic identity" (Martínez 2006, 43).

While Martínez's thesis may not undermine Alcoff's claim that *Latino* is more politically potent, it does weaken her claim that the events of 1898 support the adoption of the term Latino. In her account, the term *Hispanic* is an invention and imposition of governmental bureaucracy in 1978. Moreover, *Hispanic* connotes cultural identity and not national identity and signifies links with Spain, which obfuscates the colonial relation between the United States and Latin America.

Gracia's response to Alcoff, "A Political Argument in Favor of Ethnic Names: Alcoff's Defense of 'Latino,'" strongly objects to Alcoff's designation of 1898 as the defining moment bearing on the constitution of the identity of contemporary Hispanics/Latina/os. Gracia rightly points out that Alcoff's appeal to the French origin of the term Latino is counterproductive to her own argument. After all, as Gracia notes, the term *Latino* is a Spanish derivation of the French coinage "Amerique Latine," which antedates the Spanish–American War and undermines Alcoff's claim that 1898 institutionalizes *Latino*. Taking recourse to the French coinage of the term weakens her claim that the choice of terms has to "gel with lived experience."

Gracia's objection that the term *Latino* relies on a historical interpretation of Latin America that facts cannot bear is to some extent debatable, but his suspicion that the Walter Mignolo/Alcoff thesis (that *Latino* is marked not by the Spanish/Latin American colonial relationship but by the United States/Latin American relationship) reflects a post facto political agenda sounds right. Gracia's conclusion that Alcoff's argument is suspect and probably groundless is strongly stated and warranted.

In a sort of rapprochement, Gracia, however, concedes that there are political advantages in the use of *Latino* with respect to contemporary considerations. The term *Latino* makes a more direct reference to Latin America, and the term connotes a denigrated identity, which seems to possess greater political importance than *Hispanic*. Moreover, he offers an olive branch, signaling that there should be no conflict in the choice of the terms.

Alcoff accepts the criticism that there may be some vagueness in the language of her argument. Yet she stands fast, holding forth the claim that metaphysical arguments cannot delimit the group one wants to name. She simply reiterates her position that the choice of ethnic names has political implications and that an account starting with the 1492 Iberian/Amerindian encounter and the subsequent Spanish conquest and history of colonialism does not dovetail with the contemporary situation of Latinas/os as well as the 1898 Spanish–American war and its aftermath.

A solution, if one can be found, will have to come about historically from the consensus of Hispanics/Latinos in the United States with, of course, the cooperation of the media, schools, governmental agencies, and non-Hispanic groups. Gracia's choice of the term *Hispanic* shows a preference for an English bastardization of the Spanish *Hispano*—a term preferred by Latin American writers after the Spanish–American war of 1898. Does not the term *Hispanic*, an Anglicism, shred to some degree the association with Spain? The term *Latino* is not innocent either. Alcoff's choice is an English appropriation of the Spanish translation of *Latin*. Why does the US media use *Latino* to refer to Hispanics instead of *Latin*? *Latin* has associations with classical Latin culture, law, literature, language, and civilization. Thus, *Latino* avoids such associations but remains tangential in a "harmless" way. Neither *Hispanic* nor *Latino* really fit the variability and diversity of the ongoing and dynamic hybridization of the people loosely and casually called *Hispanic* or *Latino*. Admittedly, no other terms are suitable, and there are conventional and pragmatic reasons for continuing use of these ethnic labels. Nevertheless, these labels are underdetermining. The choice of *Latino* for the title of this work is motivated by personal aesthetics and by utilitarian concerns. *Latino* appears to gel better with discussions about art and literature, and a choice had to be made. *Hispanic/Latino* would underlie the undecidable factor concerning the choice of terms, but would not be economic. Some would argue that *Latino* is a better descriptive term for Latin Americans and their descendants in the United States. *Hispanic* denotes more broadly to include Spain and their descendants in Latin America and the United States. *Latino* derives from the Spanish *latino*, denoting the Romance countries, including Portugal, and their former colonies in the Americas. Hence, *Latino* suffices for use in the title of this work.

CHAPTER NINE

Coda

Is there some common meaning that diverse representations of the Latino Christ share? Some would answer yes. They would explain that Christ or Jesus is the common meaning or referent of the images of Christ in art, literature, and theology. In describing this ur-Christ or original Jesus, they could only offer another representation. Only representations or versions of Christ are possible. All claims about Jesus/Christ are fictitious.

Christ's representation is multiply realizable. Each particular representation reflects not only an ethos relative to place, time, and community, but also the peculiarities of individuals and their temperaments, forged in crucibles of inner psychological and emotional worlds as well as vortices of particular historical circumstances. Imaginary constructions of Christ mirror projections of self-understanding and expressions of ideas or ideals and feelings of artists, writers, philosophers, theologians, and people generally. These comments do not convey any novel ideas or declare anything controversial. The point is that all representations of Christ are imaginary.

Dalí's nuclear mystical Christ expresses the idea of beauty through the unity of the natural and spiritual, the rational and irrational, and the macrocosmic and microcosmic. Dalí's faceless Christ, at one level, is a projection of Dalí's own self-image, but at another level, represents the unity of matter and spirit in the modality of human life. The existence of one man may end, but the essence of humanity endures; and so it follows that the beauty of humanity does not pass away with the death of any one man, no matter how perfect.

Dalí's idea of Christ gives rise to the possibility of the cognition of the unity of the material and the spiritual. Seemingly antithetical opposites, matter and spirit are really one and the same. Similarly, the divine and the human appear to be separate, independent, and antithetical, while in reality the divine and the human are one. It depends on how someone looks. Looked upon in a heavenly way, it appears divine, then looked upon in an earthly way, it appears human. Viewing the figure on the cross in a human manner is to see Jesus. Viewing the figure on the cross in a divine way is to see Christ. Either way, one thing is seen in two different ways. To see the one thing at the same time as human and divine is Dalí's insight. However, Dalí's Christ does not suffer. Dalí's Christ on the cross is only feigning suffering, a semblance of suffering, and a weak semblance at that. Suffering is agony, an ugliness and a distortion of the Dalian ideal, intolerable and unacceptable for expressing the material/spiritual unity. His purported unity is a false unity because it is one-sided and abstract. Dalí's Christ is a docetic Christ, a phantom with the appearance of flesh and bone, but only appearance. Knowledge of Christ is probably restricted by appearance, a limitation Christians may not transcend.

Fray Angélico Chávez's ode to *The Madonna of Port Lligat*, a duet with Dalí, juxtaposes traditional Catholic dogma with Dalian nuclear mysticism. While the infant Jesus in the 1949 version is diminutive in comparison with the infant in the 1950 version, both pictures appear to feature the Madonna as the organizing principle for the compositions. Yet Dalí said that the paintings were really about the infant. Chávez seems aware that Dalí had made this claim. In any case, Chávez claims that the infant Jesus is the heart of the poem, even though he emphasizes the dialectical unity of Madonna and Child. For all his talk about the unity of the spiritual and the material in the Logos, Chávez relapses into a more thorough-going spiritualism in his Biblical commentary that accompanies his poem. This is especially evident in his identification of the "good things" God gives the hungry with the Eucharist, as though the hungry could be nourished or satisfied with a wafer of bread and a swig of cheap red wine from a tiny plastic cup. What both Dalí and Chávez see that most people miss is that the humanization of divinity in the Christ idea is at the same time the divinization of humanity. Unfortunately, Dalí's *Madonna of Port Lligat* is for Chávez a convenient form for conveying orthodox Catholic doctrine.

Unlike the sanitized Christs of Dalí and Chávez, Orozco's expressionist Christ gives vent to cynical and pessimistic feelings about the potential divinity in human reality. The idea Orozco expresses in the murals of the Colegio San Ildefonso, the Prometheus mural, and the Baker Library Epic of American Civilization panels reveals a cynical attitude toward the ideals and ideologies the masses attempt to realize in their struggles. Reality in gun and blood proves the illusory and utopian nature of ideals and ideologies. In this mix appears the mythological hero generously laden with gifts of knowledge, art, and industry for humankind. The hero stands at one dialectical pole, the masses at the other. Prometheus, Quetzalcoatl, and Christ represent oppositional forces against traditional religion, rebels against convention, prophets speaking out against the dehumanizing forces of so-called civilization.

Prometheus, impatient with Zeus, takes matters in his own hands and delivers to humankind the knowledge of what is potentially already theirs. Quetzalcoatl rejects the belief that humans owe a blood debt to the gods: a mutual reciprocity exists between gods and humankind, but human life is too precious for even the gods to claim. Christ rejects the stupidity of a mechanized civilization whose religion is a disguise for money and power. Like Prometheus, Christ is impatient and destroys the superficial world created by mass attitudes and ideals. Christ represents the possibility of beginning again, a second chance. The triumvirate of mythological heroes—Prometheus, Quetzalcoatl, and Christ—represent what the human being ought to be, the masses represent what human beings are and are probably destined to be. The ideal human being remains a myth or a fiction.

Cervantes's fictional character don Quixote inspires Unamuno's idea of Christ as an immortalizer, who through his agony, immortalized himself in history. Unamuno's idea of Christ is entirely symbolic of the agonic struggle between reason and faith, hope in personal immortality and the inevitability of death. Alas, the way to live with this highly individualistic struggle is to live life as if one could make oneself worthy of immortality. If Unamuno is right that one's temperament determines one's philosophy, and if there is a fundamental Spanish attitude to life, then Unamuno's moral imperative is the only possible consequence of the practical significance of the Spanish Christ. Miguel de Unamuno hides conspicuously behind St. Manuel the Good, Martyr. What Unamuno's Christ and St. Manuel share in common is the immortality they attained in history on account of the stories about them.

Every representation of Christ is a fiction. This is never more true than in Borges's fictional portrayals of Christ. For Borges, the question is, what is it possible to think about Christ? Both Judas and Baltasar Espinosa function as doubles of Christ, iterations of the Christ idea. Moreover, both characters suggest that representations of Christ are multiply possible. "Three Versions of Judas" more than "The Gospel According to Mark" raises serious theological questions, questions that are not only possible to ask but necessary as well—for theologians. However, the inherent absurdity in the story undermines any claims beyond the fictional. Borges shows that the Christ idea, while fictional, is multiply realizable, repeatable, cyclical, and eternally recurrent in similar but not identical ways

Rojas constructs the most sympathetic profile of Christ, namely that Christ represents humanity. Paintings, drawings, and sculptures of Christ render him at all stages of life, expressing the full range of human emotion and feeling. Christ reveals the sacredness of the human condition with all its virtues and vices. In Martin Scorsese's film adaptation of Kazantzakis's *The Last Temptation of Christ*, there is a ten-second sequence in which Jesus is dreaming what it would be like to be a married man making love to his wife, in this case, Mary Magdalene. Kazantzakis and Scorsese unwittingly capture a similar idea that Rojas conveyed in his Christological dialogue.

Liberation theologians echo Rojas's immanent presence of divinity in humanity with their talk about el Dios pobre. With this locution, they signify the idea that God appears in the faces of the poor and needy. In other words, the poor masses manifest and make God present. Motivated by this intuition, liberation theologians turned to the historical Jesus as a new point of departure for developing a genuine Latin American Christology. At one level, the result is Christ the Liberator. Traditional Christianity makes salvation the personal matter of an individual's relationship to God. Liberation theology expands the scope of salvation, making it collective, not individual, and turns veridical salvation ninety degrees, extending salvation horizontally. It shifts the eyes of hope from the promise of heaven to the promise of the Kingdom of God on earth—universal health care, meaningful jobs, a living wage, decent housing, clean air and water, free and universal education, a participatory democracy, the end of racism, classism, sexism, homophobia, and all other social ills.

The danger with politicizing the faith is that any ideology, political party, movement, or state can identify itself with liberation and freedom. For example, in the United States, right-wing fundamentalist theology claims that social conservativism and unrestrained capitalism offer the best chances for liberation. Jesus is a capitalist, an advocate of private property, a proponent of the free market, an opponent of Marxism, socialism, and communism. Jesus wears Pierre Chardin hand-tailored suits, buys expensive jewelry, drinks champagne, eats caviar, and so on. He is a business consultant fetching thousands of dollars for his lectures to money-hungry businesspeople yearning to learn Jesus's five steps to success and wealth. Early in the twentieth century, Bob Barton wrote a book called *The Man Nobody Knows* (1925), in which he describes a twentieth-century Jesus as a successful businessman.

Even beginning with the Jesus of the Gospels as their point of departure, people can find any aspect that suits their ideology. Frankly, there seems to be a better fit between the Jesus of liberation theology and Jesus of the Gospels than that between the Jesus of the Gospels and the Jesus of American conservative Christianity. Better fitness expresses something more genuine and authentic. Unfortunately, the Jesus of the Gospels is not the historical Jesus, but that is all we have. The Gospel narratives express the faith of the early Christians and are not a reliable source for a historical account of the life of Jesus, but the Gospels are confessions of faith rooted to some extent on the historical Jesus. Maybe Christians' only hope is to create contemporary images, ideas, and narratives of Christ that echo the Gospel narratives. In any case, as a guard against dogmatism and absolutization, the attitude toward religious symbols like Christ should recall the imaginary and factual nature of those symbols.

Hispanic/Latina/o theology interprets Christianity in light of the biological or cultural hybridity posited as the determining factor of ethnic identity subject to a social-racist hierarchy in the United States. Inversely, the Christian faith illuminates the true nature of the Hispanic condition in the United States. Out of this dialectical reading, mestizaje or mulatez emerges as a starting point for Hispanic theology and the hermeneutical key for interpreting the Latino reality. Focusing on the particularities of Hispanic/Latina/o ethnicity in the United States, Hispanic theology risks losing universal relevance. Moreover, Hispanic/Latina/o theologians share a fault with José Vasconcelos, optimistically believing that racial hybridization is a driving force of social progress. Maybe hybridization is a driving force of evolution, but neither evolution nor hybridization guarantee social progress, contrary to Herbert Spencer, Gabino Barreda, and Pierre Teilhard de Chardin. The power of Hispanic/Latina/o theology lies in its particularization, not in its universal relevance. Once, when Gustavo Gutiérrez visited Boston, he said that US Hispanics could appropriate nothing from Latin American liberation theology. For clarification he added, "Tienes que beber de tu propio pozo" (You have to drink from your own well). Gutiérrez meant, of course, that theological reflection has to begin with one's historical circumstances. As Ortega y Gasset puts it, "Yo soy yo y mis circunstancias" (I am myself and my circumstances).

There is no singular Latino Christ, but there is a multiplicity of imagined Latino Jesuses/Christs in art, literature, and theology. Each representation reflects something like a culture or an ethnicity's ethos, but also the peculiarities of individuals and their temperaments forged in crucibles of inner psychological and emotional worlds, as well as vortices of particular historical circumstances. In these imaginary constructions of Christ are projections of self-understanding and expressions of ideas or ideals that motivated artists, writers, and theologians to engage in their creative endeavors to express some particular feature or universal property as the chief characteristic of Christ.

BIBLIOGRAPHY

Ades, Dawn. *Art in Latin America*. New Haven: Yale University Press, 1989.

———. *Dalí and Surrealism*. New York: Harper and Row, 1982.

Ades, Dawn, and Fiona Bradley. *Salvador Dalí: A Mythology*. Liverpool: Tate Gallery Publishing, 1999.

Alberich, José. "Sobre el positivismo de Unamuno." *Cuadernos de la Cátedra de Miguel de Unamuno* 9 (1959): 61–75.

Alexandrian, Sarane. *Surrealist Art*. London: Thames and Hudson, 1970.

Anzaldúa, Gloria. *Borderlands/La Frontera: The New Mestiza*. 2nd ed. San Francisco: Anne Lute Books, 1999.

Aristotle. "Physics." In *Introductory Readings in Ancient Greek and Roman Philosophy*, edited by C. D. C. Reeve and Patrick Lee Miller, 266–75. Indianapolis: Hackett Publishing, 2006.

Assmann, Hugo. "La actuación histórica del poder de Cristo." In *La Nueva Frontera de la Teología en America Latina*, edited by Rosino Gibellini, 133–44. Salamanca: Sígueme, 1977. Translated as "The Power of the Poor in History: Conflicting Christologies and Discernment." In *Frontiers of Theology in Latin America*, edited by Rosino Gibellini, 133ff. Maryknoll, NY: Orbis Books, 1983.

———. *Teología desde la praxis de la liberación*. Salamanca: Ediciones Sígueme, 1973.

———. *Theology for a Nomad Church*. Maryknoll, NY: Orbis Books, 1975.

Athanasius. *On the Incarnation: The Treatise* De Incarnatione Verbi Dei. Translated by Sister Penelope Lawson. Crestwood, NY: St. Vladimir's Seminary Press, 1944.

Aulén, Gustav. *Christus Victor: An Historical Study of the Three Main Types of the Idea of the Atonement*. New York: MacMillan Publishing, 1969.

Balfour, Arthur James. *The Foundation of Belief: Being Notes Introductory to the Study of Theology*. London: Longmans, 1895.

Beck, Lewis White. *A Commentary on Kant's Critique of Practical Reason*. Chicago: University of Chicago Press, 1960.

Bergson, Henri. *Creative Evolution*. Translated by Arthur Mitchell. New York: Random House, 1944.

Bettenson, Henry, ed. *Documents of the Christian Church*. 2nd ed. Oxford: Oxford University Press, 1980.

Boff, Leonardo. *Church, Charism and Power: Liberation Theology and the Institutional Church*. Translated by John W. Diercksmeier. New York: Crossroad, 1986.

———. *Evangelho do Cristo cósmico. A busca da unidade do todo na ciéncia e na religião*. Petropolis, Brazil: Editoria Vozes, 1970.

———. *Jesus Christ Liberator: A Critical Christology for Our Time*. Maryknoll, NY: Orbis Books, 1978.

Borges, Jorge Luis. *Antología Personal*. Buenos Aires: Sur, 1961.

————. *Collected Fictions*. Translated by Andrew Hurley. New York: Viking Penguin, 1998.

————. *Ficciones*. Edited by Anthony Kerrigan. New York: Grove Press, 1962.

————. *Obras completas*. 2 vols. Buenos Aires: Emecé Editores, 2005.

————. *Selected Non-fictions*, edited by Eliot Weinberger. Translated by Ester Allen, Suzanne Jill Levine, and Eliot Weinberger. New York: Penguin Putnam, 1999.

Bossart, W. H. *Borges and Philosophy: Self, Time, and Metaphysics*. New York: Peter Lang Publishing, 2003.

Bradley, Fiona. "Dalí as Myth-Maker: The Tragic Myth of Millet's *Angelus*." In *Salvador Dalí: A Mythology*, edited by Dawn Ades and Fiona Bradley, 12–31. Liverpool: Tale Gallery Publishing, 1999.

Breton, André. *Surrealism and Painting*. Translated by Simon Watson Taylor. New York: Harper and Row Publishers, 1965.

Bultmann, Rudolf. *Jesus Christ and Mythology*. New York: Charles Scribner's Sons, 1958.

Buñuel, Luis, Salvador Dalí, Simone Mareuil, Pierre Batcheff, Albert Duverger, Jean-Louis Bunuel, Stephen Barber, Dave McKean, and Richard Wagner. 2004. *Un Chien Andalou*. [Los Angeles, Calif.]: Transflux Films.

Burns, Paul C. Introduction. In *Jesus in Twentieth-Century Literature, Art, and Movies*, edited by Paul C. Burns, 1–17. New York: Continuum, 2007.

Camus, Albert. *The Rebel: An Essay on Man in Revolt*. Translated by Anthony Bower. New York: Alfred A. Knoff, 1956.

Candelaria, Michael. *Popular Religion and Liberation: The Dilemma of Liberation Theology*. Albany, NY: SUNY Press, 1990.

————. *The Revolt of Unreason: Miguel de Unamuno and Antonio Caso on the Crisis of Modernity*. Amsterdam: Brill/Rodopi, 2012.

Cardoza y Aragón, Luis. *Orozco*. México: Fondo de Cultura Económica, 1983.

Carrasco, Davíd. *Religions of Mesoamerica: Cosmovision and Ceremonial Centers*. San Francisco: Harper, 1990.

Caso, Antonio. *Estética*. Vol. V of *Obras Completas*, edited by Rosa Krauze de Kolteniuk. México: UNAM, 1971.

Charlot, Jean. Foreword. In *The Artist in New York* by José Clemente Orozco, 9–22. Austin: University of Texas Press, 1974.

————. *Mexican Art*. Vol. II of *An Artist on Art: Collected Essays of Jean Charlot*. Hawaii: The University Press of Hawaii, 1972.

Chávez, Fray Angélico. *The Virgin of Port Lligat*. Fresno, CA: Academy Library Guild, 1959.

Cox, Harvey. *The Silencing of Leonardo Boff: The Vatican and the Future of World Christianity*. New York: Meyerstone Books, 1988.

Craven, David. *Art and Revolution in Latin America, 1910–1990*. New Haven: Yale University Press, 2002.

Dalí, Salvador. *The Collected Writings of Salvador Dalí*. Edited by Haim Finklestein. Translated by Haim Finkelstein. Cambridge: Cambridge University Press, 1998.

————. *Diary of a Genius*. Translated by Richard Howard. New York: Prentice Hall, 1986.

————. *The Secret Life of Salvador Dalí.* Translated by Haakon M. Chevalier. New York: Dial Press, 1942.

————. *The Unspeakable Confessions of Salvador Dalí.* New York: William Morrow and Company, 1976.

Descharnes, Robert, and Gilles Néret. *Dalí 1904–1989: The Paintings.* Köln: Taschen, 2001.

Didier, Jaén T. Introduction. In *The Cosmic Race/La raza cósmica* by José Vasconcelos. Baltimore: The Johns Hopkins University Press, 1997.

Echegaray, Hugo. *The Practice of Jesus.* Maryknoll, NY: Orbis Books, 1984.

Eisenstein, Sergei. "Orozco: the Prometheus of Mexican Painting (Notes)." In Elliott 1980, 74.

Elizondo, Virgilio. *The Future is Mestizo: Life where Cultures Meet.* Boulder, CO: University Press of Colorado, 2000.

————. *Galilean Journey: The Mexican American Promise.* Maryknoll, NY: Orbis Books, 1983.

Elliott, David. "Orozco: a Beginning." In Elliott 1980, 11–19.

Elliott, David, ed. *¡Orozco! 1883–1949.* Oxford: Museum of Modern Art, 1980.

Ellucaria, Ignacio. *Freedom Made Flesh: The Mission of Christ and His Church.* Maryknoll, NY: Orbis Books, 1976.

Fanés, Fèlix. *Salvador Dalí: The Construction of the Image, 1925–1930.* New Haven: Yale University Press, 2007.

Fernández, Justino. *Orozco: Forma e idea.* México: Porrúa, 1956.

Ferrater Mora, José. *Ortega y Gasset: An Outline of His Philosophy.* New Haven: Yale University Press, 1963.

————. *Unamuno: A Philosophy of Tragedy.* Translated by Philip Silver. Berkeley: University of California Press, 1962.

Feuerbach, Ludwig. *The Essence of Christianity.* Translated by George Eliot. Amherst, NY: Prometheus Books, 1989.

Fichte, Johann Gottlieb. *The Science of Knowing: Fichte's 1804 Lectures on the Wissenschafts-lehre.* Translated by Walter E. Wright. Albany: SUNY Press, 2005.

Flórez Miguel, Cirilo. "La formación del discurso filosófico de Unamuno." *Cuadernos de la Cátedra Miguel de Unamuno* 29 (1994): 23–42.

Foucault, Michel. *The Order of Things: An Archaeology of the Human Sciences.* A translation of *Les Mot et les Choses.* New York: Vintage Books, 1994.

Freud, Sigmund. *The Future of an Illusion,* edited and translated by James Strachey. New York: W. W. Norton, 1961.

Frost, Robert. "Fire and Ice." *Harper's Magazine.* December 1920, 67.

Ganivet, Ángel. *Idearium español: El por venir de España.* Libre Día General de Victoriano Suárez, 1905.

García, Mario T. "Fray Angélico Chávez: the Making of a Maverick Historian." In McCracken 2000, 25–36.

Gardner, Sebastian. "Aesthetics." *The Blackwell Companion to Philosophy.* 2nd ed. Edited by Nicholas Bunnin and E. Tsui-James, 231–56. Malden, MA: Blackwell Publishers, 2003.

Gibellini, Rosino, ed. *La nueva frontera de la teología en América Latina*. Salamanca: Ediciones Sígueme, 1977. Translated as *Frontiers of Theology in Latin America*. Maryknoll, NY: Orbis Books, 1983.

González, Justo. *A History of Christian Thought*, Vol. 1: *From the Beginnings to the Council of Chalcedon*. Nashville: Abington Press, 1970.

González, Michelle. "Jesus." In *Handbook of Latina/o Theologies*, edited by Edwin David Aponte and Miguel A. De la Torre, 17–24. St. Louis: Chalice Press, 2006.

González Mello, Renato. "Orozco in the United States: An Essay on the History of Ideas." In González Mello and Miliotes 2002, 22–61.

———. "Public Painting and Private Painting: Easel Paintings, Drawings, Graphic Arts, and Mural Studies." In González Mello 2002, 62–97.

González Mello, Renato, and Diane Miliotes, eds. *José Clemente Orozco in the United States, 1927–1934*. New York: Hood Museum of Art, Dartmouth College, in association with W. W. Norton, 2002.

Goodman, Nelson. *Ways of Worldmaking*. Indianapolis: Hackett Publishing Company, 1978.

Gracia, Jorge. *Hispanic/Latino Identity: A Philosophical Perspective*. Malden, MA: Blackwell Publishers, 2000.

———. *Painting Borges: Philosophy Interpreting Art Interpreting Literature*. Albany: SUNY Press, 2012.

Gutiérrez, Gustavo. Preface. *The Practice of Jesus* by Hugo Echegaray, xii–xx. Maryknoll, NY: Orbis Books, 1984.

———. *Teología de la liberación: Perspectivas*. Salamanca: Ediciones Sígueme, 1985.

Hampshire, Stuart. *Spinoza*. Baltimore, MD: Penguin Books, 1951.

Harnack, Adolf von. *What is Christianity?* Translated by Thomas Sanders. Philadelphia: Fortress Press, 1986.

Harth, Marjorie, ed. *José Clemente Orozco: Prometheus*. Pomona, California: Pomona College Museum of Art, 2001.

Hurlburt, Laurence P. *The Mexican Muralists in the United States*. Albuquerque: University of New Mexico Press, 1989.

———. "Notes on Orozco's North American Murals, 1930–1934." In Elliott 1980, 51–58.

Ilie, Paul. *Unamuno: An Existential View of Self and Society*. Madison: University of Wisconsin Press, 1967.

Jaksic, Iván, ed. *Debating Race, Ethnicity, and Latino Identity: Jorge J. E. Gracia and His Critics*. New York: Columbia University Press, 2015.

James, William. *Pragmatism: A New Name for the Old Ways of Thinking*. Indianapolis: Hackett Publishing, [1907] 1981.

———. *The Will to Believe and Other Essays in Popular Philosophy*. Cambridge, MA: Harvard University Press, 1979.

Janik, Allan, and Stephen Toulmin. *Wittgenstein's Vienna*. New York: Simon and Schuster, 1973.

Johnson, Jennifer. *Albion Monitor*. September 4, 1998, modified October 25, 2013. monitor.net/monitor//9804a/nea.html.

Johnson, Roberta. *Crossfire: Philosophy and the Novel in Spain, 1900–1934*. Lexington, KY:

University of Kentucky Press, 1993. Translated as *Fuego cruzado: Filosofía y novela en España (1900–1934)*. Madrid: Ediciones Libertarias/Prodhufi, 1997.

Kamen, Henry. *A Concise History of Spain*. London: Thames and Hudson, 1973.

Kant, Immanuel. *Critique of Judgement*. Translated by J. H. Bernard. New York: Hafner Publishing Company, 1966.

———. *Critique of Practical Reason*. Translated by Lewis White Beck. 3rd ed. Upper Saddle River, NJ: Prentice-Hall, 1993.

———. *Critique of Pure Reason*. Translated by J. M. D. Meiklejohn. Amherst, MA: Prometheus Books, 1990.

Kerrigan, Anthony, and Martin Nozick, eds. *The Selected Works of Miguel de Unamuno*. Princeton: Princeton University Press, 1974.

Kettner, Frederick. *Spinoza: The Biosopher*. New York: Roerich Museum Press, 1932.

Lautréamont, Comte de. *The Songs of Maldoror*. Illustrated by Salvador Dalí. Translated by R. J. Dent. Solar Books, 2011.

Lloyd-Jones, Hugh, ed. *Sophocles: Ajax, Electra, Oedipus Tyrannus*. Translated by Hugh Lloyd-Jones. Cambridge, MA: Harvard University Press, 1994.

Locke, John. *Essay Concerning Human Understanding*. In *Modern Philosophy: An Anthology of Primary Sources*, edited by Roger Ariew and Eric Watkins, 316–420. 2nd ed. Indianapolis: Hackett Publishing, 2009.

Mackay, John. *The Other Spanish Christ: A Study in the Spiritual History of Spain and South America*. New York: Macmillan, 1932.

Maclachlan, Colin M., and William H. Beezley. *El Gran Pueblo: A History of Greater Mexico*. 2nd ed. Upper Saddle River, NJ: Prentice Hall, 1994.

Malvido Miguel, Eduardo. *Unamuno a la busca de la inmortalidad: Estudio Del sentimiento trágico de la vida*. Salamanca: Ediciones San Pío X, 1977.

Marcos, Luis Andrés. *"Presupuestos fundamentales para una lectura filosófica de la obra de Miguel de Unamuno." Cuadernos de la Cátedra Miguel de Unamuno* 29 (1994): 91–110.

Martínez, Ignacio. "Hispanidad and the Weltanschauung of the Pan-Hispanic World: Intellectual and Cultural Foundations." Master's thesis, Department of Latin American Studies, University of New Mexico, 2006.

Martín-Rodríguez, Manuel. "Painting the Word/Wording the Painting: Allegory and Intertextuality in *The Virgin of Port Lligat* by Fray Angélico Chávez." In *Fray Angélico Chávez: Poet, Priest, and Artist*, edited by Ellen McCracken, 91–100. Albuquerque: University of New Mexico Press, 2000.

McCracken, Ellen, ed. *Fray Angélico Chávez: Poet, Priest, and Artist*. Albuquerque: University of New Mexico Press, 2000.

———. *The Life and Writing of Fray Angélico Chávez: A New Mexico Renaissance Man*. Albuquerque: University of New Mexico Press, 2009.

McMurray, George R. *Jorge Luis Borges*. New York: Frederick Ungar Publishing, 1980.

Meille, Giovanni. *Christ's Likeness in History and in Art*. London: Bergamo, 1924.

Miranda, José. *Marx and the Bible: A Critique of the Philosophy of Oppression*. Maryknoll, NY: Orbis Books, 1974.

Monegal, Emir Rodríguez. *Jorge Luis Borges: A Literary Biography*. New York: E. P. Dutton, 1978.

Nozick, Martin. *Miguel de Unamuno*. New York: Twayne, 1971.

Okafor, Udoka. "Exclusive Interview with Andres Serrano, Photographer of 'Piss Christ.'" *Accessed on 6/4/14, updated on 8/4/14. Huffington Post.* www.huffingtonpost.com/udoka-okafor/exclusive-interview-with-_18_b_5442141.html.

Orozco, José Clemente. *The Artist in New York: Letters to Jean Charlot and Unpublished Writings, 1925–1929*. Translated by Ruth L. C. Simms. Austin: University of Texas Press, 1974.

———. *José Clemente Orozco: An Autobiography*. Austin: University of Texas Press, 1962.

Pascal, Blaise. "*Pensées sur la Religion*: Excerpts." In *Fifty Readings Plus: An Introduction to Philosophy*, edited by Donald C. Abel, 116–21. 2nd ed. New York: McGraw Hill, 2010.

Paz, Octavio. *Essays on Mexican Art*. Translated by Helen Lane. New York: Harcourt, Brace & Company, 1993.

Pelikan, Jaroslav. *Jesus through the Centuries: His Place in the History of Culture*. New Haven: Yale University Press, 1999.

Prothero, Stephen. *American Jesus: How the Son of God Became a National Icon*. New York, NY: Frarrar, Straus and Giroux, 2003.

Reiman, Karen Cordero. "Prometheus Unraveled: Readings of and from the Body: Orozco's Pomona College Mural (1930)." In González Mello and Miliotes 2002, 98–117.

Rochfort, Desmond. "A Terrible Beauty: Orozco's Murals in Guadalajara 1936–1939." In Elliott 1980, 74–96.

Rojas, Ricardo. *El Cristo invisible*. Buenos Aires: Librería La Facultad, 1928.

Rudd, Margaret. *The Lone Heretic: A Biography of Miguel de Unamuno y Jugo*. Austin: University of Texas Press, 1963.

Ryan, Jerry. "Artist, Activist, Martyr: The Priest Behind the Hammer and Sickle Crucifix." *Commonweal* 142, no. 12 (2015). https://www.commonwealmagazine.org/artist-activist-martyr.

Salcedo, Emilio. *Liberación de la teología*. Buenos Aires: Carlos Lohlé, 1975.

———. "Unamuno y Ortega y Gasset: Diálogo entre dos españoles." *Cuadernos de la Cátedra Miguel de Unamuno* 7 (1956): 97–130.

Schopenhauer, Arthur. *On the Basis of Morality*. Translated by E. F. J. Payne. Indianapolis: Hackett Publishing, 1995.

———. *The World as Will and Idea*. Edited by David Berman. Translated by Jill Berman. London: Everyman's Library, 2002.

———. *The World as Will and Idea*. In *Masterworks of Philosophy*, vol. 3, edited by S. E. Frost Jr. New York: McGraw-Hill, 1972.

Scott, David. "Orozco's Prometheus: Summation, Transition, Innovation." In Harth 2001, 13–26.

———. "Prometheus Revisited." In Harth 2001, 27–47.

Segundo, Juan Luis. *Church and Community*. Maryknoll, NY: Orbis Press.

———. *Liberación de la teología*. Buenos Aires: Carlos Lohlé S.A.I.C, 1975.

Shanes, Eric. *The Life and Masterworks of Salvador Dalí.* New York: Parkstone Press International, 2010.

Shestov, Lev. *Athens and Jerusalem.* Translated by Bernard Martin. Athens: Ohio University Press, 1966.

———. *La Nuit de Gethsémani: Essai sur la Philosophie de Pascal.* Paris: Grasset, 1923.

Sierra, Justo. *Prosas de Justo Sierra.* Mexico City: UNAM, 1939.

Sobejano, Gonzalo. *Nietzsche en España.* Madrid: Editorial Gredos, 1967.

Sobrino, Jon. *Christology at the Crossroads: A Latin American Approach.* Translated by John Drury. Maryknoll, NY: Orbis Books, 1978.

Spinoza, Baruch. *The Ethics.* In *Modern Philosophy: An Anthology of Primary Sources,* edited by Roger Ariew and Eric Watkins, 144–96. Indianapolis: Hackett Publishing, 1998.

———. *The Ethics.* In *The Rationalists.* Garden City, NY: Dophin Books, 179–406.

Starnes, Todd. "WH Silent over Demands to Denounce 'Piss Christ' Artwork." 2012. radio.foxnews.com/toddstarnes/top-stories/wh-silent-over-demands-to-denounce-piss-christ-artwork.html.

Stewart, Matthew. *The Courier and the Heretic: Leibniz, Spinoza and the Fate of God in the Modern World.* New York: W. W. Norton, 2006.

Stirner, Max. *The Ego and Its Own.* Edited by David Leopold. Cambridge: Cambridge University Press, 1995.

Taylor, Michael, ed. *The Dalí Renaissance. New Perspectives on His Life and Art after 1940.* New Haven: Yale University Press, 2008.

Taylor, Richard. *Metaphysics.* Englewood Cliffs, NJ: Prentice Hall, 1974.

Teilhard de Chardin, Pierre. *The Phenomenon of Man.* New York: Harper and Row, 1959.

Tertullian. "On the Flesh." In *Ante-Nicene Christian Library: Translation of the Writings of the Fathers,* vol. 3, edited by Alexander Roberts and James Donaldson, 5. Edinburgh: T & T Clarke, 1867–1873.

Thiselton, Anthony C. *The Two Horizons: New Testament Hermeneutics and Philosophical Description with Special Reference to Heidegger, Bultmann, Gadamer, and Wittgenstein.* Grand Rapids, MI: William B. Eerdmans, 1980.

Unamuno, Miguel de. *The Agony of Christianity and Essays on Faith. Selected Works of Miguel de Unamuno.* Vol. 5. Edited by Anthony Kerrigan and Martin Nozick. Translated by Anthony Kerrigan. Princeton: Princeton University Press, 1974.

———. *Del sentimiento trágico de la vida en los hombres y en las naciones.* In *Obras selectas.*

———. "Mi religión." In *Obras selectas,* 255–60.

———. *Obras selectas.* Madrid: Editorial Plenitud, 1965.

———. *Our Lord Don Quixote: The Life of Don Quixote and Sancho, with Related Essays,* vol. 3, edited by Anthony Kerrigan and Robert Nozick. Princeton: Princeton University Press, 1967.

———. "San Manuel the Good, Martyr." In *Selected Works of Miguel de Unamuno.* vol. 7. Edited by Anthony Kerrigan. Princeton University Press, 135–82.

———. *The Tragic Sense of Life of Men and of Nations.* Translated by J. E. Crawford Flitch. New York: Dover Publications, 1954.

Vaihinger, Hans. *The Philosophy of 'As If': A System of the Theoretical, Practical, and*

Religious Fictions of Mankind. Translated by C. K. Ogden. New York: Barnes and Noble, 1966.

Valle, Luis G. del. "Hacia una prospectiva teológica a partir de acontecimientos." In Gibellini 1977, 82–103.

Vasconcelos, José. *The Cosmic Race/La raza cósmica.* Translated by Didier T. Jaén. Baltimore, MD: Johns Hopkins University Press, 1997.

Vidales, Raúl. *"Cuestiones en torno al método en la teología de la liberación."* In Gibellini 1977, 41–62.

Viramontes, Helena. *Under the Feet of Jesus.* New York: Penguin Books, 1996.

Wallis, Jonathan. "Holy Toledo! Saint John of the Cross, Paranoiac-Critical Mysticism, and the Life and Work of Saint Dalí." In Taylor 2008, 37–52.

Wolfson, Harry Austryn. *The Philosophy of Spinoza: Unfolding the Latent Processes of His Reasoning*, vol. 2. New York: Schoken Books, 1969.

Woodall, James. *Borges: A Life.* New York: Basic Books, 1996.

INDEX